THE TANGO OF ETHICS

INTUITION, RATIONALITY AND THE PREVENTION OF SUFFERING

Jonathan Leighton

imprint-academic.com

Copyright © Jonathan Leighton, 2023

The moral rights of the authors have been asserted.
No part of this publication may be reproduced in any form
without permission, except for the quotation of brief passages
in criticism and discussion.

Published in the UK by
Imprint Academic, PO Box 200, Exeter EX5 5YX, UK

Distributed in the USA by
Ingram Book Company,
One Ingram Blvd., La Vergne, TN 37086, USA

ISBN 9781788360883 Paperback

A CIP catalogue record for this book is available from the
British Library and US Library of Congress

Contents

	Acknowledgements	viii
1.	Ethics as an Authentic Dance	1
	The path of truth and compassion	1
	Post-Battle assessment	2
	Can ethics help us improve the world?	4
	Rethinking ethics	8
	The tango of ethics	10
	Can one be too transparent about ethics?	13
	Adjusting priorities	14
2.	Intuition and Rationality	15
	Intuition and its roots	15
	The role of rationality	16
	Managing expectations: the limits of rationality	19
3.	Ethics: What is the Question?	21
	Understanding oughtism	21
	Consequentialism: impact matters	27
	Utilitarianism: impact on wellbeing matters	29
	Deontology: follow the rules	31
	Virtue ethics: be good	32
	Can any one theory be correct?	32
4.	Ethics and Subjective Experience	36
	Hedonic states and wellbeing	36
	Preference satisfaction	39
	Interests	40
	Suffering	41
	The notion of urgency	43
	The significance of extreme and unbearable suffering	45
	Buddhism and craving	49
	Voluntary suffering	49
	Happiness and wellbeing	51
	Capturing the dynamics of hedonic states	55
	Absence of suffering: from hedonic zero to bliss	56

5.	Evaluating Value	60
	The confusion about value and the compulsion to create it	60
	The fundamental ethical asymmetry between suffering and happiness	64
	Negative utilitarianism	67
6.	The Map and the Territory	72
	The mathematics of suffering	73
	Measuring suffering	75
	The hedonic delusion	76
	Lost in aggregation	79
7.	Determining Priorities	82
	Intensity vs. instances: the essence of uncertainty	82
	Comparing physical pain and psychological suffering	86
	Unbearable suffering as an ethical tipping point	88
	Expected value and cause prioritisation	93
8.	Suffering and the Illusion of Separateness	95
	The true nature of personal identity	95
	The Golden Rule	99
	Rawls's veil of ignorance	100
	Anti-speciesism	101
	Awakening awareness	102
9.	Our Complex Relationship with Suffering	104
	The fleetingness of momentary decisions	104
	Voluntary personal sacrifices don't justify imposing suffering on others	106
	Tolerating the intolerable	107
	The need for systems that are more rational and compassionate than we are	113
	The intuition towards fairness and against the concentration of suffering	114

10.	Existence	118
	A life worth living	118
	Escaping the Repugnant Conclusion	121
	Why non-existence isn't a bad thing	122
	Reducing existential risk: an intuition with conditions	123
	Preserving consciousness	127
11.	A Holistic Ethical Framework	129
	Key principles	129
	xNU+	131
	How xNU+ compares to prioritarianism	137
	How xNU+ responds to common objections to negative utilitarianism	137
	Consistency: being truthful and rational	139
	How everything is connected by utilitarianism	140
	How obsessive utilitarianism can be self-defeating	140
12.	Current and Potential Causes of Intense Suffering	146
	Human suffering	146
	Abuse and torture of non-human animals	147
	Nature and wild animal suffering	148
	Insect and other invertebrate suffering	149
	Far future suffering	155
	Artificial/machine suffering	156
13.	A Tangible Tango: Resolving Ethical Conflicts	159
	Helping those closest vs. helping strangers	161
	War	162
	Animal experimentation	164
	The grey zone of animal exploitation	168
	Veganism vs. reducing suffering: is eating animal products ever justifiable?	169
	Eating oysters and other brainless invertebrates	172
	Painlessly killing happy animals	174
	Euthanasia of suffering animals	176
	Euthanasia and assisted suicide in humans	177
	Saving lives vs. preventing suffering	179
	Anti-natalism	181

	The meat-eater problem	182
	Preserving the environment vs. reducing wild animal suffering	183
14.	From Ethics to Action	186
	Reflections on the ethical tango	186
	Creating a new suffering metric for health economics	187
	Impacting the far future	190
	Designing compassionate blueprints for governance based on xNU+ ethics	192
	The last tango: embedding xNU+ ethics into AGI	195
	Balancing personal initiative and collective action	203
	Activism and the desire to see impact	207
	How much empathy do we need?	208
	The fractal-like nature of ethical action	208
	Spreading love, empathy, rationality and compassion	209
References		211
Index		230

"Humans may crave absolute certainty; they may aspire to it; they may pretend, as partisans of certain religions do, to have attained it. But the history of science—by far the most successful claim to knowledge accessible to humans—teaches that the most we can hope for is successive improvement in our understanding, learning from our mistakes, an asymptotic approach to the Universe, but with the proviso that absolute certainty will always elude us."
—Carl Sagan, American astronomer

"The tango is a direct expression of something that poets have often tried to state in words: the belief that a fight may be a celebration."
—Jorge Luis Borges, Argentinean writer

"The tango is the man and woman in search of each other. It is the search for an embrace, a way to be together…"
—Juan Carlos Copes, Argentinean tango dancer

"The tango is the ultimate communication between two people. It begins with an embrace, an initial sharing of affection, yet stresses individual balance… The mastering of one's individual balance is what allows two bodies to dance as one…"
—Miguel Angel Pla, Argentinean tango instructor

Acknowledgements

I would like first of all to express my gratitude to Alex Nil Shchelov, Brian Tomasik, Catia Faria, Emma Tulanova, Magnus Vinding, Manu Herrán, Robert Daoust, Robert McNeill, Roger Crisp and Teo Ajantaival for providing feedback on all or parts of the manuscript and offering many valuable comments and suggestions. Magnus provided particularly detailed comments throughout, challenging many of my phrasings and arguments, which led to greater clarity. I would also like to thank Ilianna Skoulaki for her brilliant artistic interpretation of the cover concept.

Many of the ideas in this book evolved through various interactions and discussions over the years, especially with members of the effective altruism community who are deeply concerned about suffering. Aside from those mentioned above, I would like to acknowledge in particular (though non-exhaustively) David Pearce, Adriano Mannino, Lukas Gloor, Lucius Caviola, Jonas Vollmer, Andrés Gómez Emilsson, Olivier Bertrand, Rupert McCallum, Laura Green, Guillaume Chauvat, Max Carpendale, Ruth Freiling and Sille Juul Kjærbo. Janique Behman was an early OPIS supporter with whom I co-organised a workshop for suffering-focused effective altruists in the Swiss Alps in March 2019. Greg Colbourn kindly welcomed me for a productive stay at the EA Hotel in Blackpool. Thanks also to Roman Yampolskiy and Thomas Metzinger for their interest in this project.

I would like to thank my Patreon supporters, as well as the many supporters of OPIS. Particular thanks in this regard to Alex Nil Shchelov, Manu Herrán, Tom Marty, Dani Sieber, Marieke de Visscher, Danny Hayter, Hannah Masson-Smyth, Paul Louyot, Stijn Bruers, Zack Eagleton and Matthew Goodman, as well as the many others who contributed to the Burkina Faso initiative, including Mike McIntosh, Hugh Panton, Sujatha Der and Adrian Crimmen. Special thanks to Peter Singer for his public support for OPIS and our projects. Apologies to anyone I neglected or didn't have space to mention in these last two paragraphs—I am grateful to everyone I have interacted with who has contributed in some way to our mission.

I wrote this book while engaged in initiatives focusing on specific causes of suffering that poignantly illustrate the urgency of the problem. A collaboration with Sebastian Saville of International Doctors for Healthier Drug Policies (IDHP) allowed us to advocate at the UN Human Rights Council for better access to morphine. Dr. Martin Lankoandé, founder of Hospice Burkina, has been a close collaborator in an initiative to ensure that terminal cancer patients in Burkina Faso can access morphine and palliative care, and Dr. Anne Merriman of Hospice Africa Uganda provided invaluable support. I would like to thank my friends in the cluster headache community for their trust and collaboration, especially Tony Taipale, Ainslie Course, Eileen Brewer, Cindy Reynolds, Shellie Clark Masini and Miguel Angel de Pascual, as well as our partners at TheraPsil, Spencer Hawkswell and Holly Bennett.

I would like to express my deep thanks to my OPIS colleagues for their collaboration, friendship, support and dedication to preventing intense suffering in the world, including Jean-Christophe Lurenbaum, Robert Daoust, Manu Herrán, Sorin Ionescu, Alyssa Berris, Zoë Gumm, Axelle Playoust-Braure, Marieke de Visscher, Samah Atout, Sandeep Sibal, Tobias Leenaert, Nell Watson, Corin Ism, Oscar Horta, Joe Brewer and Jamie Catto. Jean-Christophe and Robert, who invited me to join the Algosphere as one of its first allies, have been close and trusted colleagues for nearly a decade, and I am grateful for this.

On a more personal note: Christine Eberhard, who tangoed with me during an important phase of my life journey, impressed me with her intuitive ability to communicate empathetically with non-human animals, and to gauge their will to live when suffering. Dominique Radas gave me greater insight into Buddhism and the centrality of balance through many discussions we had in Mallorca. Jem Bendell, a friend for many years and now also a collaborator, gave me the opportunity to bring a suffering-focused perspective to the Deep Adaptation community and reflections on societal collapse. Pete Lawrence has given my ideas an outlet within the Campfire Convention community and also invited me to run a panel discussion on citizens' assemblies and ethical governance. Sebastian Schlueter facilitated a case clinic for an ethical governance project being developed. Matt Coldrick has provided informal coaching and we have had many stimulating and valuable conversations by the sea in Paros. Anders Hsi introduced me in greater depth, through his writings and many discussions, to the Dao De Jing, which embodies the concept of yin and yang and the dance between them. Natasha Georgiadou has brought me balance and joy during the final stages of preparing the manuscript. My parents, as always, have been highly supportive over the years. Finally, the Tango Paros group gave me the opportunity to experience first-hand what it's actually like to dance the tango.

One

Ethics as an Authentic Dance

The path of truth and compassion

A book like this ultimately aspires to have some influence on the world. And in the spirit of intellectual inquiry with which it was written, I would like to begin, perhaps unusually, by questioning that very aim. Given the intense competition among ideas, what reason would one have for giving greater weight to the ideas expressed here than to others? For the rationally minded, truthful starting assumptions and solid logic would make a persuasive case. Whether or not I have succeeded, I have striven to be meticulous about both. But rational arguments can still serve hidden motivations, such as a rebellious desire to question conventional wisdom. If the ideas developed here, in which people are challenged on their deepest intuitions about existence and morality, were to become highly influential, would that necessarily be a good thing?

Fundamentally, everything that happens in the world is the result of subatomic particles interacting according to the laws of physics. Even the decision to write this book is based on motivations and intuitions that, through some combination of randomness and emergent order, happened to arise in one individual's brain. What makes one random world where more people take these ideas seriously better than another random world where fewer do? This question expresses both an essential focus of ethical thinking—how do we know what would ideally be the best thing to do?—and the fact that this ethical thinking itself is a product of the universe. And so I can also ask the question with a more philosophical framing: is it a good thing that the universe causes a book like this to be written?

What I can honestly say is that the main motivations for writing this book, as for my previous one, without expanding on the upstream causes of these motivations, are a combination of compassion—a desire to alleviate suffering in the world—and a search for the truth. Even if these motivations developed independently, they are closely related, because the truths about suffering and about the nature of personal identity can also lead to compassion, as I will argue. I therefore have reason to hope that a world that is in any way influenced by these ideas will be a world that is more aware and respectful of the truth, and more compassionate. And I do hope this is the path the universe happens to take.

Post-Battle assessment

My first book, *The Battle for Compassion: Ethics in an Apathetic Universe* (Leighton, 2011), was an exploration of the basis of ethics from a big-picture perspective, an attempt to methodically answer the question "what matters?" To briefly summarise some of the main points:

- Things just happen in a world that operates according to the laws of physics, and if we want (from inside this system) to change things for the better, we need to understand the world as best we can and change the environment in which people find themselves, rather than blaming them for actions we don't like.
- Everything that matters comes down to the subjective experience of sentient beings,[1] and alleviating intense suffering is the one thing that matters most.
- We are all variations on a theme, with personal identities that have much in common with one another and that shift over time, and intense suffering is equally important no matter where, when and by whom it is experienced.
- Although it is impossible to achieve an ethical framework that provides absolute, rigorous, non-arbitrary prescriptions, we can continuously aim to promote compassion and rationality in the interest of reducing suffering in the world.

I also proposed the term "negative utilitarianism *plus*" (NU+) to describe an approach to ethics that prioritises the alleviation of suffering but, with the addition of the "+", also acknowledges the human urge to live and to thrive.

---

[1] In this book, I use the terms "sentient" and "conscious" interchangeably. Some consider sentience to mean more specifically the ability to have hedonically positive or negative experiences. While the ability to experience pain and suffering may be what matters ethically, I prefer a more general use of the term "sentience" that corresponds better to the traditional definition, which is the ability to perceive and feel—the key feature of consciousness. Even if a human being could not feel pain or pleasure, I would still consider them to be sentient.

My main stances haven't changed much and have been largely strengthened as I see their relevance to our rapidly changing world. Soon after *The Battle for Compassion* came out, I was pleased to discover a strong convergence between my ideas and those of other thinkers and advocates for societal change, in particular within the effective altruism movement, aiming to relieve suffering in the world. A few of my stances have changed, in part through conversations, reading and reflecting, and a greater willingness to challenge my own previous beliefs. For example:

- I no longer believe that simply tweaking our existing capitalist economic system will bring about the changes we need in society, and I feel much more strongly that we need to rethink the ways not only that we distribute but that we create wealth, while respecting individual freedoms.
- I no longer believe in encouraging people to have children, but rather, in ensuring that those children who are brought into the world are protected from avoidable suffering, instilled with a sense of compassion and encouraged to become forces for positive change.
- On a personal level, I soon afterwards adopted a vegan diet when I could no longer resist the cognitive dissonance between my ethical beliefs and my omnivorous lifestyle. The massive torture of animals for human consumption is the largest-scale moral catastrophe of our times, and I am now dedicated to spreading awareness of this fact and doing what I can to help change things.

This book addresses many of the same issues as *The Battle for Compassion*, but I take the thinking further, exploring with greater clarity and precision what a coherent, more holistic ethical framework could look like. I also identify what I see as serious flaws in some of the arguments frequently proposed on how to provide quantitative prescriptions for our actions. In particular, I will be arguing:

- There are inherent limits to the use of rationality in ethics that many rationalists overlook, including in the use of numbers to represent hedonic states and to determine priorities.
- The vague concept of "value" has distorted rational thinking about ethics by being implicitly conflated with an inherent need to be created.
- The strong intuitions about preserving life and existence need to be explicitly acknowledged but also challenged, rather than simply accepted.
- We can't expect most people to live and act in contradiction with some of their deepest intuitions.

In a chapter on determinism in *The Battle for Compassion*, I wrote: "Each explanation may be useful, and different ways of viewing the world can therefore each have validity, provided they do not lead to conflicting conclusions." When it comes to ethics, I would adjust the last part to read, "*even if* they lead to conflicting conclusions". We are faced with the fact that there often isn't one single "right" conclusion. And our challenge is often to hold two different perspectives or levels of understanding in our minds at the same time.

Can ethics help us improve the world?

We face colossal challenges today, among them climate change, pandemics, armed conflict, political and religious extremism, human rights abuses, massive cruelty to animals, widespread poverty and disease, the concentration of wealth and political power, growing authoritarianism and the threat of irreversible totalitarianism, the risks of artificial general intelligence (AGI), and various other causes of harm and catastrophic/existential threats. All of these problems demand addressing and need to be worked on in parallel. But some of them might be especially urgent to try to solve now because of their greater potential long-term impact. There is also the risk that some solutions might make other problems worse. It would be extremely helpful to know with greater certainty how to determine our priorities.

Yet when we talk about the details, differences emerge that can lead to fractures and conflicts even between well-meaning people. Activists and others promoting societal change, including those with apparently similar values, may have dramatically conflicting priorities. People seem to choose their camp based on affinity to the problem and how salient it seems to them. For many, climate change is the dominant spectre that threatens the collapse of our civilisation (for an ethical perspective, see Leighton & Bendell, 2022). For others, it's the emergence of an AGI that doesn't understand or respect human values and similarly threatens us with extinction, or with a long-lasting dystopia filled with suffering. Both of these threats may play out on similar timescales, over the next decades, and we may even face a superposition of these scenarios. Many people are more focused on current suffering, including the massive torture of factory-farmed animals and the various sources of human misery. As I finalise this book in early spring 2022, it is the tremendous suffering caused by Russia's brutal invasion of Ukraine that dominates much of the world's consciousness. The dimensions of each problem are so different, and as we focus on one we tend to neglect the others.

Definitive prioritisation may be impossible, but a solid ethical framework can help us reshuffle our priorities. Concrete issues to resolve range from the philosophically existential to the very detailed and practical:

- Most fundamentally, how do we prioritise the prevention of suffering vs. the preservation of existence?
- How can we reconcile utilitarian, numerical, impact-based thinking with deontological, morally intuitive thinking, within a more comprehensive ethical framework?
- What values do we prioritise as we seek to limit the risks due to an AGI?
- On what basis would we ideally organise our societies socially, economically and politically?
- How can our governments and institutions better embed ethics into decision-making?
- How do we build a consensus around core ethical ideas?
- Is it OK for humans to eat animals – even if there is no suffering?
- Is it OK to cause harm to a few in order to prevent harm to many?
- How do we address the vast amount of suffering of animals living in the wild?
- How significant is insect suffering and how do we take it into account?
- How do we prioritise alleviating ongoing suffering vs. potential suffering in the far future?
- And at the most personal level, what kind of balance can we find between our role as agents of ethical change and our desire to thrive? What does it mean to live ethically, and how can we best make a difference?

We need a rational approach to trying to resolve these questions and determine rules or guidelines for how to live as individuals and as a society. Ethics can provide an intellectual foundation for decision-making and serve as a driving force for positive change in the world, offering principles that may override what our intuitions alone might tell us.

While we tend to agree that ethics is about things like happiness, suffering, truth, meaning and existence, we don't seem to reach much consensus on the relationship between these concepts and what importance to give them. Some deep truths about existence are so counterintuitive or terrible to contemplate that they get ignored altogether in ethical reflections, including by people who take pride in their own rationality. Ethics requires comprehensively and systematically reflecting on what matters, and what this implies about our aims and priorities, rather than simply doing what intuitively feels right.

Ideally we would want a transparent, internally consistent ethical framework that is all-encompassing and manages to reconcile different perspectives. Such a framework would provide essential reference points as we search for a way forward, and serve as the basis for new blueprints for long-term ethical governance. To be universally relevant and applicable to all foreseeable situations and technologies, it needs to be based on a big-picture perspective on existence.

But even if ethics could theoretically be solved, who would actually use it? Most political leaders don't seem to care that much about applying deep ethical thinking to big issues. What are the prospects for ethical reasoning being used to improve society, when politics is largely driven by power alliances, financial interests and pandering to populous bases? In the face of the dramatic problems we are facing, are ethical reflections akin to bean counting while the world burns?

Even as it relates to general advocacy, it's been argued: "Our policy arguments should be empirically-based with references to ideology and philosophy minimised to the greatest extent possible. People tend to disregard arguments that are perceived to be in conflict with their underlying values and partisan and ideological group-identities" (Taylor, 2015). If this view is correct, it might suggest that an ethical framework is not actually very useful for persuading most people.

Fortunately, many people are responsive to rational arguments, especially if compatibility with their own values is emphasised. And there are several concrete and important ways that an ethical framework can be applied by rational people, with potentially far-reaching implications:

- Activists and organisations using the framework to decide where to devote their efforts and incorporating the ideas into advocacy work.
- Foundations and other philanthropic sources using it to decide where to focus their spending.
- Ethically motivated politicians drawing on it in deciding on priorities and new legislation.
- Political philosophers and others designing new blueprints for societal decision-making and governance.
- Programmers attempting to ensure that a powerful AGI is aligned with ethical values before humans lose control.

I believe that one of the key elements of a better future for our world lies in spreading compassion and rationality, and embedding a solid ethical framework based on these values into decision-making systems. It is essential that we be as clear as possible in defining the ethical framework, and that we eliminate flaws in the reasoning that supports it. If the reasoning is faulty, the policy implications could be dramatic. Even apparently similar aspirations to improve the wellbeing of all our planet's inhabitants could lead to very different courses of action and outcomes, based on significant differences in some of the underlying assumptions. The need to think systematically about ethics is not only about optimising impact within the space of positive outcomes, but also about ensuring we do not unknowingly make things worse.

If we are grappling with issues that may affect the long-term future of life and consciousness on this planet and possibly even in other parts of the universe, it is essential that we think very deeply about what matters, fully understand the roots of any intuitions that are driving or influencing our decisions and challenge these intuitions if necessary, but also acknowledge potential flaws in our rational arguments.

Phil Torres, an author and researcher who focuses on existential risk, wrote with respect to the dangers of AI, "As numerous AI safety experts have pointed out, it may not be enough for humanity to align the value system of a superintelligence 90 percent, just as dialling 9 out of 10 phone number digits won't get you someone who's 90 percent similar to the person you're trying to call. In other words, our values are 'fragile', meaning that we may have to solve the age-old philosophical question of what our values should be entirely, rather than partially, by the time AI reaches a human level of general intelligence" (Torres, 2017; the phone number reference is from Yudkowsky, 2013). I don't think we can actually meaningfully answer the question what our values "should" be without specifying more narrowly what we mean by the term, as I will explain in detail further on. However, in line with Torres's point, if we can't clearly say or define what we want, we may end up with some very bad surprises. As I will argue in this book, I don't think that anything can be said to matter as much as preventing intense suffering, and our challenge is how to do this as effectively as possible, given the various possible paths and outcomes, and also the conflict with some of our deepest intuitions.

Although ethical reasoning can only be fully persuasive for people who are open enough to rational argumentation to put their own beliefs and values into question, the reasoning has to underlie our goals and our efforts at social change, regardless of what methods we then use to effect that change. As advocates for a better world, we need to be clear about what we are fighting for and why. A rational ethical framework is still useful for advocacy purposes, because transparent, rational arguments are more credible. Rational thinkers will want to see the detailed argumentation for a change of course. The arguments can still be summarised in a simpler form, or depicted through images and films that help communicate them to a larger audience, but the underlying reasoning needs to be transparent, including the motivation behind the framework.

Rethinking ethics

One of my goals with this book is to urge people to reconsider how they think about ethics, and to put into question some of their existing assumptions. This is more challenging than, for example, a mathematician demonstrating a flaw in another mathematician's proposed proof of a theorem. Logical errors in a mathematical proof are relatively straightforward to demonstrate, as the rules of the game are already relatively clear and people largely agree on them. And secondly, finding a flaw in a long proof is not unexpected and unlikely to be a cause for major embarrassment. On the other hand, trying to persuade people who are already engaged in some way with ethics that some of the ways they are applying rationality and using numbers might be flawed is akin to trying to change their worldview—something that is difficult enough when people don't have a vested professional interest in maintaining their current perspective and set of priorities.

Consciousness researcher Mike Johnson (2018) has written, "…if philosophy's established ways of framing the problem of consciousness could lead to a solution, it would've been solved by now, and by using someone else's packaged ontology, I'd be at risk of importing their confusion into my foundation. With this in mind I decided that *being aware* of key landmarks in philosophy was important, but *being uncorrelated with philosophy's past framing* was equally important, so I took a minimalist first-principles approach to building my framework and was very careful about what I imported from philosophy and how I used it." If you substitute "ethics" for "consciousness", these thoughts capture some of my concerns about ethical thinking and why I am interested in taking a different approach.

An argument full of false assumptions or riddled with holes is immediately recognised as worthless. But even an argument with just one false assumption can potentially lead to an equally false conclusion. A single negative sign can change the value and significance of a formula more dramatically than getting the value of any number of constants wrong. This weakness is, in my opinion, one of the problems with much of contemporary ethics and especially aggregative classical utilitarianism (discussed shortly), which has become influential in efforts to bring more rationality into improving the world. Much of the reasoning carried out is methodical and logical, but some of the assumptions are, I believe, untenable.

Truth encompasses facts about the world, including metaphysics and the reality of subjective experience, and logical statements arrived at through rationality. So in principle, discovering truths — though not actual "moral truths", as I will argue shortly — is at the core of ethics, and ethical thinking requires nudging ourselves in the direction of certain fundamental truths about reality and existence.

My mission for this book is to offer a holistic framework for thinking about ethics that sheds the unclear terminology, moral framing and questionable assumptions often encountered in other frameworks. For clarification, I mean "holistic" not in the spiritual sense in which the word is sometimes used, nor in the sense of "ethical holism", which has a very different, specific meaning — that the group matters more than the individuals that compose it, which is actually the opposite of the view I defend. Rather, I mean that it takes a big-picture perspective that encompasses very different ways of seeing and thinking about the world. While I recognise that use of this term could lead to confusion, I haven't found an alternative that captures this meaning equally well.

The approach is centred on phenomenal or subjective experience — the most ethically relevant facts about the universe — as well as compatibility with metaphysical truths about identity and existence. I aim to distinguish between assumptions that have axiomatic truth value and others that do not, and how they can both be used to build up logical ethical arguments. I examine how rationality interfaces with our intuitions and biases, the constraints that our intuitions and biases impose, as well as the limits of rationality itself, and try to reconcile rationality and intuition in a reasonable and transparent way. The balance between rationality and intuition is, in fact, also the sense, if inherently imprecise, in which I tend to use the word "reasonable". Through this inquiry I seek a basis for identifying the most urgent actions in the interest of a better world. I don't claim to have arrived at a framework with the solidity and precision of a mathematical proof, but I hope to have shown with a little more clarity what the key elements of such a framework might be.

A fundamental question that much of this inquiry boils down to is about filling the void of non-existence. Do we choose to do it, even when there will be horrible suffering as a result? Most ethical thinking going back millennia is within the context of an existing society and is restricted to questions about how to live well with one another. But this framing can preclude taking a bigger-picture perspective and questioning existence itself. This is something of a taboo, but if we don't confront it we may be unable to fully account for the ethical dilemmas we find ourselves in and address them adequately.

Big-picture reflections on intense suffering give everything else that people typically discuss and argue about much less importance. Intense suffering is on a whole different level of seriousness than someone having their feelings hurt because of an article someone wrote or an insensitive comment made online. And so while much of societal decision-making is incredibly messy and often involves negotiations between competing interests, I am seeking to focus much of the attention on the extreme end of the scale of suffering, where all the other considerations pale in comparison.

Some of the ideas presented in this book may appear to reflect an unusual, outlier perspective that doesn't sit well with how we normally view the world, because it puts into question many of the things we value as human beings and would risk upending our current priorities. Ultimately, though, I hope this book can serve as a guide towards greater convergence and unity, showing how we can retain many of our existing values while becoming more effective agents in the pursuit of a world without intense suffering.

The tango of ethics

One of the biggest challenges in ethics is to better understand the yin and yang relationship between intuition and rationality. Both play a critical role in ethical thinking, and we may sometimes be confused about which of the two we are dealing with. Yet when thinking and debating about ethics, people can make logical errors about some of the fundamentals while believing they are being rational, because they are unknowingly relying on faulty intuitions. They may also dismiss deep-rooted intuitions that contradict their reasoning, insisting that we need to bite the bullet and act on the rational conclusions. Alternatively, they may refuse to accept the conclusions of rational arguments because they are counterintuitive.

We can see ethics as a tango between intertwined, complementary and often opposing ways of seeing and even being in the world, with intuition and rationality often associated with subjective and objective perspectives, respectively. These different ways of being in the world, or modes, can be symbolised by various metaphors and archetypes, such as the feminine and the masculine,[2] the romantic human and the "God-like" agent, analogue and digital. The intuitive side may resist systematisation and the obsession with numbers and optimisation. The rational side insists that if you can't explain a problem with numbers, you can't solve it.

Mathematically these different modes might also be seen as different hierarchical levels—not of superiority or importance, but of complexity, with some intuitions corresponding to rawer, more primeval urges and emotions, and rationality being about understanding the relationship between ideas. Yet one mode is not clearly at a higher level of complexity than the other. Feelings may have appeared longer ago in our evolutionary past and be more central to our functioning than the ability to carry out rational thought. Yet the meaning we attach to existence is itself a function of complex thought, and the happiness and suffering that meaning can give rise to are the products of much greater complexity than the simple triggering of a pain receptor or a fight or flight response.

These modes interact in an endless tango between existing and acting, feeling and thinking, experiencing love and problem-solving, seeking bliss and alleviating suffering. And this tango plays out in so many ways relevant to ethics, with the confrontation between distinct modes of being that are both relevant. One may feel obliged to take sides, as if the tango were a contest to be won between two dancers, rather than a search for understanding and balance. One may even find oneself switching perspectives on the world, as if the one that was leading has now become the follower, without even realising it. For example:

- Subjectively it feels like we have free will, and we are most effective personally when we act as if we do, yet objectively—if we understand free will in the sense of our minds being the ultimate, undetermined sources of our desires and actions—we don't, and we can be more effective at changing things in the world when we apply this level of understanding to other people and their environments.
- Subjectively an action can feel very "wrong", yet objectively we can understand that terms such as this are not meaningful in the way we often think they are.
- Subjectively we are each unique beings with our own stable identity that provides our lives with meaning, yet objectively the whole notion

---

[2] I emphasise that I use these terms in the archetypal sense, not to suggest that biological sex need determine an individual's propensity towards intuitiveness or rationalism.

of identity is fluid, and our own sense of having a distinct, continuous personal identity is an illusion.
- Subjectively it feels like the deep meaning and even spirituality we can experience are central to understanding existence and imbue it with unique value, yet this view can conflict with a more detached perspective that questions whether this meaning justifies existence itself.

The conflict between rationality and intuition and, more generally, the head and the heart, is hardly a novel theme. The now-classic trolley problem — one of the best known modern philosophical thought experiments, introduced by British philosopher Philippa Foot — encapsulates the core problem of how numerical, utilitarian reasoning conflicts with our deepest moral intuitions. In this scenario, one has to decide whether to divert a runaway trolley car, heading towards a track on which several people are lying, to another track with just a single person. The trolley problem has been transposed into endless variations (including a popular genre of philosophical humour; Trolley problem memes, n.d.; see also Zhang, 2017, and Feldman, 2016), each with added complexities, each making the utilitarian, strictly numerical answer appear more or less reasonable, depending for example on whether or not one has to actively kill someone in order to save lives. Psychologist, philosopher and neuroscientist Joshua Greene (2015) has provided a description of the neurological roots of the conflict in terms of a "dual-process framework" with an automatic, emotionally-driven pathway and a controlled, calculating one. Various explanations have been offered for the choices people tend to make in different variations of the problem, including perceptions of intention and directness of harm. But the conflict hasn't been resolved in a way that offers any kind of clear, objective prescriptions — normative solutions — despite hopes from some philosophers, including Greene himself.

There are some other important ways that intuitions conflict with rationality in modern ethical thinking that I believe have not been adequately addressed, or even clearly and widely identified. I think these conflicts are essential to reflect on in order to see the ethical project in its entirety.

Paradoxically, while the degree to which we use rational thought may distinguish us from most non-human animals, if it dominates it can also make us less "human", less present, less feeling. What many of us most deeply value about ourselves and about life is not actually what distinguishes us from other animals, but that which we have in common with them.

Our intuitions are both a source of meaning and a source of suffering. We need our intuitions to sustain meaning, but we need rationality to spare ourselves the suffering.

The tango is a dance, not a competition between partners, and so is the interaction between intuition and rationality, despite the inherent conflict. But while the tango is a metaphor for the tension between two perspectives that both have apparent validity, it does not imply equality in the distribution of responsibility—that a correct answer lies at the midway point between the two. Neither can we expect an ethical framework to give unequivocal, objectively valid guidance or prescriptions on what to do in any given situation.

I see ethics as a process of trying to exercise compassion more effectively. I wrote this book to study this multi-layered tango, to see if we can learn to dance better through the chaos. While we may not have chosen this dance, I believe we have no alternative but to embrace it.

Can one be too transparent about ethics?

Truth and transparency are widely valued, at least in principle, although the political choices many people make these days suggest they are not valued by everyone as highly as we might like. We especially want to know facts that have a possibility of affecting us, and when we feel others are truthful and transparent with us it builds trust. But can writing truthfully and transparently about ethics be counterproductive, reducing the likelihood of achieving whatever goals the thinking points to?

I've thought about this question because some of the ideas I express are counterintuitive, and I have had concerns not only that those ideas might be rejected, but some of the more intuitively reasonable ones as well, by association. Being truthful and being persuasive regarding your goal are not always aligned. For example, there is research showing that people with strong views can actually become more certain about their views in the face of facts undermining them (Jarrett, 2018). And there is evidence that getting people to believe that there are objective moral facts may lead them to behave more "morally"—a reason to persist in using moral language and words like "ought" for the purposes of persuasion, even though it can undermine the ethical reasoning (Young & Durwin, 2013).

To the extent that there is a risk of counterproductive consequences, this again raises a question I hinted at above: what is writing such a book primarily meant to achieve? Is it about revealing the truth for truth's sake? Or is it about spreading ideas in the belief that they are actually more likely to lead to reduced suffering in the world? By writing this book, I implicitly have faith in transparency usually being the best approach, and that by fleshing out uncomfortable truths we can deal with them more authentically.

Adjusting priorities

The effective altruism movement has attracted mainly young adults aiming for a world with less suffering, fewer lives lost to preventable causes and a future of flourishing, and using their brains to make this process as efficient, rational and evidence-based as possible. Many of them are dedicating their careers and pledging a significant percentage of their income to doing the most good they can. And many philanthropists see charities run by or recommended by effective altruists as the best donation opportunities. I am closely connected to this movement and see it as a major force for good in the world, even though it has received some legitimate, sometimes harsh criticisms.

But there is a persistent, implicit conflict among members of the movement between two very different views about what matters: the reduction of suffering vs. the preservation and creation of life and happiness. These different perspectives could, in principle, lead to wildly diverging and ultimately opposing goals. Furthermore, the ethical reasoning employed in some of the arguments made by rationalists who are affiliated with this community seem in places to be based on questionable assumptions, leading to prescriptions that could potentially de-prioritise the things that matter most. This is, of course, in no way limited to the effective altruism movement, which has largely adopted mainstream consequentialist thinking focused on achieving the best outcomes.

An influential movement that places so much emphasis on rationality would ideally base its principles on a transparent, universally applicable ethical framework that roots out vestiges of conventional but potentially flawed ways of thinking about the world. And to the extent that a fully consistent ethical framework is impossible to achieve, it would be helpful to provide reasoning or guidance on how the inconsistencies within it might be addressed.

Two

Intuition and Rationality

Intuition and its roots

Intuitions can be understood as thoughts or feelings about truth, "rightness" or what matters, that arise when exposed to or assessing a situation or making a decision, without conscious reasoning. They can be deeply hardwired genetically, but they can also be acquired through both cultural exposure and life experience, and internalised as if they were hardwired. Different cultures thereby nourish moral intuitions of different strengths about what is "right" and "wrong". The very notion that there are things that we "ought" to do is perhaps our strongest moral intuition altogether.

Many of our intuitions were shaped by blind, ruthless evolutionary pressures that favoured survival, reproduction and continuity, including both the direct pursuit of self-interest (e.g. seeking mates, resources and social capital, and avoiding suffering) and pro-social behaviour (caring for others). Psychologist Jonathan Haidt's (2012) Moral Foundations Theory has been one influential attempt to identify distinct kinds of moral intuitions that vary between political tribes and cultures, with axes of care, fairness, loyalty, authority, purity and liberty. Others have attempted to develop a theory of moral intuitions that is more strongly grounded in the mathematics of cooperation and well-established behaviours with evolutionary roots, such as kin selection, tribalism and conflict resolution.

One of the most striking consequences for philosophy of the evolutionary origins of many intuitions is that it is very difficult for a brain, designed by spontaneous processes that intrinsically favour existence, to escape its own biases and arrive at counterintuitive conclusions that put its own value into question. The intuition that existence is a good thing pervades ethical inquiry, even though the intuition was not created through inherently benevolent forces. As I wrote in *The Battle for*

Compassion, "Philosophical enquiry is often constricted by an implicit need for arguments that are consistent with life being intrinsically worthwhile—a conclusion that we obviously want to arrive at but, if we are to be honest, is not foregone. This is one of our greatest taboos" (Leighton, 2011, p. 131).

We need to be transparent about our intuitions and biases whenever we identify them, no matter how self-evident they may seem, and be prepared to challenge them, especially when they conflict with arguments that we recognise as valid. In particular, we need to be wary that these biases do not cause our argumentation to become a post hoc defence of the psychological relics of past evolutionary processes. We cannot simply rubber-stamp our acting on our intuitions as "moral", nor define our acting in opposition to them to be "immoral", if we want our ethical explorations to be more meaningful than simply descriptions of actual human behaviour.

At the same time, some of these intuitions feel so essential to what it means to be human that overriding them would cause huge cognitive dissonance and frustration. There are many kinds of such intuitions that influence people's decisions and motivations, and the very strong ones obviously need to be taken into account in policy-making in order to avoid intense resistance. In this book, I will be focusing especially on our intuitions about existence, about directly causing harm and about concentrating suffering, because these are the ones that can create some of the most difficult conflicts with a rational framework with the overall aim to prevent suffering. I will also discuss intuitions that can lead us to make faulty arguments, as well as intuitions that we do indeed require for making decisions, especially when rationality runs up against a wall.

The role of rationality

Rationality is essentially the process of thinking in a way that leads to truthful conclusions. It combines the use of logical steps with the incorporation of evidence from the world in a way that is statistically valid.

Rationality is sometimes divided into "instrumental rationality", which is about achieving goals most effectively, and "epistemic rationality", which is about achieving accurate beliefs about the world (Rationality, n.d.). While this distinction may be practically relevant because it points to two often distinct ways in which rationality is used, I don't see a fundamental difference in the underlying principles. In fact, instrumental and epistemic rationality can also be seen as specific examples of each other. For example, instrumental rationality can be understood as using logic to get from A to B most effectively—

"systematised winning", as Eliezer Yudkowsky (2009) has called it. But getting from A to B could be to create an accurate model of the world, such as a universal theory of physics or a complete description of the phenomenon of consciousness. Conversely, determining the most effective way of getting from A to B could be seen as determining a very specific truth relevant to a specific situation. In other words, knowing the truth can be seen as a goal, and finding out the best way of achieving a goal can be seen as a form of truth-seeking. And in most cases we are making use of overlapping sets of tools from the same rational toolkit.

Rationality cannot provide a definitive answer to how to choose B entirely independently of intuitions. No matter how seemingly rational the process of defining B, it ultimately starts with and incorporates some intuitive motivations and assumptions, including the axioms and other principles used to build up the argument, but also—and I think this is a crucial point, especially when it comes to existential deliberations—the very decision to employ rationality altogether, and to what degree. Nonetheless, we can use a rational, more complete understanding of reality to determine goals that are as consistent as possible with that understanding, and therefore inherently more rational from a big-picture perspective. This approach could be termed "big-picture rationality", and it is often in this sense that I simply use the term "rationality". Ethics can be seen as thinking about how to live, which is about how to make decisions, and this requires using rationality to think in the largest sense possible about which goals to aim for. Goals that are inconsistent with metaphysical truths or based on an incomplete awareness of the most relevant aspects of reality could be considered irrational in a big-picture sense. Again, this is often how I am using the term "irrational". The context should make it clear when I am referring to rationality and irrationality in this deeper, existential sense, which can depart from how we label everyday decisions and actions.

What is the basis for our trust in rationality, or its incarnation in the scientific method? There is a video of Richard Dawkins explaining the justification for science—the use of rationality to understand the world, including through experimentation to generate evidence—in two or three words: "It works... bitches" (Farhad, 2013). At a purely theoretical level there is a certain circularity in his answer, since we need elements of a rational framework itself to properly determine whether something works, i.e. whether an event has been caused by a certain upstream action. The whole process of gaining trust in science was bootstrapped by our primal intuitions.

But those primal intuitions that allow us to infer causality themselves embed a rational perception of causality. This reflects the fact that some degree of rationality was hardwired into our brains through the process of evolution as an effective means of navigating and surviving in the world we live in, and is revealed through many of our intuitions. For example, that a statement cannot be both true and false at the same time, or that if A is larger than B and B is larger than C, then A is also larger than C. In other words, some simple kinds of rationality are themselves intuitive. While the intuition of causality is often mistaken, such as when people wrongly infer it from correlation, there are cases where its correctness is trivially obvious.

So people can indeed claim with certainty that the scientific method allows them to create things they would never have been able to create otherwise—that it produces results. Just as we can be fairly certain, even without conducting a large randomised trial, that jumping out of a plane without a parachute is more likely to lead to death (Alexander, 2020), we can conclude that without rational thinking and the conclusions drawn from countless scientific experiments, we would never have been able to build planes. So of course Dawkins was right.

But not all rationality is strongly intuitive, as our ancestors were not faced with complicated problems that warranted the development of a brain with more sophisticated intuitive reasoning. This kind of rationality is typified by psychologist and economics Nobel laureate Daniel Kahneman's "System 2" reasoning—a slower, more calculating mode of thinking than the intuitive "System 1" reasoning (Kahneman, 2011).

Arriving at a rational answer to a question requires that the question be clear and meaningful. Without this clarity, we might still be able to apply logical thinking in our attempt to answer it, but the answer itself might not be fully meaningful. As I will discuss shortly, I believe that the field of ethics has been plagued by the attempt to answer a question that has not been clearly defined. "What ought we to do?" already suggests that there is something we "ought" to do and we need to just find out what it is. By asking clearer questions we can arrive at clearer answers that can actually be used to stake out the ethical terrain with greater certainty.

What might appear to be the rational thing to do for oneself—for one's own wellbeing—might not be the most rational thing to do from a big-picture perspective that takes into account the metaphysical nature of reality. To the extent that ethics is based on a rational understanding of reality, it can thus conflict with a more limited kind of rationality that serves our own interests, and with our deep intuitions for self-preservation. Our desire for social status and the use of signalling to improve it may manifest itself in questionably rational positions we hold and actions we carry out, even in the name of ethics. If we keep asking "why?", we may often find the underlying ego laid bare, with its need to be loved, admired and cared for. A fully rational approach to ethics does not limit itself to thinking in terms of personal identity, but transcends any associated illusions to arrive at a more general, more universal perspective that is metaphysically coherent.

Managing expectations: the limits of rationality

Even a methodical, rational approach to ethics is fundamentally constrained by the need for some arbitrariness in deciding on specific priorities or courses of action, because there are questions — especially ones that are vaguer than they might appear — that pure rationality cannot provide unambiguous answers to, and where we still need our intuitions to help plug the holes. I will address this very important point later on in a section on comparing intensity of suffering and number of individuals suffering, where we are confronted head on with the limits to what rationality can do, despite our expectations.

More generally, attempts to apply rational decision-making to the big picture can lead down endless rabbit holes, where it seems that each answer depends on the answers to further questions related to decision theory and related mathematical disciplines. It can all be seen as a big mathematical puzzle where we are never quite sure if we have come close to solving it, or that there isn't some hidden flaw in our reasoning that falsifies our conclusions.

Additionally, as I suggested above and argued in *The Battle for Compassion*, an ethical theory with prescriptive aspirations cannot have the purity of a mathematical proof because the leap from description to prescription depends on moral intuitions, which do not have the logical status of mathematical axioms. However, I would qualify a statement I made in that book, where I wrote, "In a universe where nothing 'matters' and things just happen, the importance of relieving others' suffering cannot be proven. Unlike the self-evident importance of subjective experience to those having it, it is not even axiomatic" (Leighton, 2011, p. 82). In fact, as I will argue in these pages, the inherent need — the urgency — for others' suffering to be relieved is equivalent to the need to have one's own suffering relieved, and both needs have an axiomatic character. Whether one considers it important *to take actions* to relieve others' suffering can depend on how consistently one applies rationality, as rationality can argue for the objective importance of action and serve as a strong motivator for some people. But there is a clear sense in which the importance of relieving the suffering is inherent to the suffering itself and independent of one's own adherence to rationality.

A way out of the dilemma of not being able to arrive at pure, absolute prescriptions with a moral character is to avoid seeking morally prescriptive formulations altogether and to methodically stick to facts about reality—including subjective experience—a few ethical axioms that are self-evident, and logic. As long as we keep to this kind of argumentation, we can draw rational conclusions that will have a purely descriptive character, including determining whether an action appears consistent with rationality, and identifying the inherent urgency of a situation. Setting out this argumentation is one of the main goals of this book. Yet as soon as we confront a narrow, theoretical ethical framework with the real world to which it is meant to apply and provide guidance, intuitions come more fully into play and a passionate tango begins. A more holistic ethical framework accounts for these intuitions as part of the reality being described—though a different level of reality—and subsumes the dance itself.

One might ask, does more rationality and less intuition make the ethical framework stronger? One faulty premise can invalidate a mathematical proof or ethical framework, but what about intuitions? Is an ethical theory that depends on one unprovable intuition any more solid than an ethical theory based on two or three?

Again, I think we need to be clear about the nature of the exercise and what our expectations are. As long as we stick to the realm of facts, axioms and logic, we can draw conclusions we are reasonably certain of. As soon as we introduce intuitions that don't have a solid axiomatic quality, we are no longer in the realm of pure logic but in the messy realm of human nature. Yet we can pinpoint these intuitions and understand the role they are playing, in order to try to determine how to deal with them rationally. The intuitions will still resist any attempt to limit them, and maybe even cause us to question the basis of our rationality.

So again, ethics is still fundamentally dependent on intuitions. Even when we use logical reasoning along the way to determine priorities and make decisions, the starting point for our reasoning itself still includes intuitions of varying strengths, including about the truth and about what feels "right". It all ultimately begins with subconscious, pre-rational intuition, and intuition will still generally have the final say when it comes to implementing the conclusions, because of the huge resistance to carrying out actions that are strongly counterintuitive. This seems to be the essential nature of the tango.

Three

Ethics: What is the Question?

Understanding oughtism

To put the subsequent ideas into context, I would like to first look at some of the main ways that philosophers traditionally think about ethics and their relevance to the problem we are trying to solve. I think that a crucial starting point is to look at the use of language and how it allows moral intuitions to creep into rational discussions without being recognised as such.

It is standard in the field of ethics to use terminology like "ought" and "should", "right" and "wrong", "duty", "obligation" and "permissible", etc. In fact, ethics itself is often described as being about determining what we "ought" to do. This framing reflects our deep intuition that there is something objective called "morality" and, more specifically, that certain acts are inherently "moral" or "immoral", "right" or "wrong", and we often use these kinds of words to reflect our moral intuitions. This intuition towards endorsing moral objectivity or moral realism — the idea that there are objective moral facts or truths — is very strong.

But we need to remember that this intuition was created by the forces of evolution to shape our behaviour in ways that favoured survival and continuity. We are capable of experiencing feelings such as guilt, shame, indignation and disgust because certain behaviours were not adaptive over the course of evolution, and these feelings helped to ensure the prevention of such behaviours. These are the roots of our moral intuitions. Words like "ought", "should", "right" and "wrong" are often used to express our moral intuitions and our individual feelings. And as Jonathan Haidt has documented, different people have very different ideas about what constitutes "right" or "wrong" and may have their sense of righteousness triggered in very different situations, depending on their culture and socioeconomic class.

Morality is a product of human minds, not something that exists independently in the universe. Even mathematics, a discipline that strongly relies on logic and also stems from human minds, takes care to use "axioms" as its starting points rather than claims to absolute truth — even though axioms are about abstract concepts that appear to have obvious truth value. A discipline like ethics that is partly based on how we feel about things cannot aspire to make objective, mind-independent statements about absolute moral "rightness" or "wrongness". As philosopher Thomas Metzinger (2017a) has written, "Normative sentences have no truth-values. In objective reality, there is no deeper layer, a hidden level of normative facts... We have evolved desires, subjective preferences, and self-consciously experienced interests."

I believe that the field of ethics has been intellectually skewed by the antiquated constructs of authoritarian societal structures, including Biblical notions of "right" and "wrong". These constructs tap into our moral intuitions but obscure a larger truth, condemning us to wandering without ever reaching the Promised Land — the supposedly "correct" ethical theory. This framing of ethics, employing colloquial words that we use every day in imprecise ways, has very possibly discouraged some philosophers from taking a more scientific approach to ethics that can lead to clear, unambiguous claims. Arguments about whether the "rightness" and "wrongness" of actions lie with virtuous intentions, abidance by rules or optimal consequences can be a distraction because they place the emphasis on the labels, partly in a concurrent attempt to use the language of morality to persuade people to act in a certain way.

This thinking also imposes a perspective in which actions have a binary ethical value. Phrasing situations in terms of "moral obligation" or "duty" already influences the reflections with the assumption that there is often one "right" way to act, as if actions can be tidily sorted into one of two boxes, and only the one optimal action is "morally right". Use of the term "morally permissible" makes a similar assumption, with parallels as well to the binarity of legality and illegality.

There is a key related point, which is that labelling actions as morally "right" or "wrong" implies that every single action we take warrants moral judgement. While it's true that virtually everything we do has consequences, and that ethical thinking provides an essential basis for how we conduct our lives in general, it would be absurd to seek to label every decision and action we take, including ordinary self-interested pursuits that do nothing directly for the world, with the moral language of "rightness" and "wrongness". There are always alternative actions we could be taking, such as other ways of spending our resources that would benefit others. And limiting the use of moral labels to situations where the choices available are explicit would be arbitrary.

The whole nature of the exercise of trying to determine "right" and "wrong" seems wrong—not in a moral sense (although it might well be counterproductive), but in a rational one, in that it asks questions for which there are inherently no clearly meaningful answers.

Philosopher and author Sam Harris (2010) has claimed that science can tell us how to be moral. He is absolutely right that facts and logic can guide us in deciding what to value, and determining goals and how to go about achieving them. But in talking about the existence of right and wrong answers to questions of human flourishing, he has already defined a specific goal and then interpreted the instrumentally rational answer to how to achieve that goal as being what we "ought" to do. It's this use of moral language that, I argue, can interfere with reaching more precise and meaningful claims.

People can be rational, intuitive and compassionate to different degrees and act accordingly. To tell someone "you should do this" in a supposedly objective, moral sense isn't any more meaningful than saying "you should be more rational", "you should be more intuitive" or "you should be more compassionate". Or, for that matter, "you should be more hard-working, more effective, less depressed..." It is essentially equivalent to expressing a desire. This is very different from saying, *if* you want to be rational (and compassionate, and respect intuitions), *then* this would be a consistent action to take. We can talk about the "right" action for a specific goal, in a rational sense. If we use rationality to try to determine the goal as well, we can talk more generally about what the "right" action might be. But it's still "right" in a strictly rational sense, and needs to be qualified as such. To imply more than that—that it is objectively "right" in a moral sense—would suggest that one has a moral duty to be rational. This again falls into the trap of using moral language to try to say something more powerful but without a clear, objective meaning.

Someone adhering to moral realism might make the opposite argument and claim that being rational is precisely what one "should" do (e.g. Lord, 2017). But then I would again question what such a statement really means. Being rational *is rational* (tautologically), and it is, by definition, required for reasoning about ethics and anything else. But it doesn't follow that there is an objective "moral requirement" to be rational.

Note that a word can still *have meaning* without the meaning being *logically* precise or meaningful. Even literally meaningless words, such as in Lewis Carroll's (1871) nonsense poem "Jabberwocky", have meaning for the feelings they convey due to similarity to other words. In this respect, the word "ought", even when intended to express an objective moral judgement of an action, is not meaningless—it's just not meaningful in the objective way many people think it is. We can have a strong intuitive sense of what people mean when they use such words, but when we examine the words more rigorously, we find that they map onto something much narrower.

Words like "ought", "should", "right" and "wrong" can, indeed, still be interpreted to have more specific meanings and uses, even in an ethical context. The different uses are not mutually exclusive, and suggestions to the contrary are another example of how so much of philosophy seems to be about false disputes about the meaning of words (Leighton, 2011, pp. 12–13). For example:

- They can connote a *feeling* of moral duty and the desire to do "the right thing", including acting in alignment with one's own moral intuitions and with one's society's values. This is probably the most frequent mental phenomenon occurring when these words are used. This is not the same as simply expressing like or dislike, which is what some emotivists would claim a moral statement means. Moral intuitions feel different from simple likes or dislikes, even if they do not have an objective truth about them. A certain act can *feel* like the "right" or "wrong" thing to do. This use of the words is aligned with what expressivists and quasi-realists (van Roojen, 2018) claim moral statements actually mean.
- They can be used to persuade people to act in a certain way by appealing to their moral intuitions. This is similar to what the prescriptivist view (a form of expressivism; van Roojen, 2018) claims moral statements actually mean. This usage can be seen as a subset of the previous one, unless the attempt at persuasion is insincere and not based on actual moral intuitions.
- They can be used to indicate what course of action appears to have the most reasonable or persuasive ethical arguments—a combination of moral intuitions and rationality.
- They can also be used to indicate whether an action complies with a specific ethical theory or framework.

Once we acknowledge that these words are only meaningful in these specific ways, we can better resist the temptation to interpret them as representing broader objective truths. We might also see motivated reasoning in labelling actions with these words and then trying to establish a solid ethical framework to which they can potentially refer.

It's the last usage in the list above that may be the most precise way that the word "ought" can be used in ethics. This is the way philosophers sometimes claim to use it, although in practice it can be unclear if it is really being meant in this very narrow sense, or in a more absolute one of moral "rightness". It seems that even many philosophers use the term loosely, implying that there are objective moral truths waiting to be discovered (which appears to be a majority stance among philosophers; Bourget & Chalmers, 2020). Philosopher William MacAskill, in a Facebook post (2015) defining effective altruism, acknowledged that some are uneasy with this usage: "I'm happy, if you don't like the term 'ought', to put in some other similar word, but it's the language philosophers speak in."

This is perhaps one of the biggest problems of ethical philosophy: the fact that the word "ought" is so central to arguments and discussions, used as if the notion itself exists separately from any specific theory but with which the "correct" theory must be aligned, when in fact it is more meaningful as a specification of what a specific theory or framework concretely *implies*. For example, the brilliant philosopher Derek Parfit (1984, p. ix) wrote in the introduction to his classic book *Reasons and Persons*, "We *ought* to act in certain ways, and some ways of acting are *morally wrong*." This is very different from saying, "This ethical framework provides rules or prescriptions about how to act, and these ways of acting conflict with those prescriptions." Rather, it frames ethics as an exercise in applying labels and hugely influences the way we think about ethical issues and scenarios.

The problem is that even talking about the prescriptions of a hypothetical "true" theory of ethics implies that there *is* one such theory with clear prescriptions. Use of "ought" language also biases us towards thinking in terms of duty or obligation. We may *wish* for people to *feel* a duty or obligation, but creating that feeling is different from understanding the basis for wishing it.

It's a subtle enough point that I have also found myself doubting it at times. Can't we just talk about what we "should" ideally do in a situation where we have a moral dilemma? There are certainly situations where the answer appears glaringly obvious what the "right" thing to do would be. Furthermore, a logically correct ethical framework would presumably point to this action.

But this is what ethics feels like from the inside, from within a situation. If we really want to understand ethics more objectively, we need to resist the temptation to use this language. As we observe the often opposing pulls of rationality and intuition in even everyday situations and not just with hypothetical trolley-type problems, and also when thinking more largely about existence, we will be able to ask better questions about the ethical decision-making process if we don't expect there to be an objectively correct answer to "what ought I to do?"

An ethical framework we can have confidence in—one that is transparent, universally applicable and as precise as possible—needs to be grounded in well-defined concepts and relatively concrete notions such as happiness, suffering and even compassion. Of course, in practice it is very hard to write passionate or prescriptive texts aimed at persuasion without using words like "should". But if we do use them in an ethical context, we at least need to be clear what we mean.

Causing extreme suffering to another sentient being when it is unnecessary, such as carrying out torture out of sadistic pleasure, is as strong a candidate as any for the term "wrong". But, although we may feel outrage, if we are to be intellectually honest we must acknowledge that this framing is only meaningful as an expression of this outrage, or to convey the fact that this action contravenes essentially any existing ethical code of conduct, or in a similarly specific sense. This is not merely splitting hairs: this is being clear about what the term "wrong" really means so that we don't get drawn into using it imprecisely, especially in the usually more complex, more ambiguous situations in which we need to make decisions, and where we find ourselves heavily dependent on our intuitions rather than pure logic.

Extreme situations like the one evoked are still highly relevant as ethical reference points. In fact, ethical debates about trade-offs between suffering and happiness often focus on scenarios with low significance and then extrapolate to the extremes, rather than starting with cases that really matter and working out the most essential principles. Philosopher Peter Singer (2013), in an article in *The Guardian* on the world's first cruelty-free hamburger, wrote, "Even a staunch conservative such as Roger Scruton, who vigorously defended hunting foxes with hounds, has written that a true morality of animal welfare ought to begin from the premise that factory farming is wrong." What I am contesting is the imprecise meaning of words like "wrong" and "ought", rather than the ultimate (from a big-picture perspective) irrationality, lack of compassion and deep intuitive unacceptability of unnecessarily causing harm to others.

The perspective I am arguing for might seem closest to moral nihilism —the view that nothing is morally "right" or "wrong" (Sinnott-Armstrong, 2019), which is a form of moral anti-realism (Joyce, 2021). Not just that the truth of moral statements is culturally dependent, a view known as moral relativism (Gowans, 2021), but something much stronger, that moral statements have no truth value. Note, however, that I am not claiming that nothing matters! Or that different states of the world are equally good. "Good" and "bad", while also open to debate about how to use them, are basic descriptors of situations and subjective experience that often map directly to happiness and suffering. As philosopher Jamie Mayerfeld (1999, p. 19) wrote, "We know what it means to 'feel bad' without breaking it down into simpler elements, and we know that 'feeling bad overall' means the same as 'suffering.' That may be as far as the search for a definition can take us."

A situation that is identical to another situation except that it contains less suffering can be described as "better": it would be objectively preferable (as I will discuss in greater depth) to have a situation with less suffering. In fact, defining more broadly what constitutes "better" and "worse" is one of the main tasks of ethics. (We may, of course, also use these words in a more colloquial way, where they represent more of an emotional reaction than an ethically relevant descriptor.) It is the use of moral language to make objectively meaningful, often binary statements about people's *actions* that I object to as not having the truth value that many philosophers seem to think they have. There is a huge difference between evaluating two *situations* and determining that one is objectively better than the other, and labelling someone's *actions* as either "right" or "wrong" in a morally judgemental way—even if a situation was improved or made worse by their actions. We still need to explore what makes situations better or worse, but this is ultimately an exercise in description, not prescription in the moral realist sense I just described.

For the purposes of clarity and consistency, throughout the rest of this book I have avoided any use of the words "should", "ought", "right" or "wrong" without quotes, except where I am citing others, using them in a strictly instrumentally rational sense where a decision or action is evaluated with respect to specific goals (for example, "These are the wrong clothes for this weather" or "You should exercise to keep in shape") rather than in the sense of a moral "duty", or in a similar way.

In the rest of this chapter, I will discuss some of the most prominent ethical theories and analyse them from the perspective I have been arguing for here.

Consequentialism: impact matters

Consequentialist theories of ethics focus on the consequences of actions in determining whether actions are morally "right" or "wrong", rather than the intent behind them (Sinnott-Armstrong, 2021). As I explained in the previous section, I don't think that this moral framing is objectively meaningful if it's intended as more than an indicator of compliance with a specific theory. Even practically, there may be little objective interest in labelling an action morally or ethically "wrong" because, for example, a well-meaning donor could have had more impact elsewhere, or unwittingly did more harm than good. But what these theories are correct about is that, if we want to improve things in the world, we need to look at the consequences of our actions. Consequentialism focuses on impact.

Corporations look at consequences very carefully in measuring the impact on their bottom line of how they spend resources. NGOs are urged to measure impact as carefully as they can and are evaluated on this impact to determine their effectiveness, whatever their goal happens to be. Any effort to improve the world, however we determine the meaning of the word "improve", means focusing on consequences. And if ethics is to provide guidance on improving the world, it has to be largely focused on consequences of actions. This is true whether the measured impact is directly on what we consider to matter, or indirectly on other metrics that we expect to influence what matters. In principle, any positive impact is measurable at some level.

Actions with favourable consequences may also have some unfavourable ones that also need to be taken into consideration. If we think of consequences more broadly, some people may be very upset with certain actions otherwise considered optimal, perhaps because these actions run strongly against their moral intuitions, and these negative reactions potentially also need to be taken into account in determining the consequences of actions. This is one major reason why determining the optimal action is so difficult, and also a reason why respecting moral intuitions, translated into formal or informal rules, may be necessary for achieving optimal outcomes.

But the core principle is clear: if we want to change things for the better—even if we aren't (yet) clear what "better" actually means in practice—we need to focus on consequences. The importance of impact to ethics is practically tautological: reality matters and not just ideas. Any conception of ethics aimed at improving things in the world therefore has to be in some way consequentialist—even if we draw on ideas from other ethical theories to actually make it happen.

What consequentialism also implies is that we need some way of evaluating impact, of being able to compare two hypothetical situations and determine any improvement moving from one to the other. If this is done rigorously, it ultimately means being able to convert situations into numbers, or at least aspects of situations. We may not know *what* to count, but there will have to be something we can count, or that we can convert into numbers. This step is one of the greatest sources of messiness and confusion in ethics. I'll explore this problem in more detail further on. Next, though, let's look at utilitarianism, where numbers play an even more explicitly defined role.

Utilitarianism: impact on wellbeing matters

Utilitarianism is a more specific form of consequentialism that assesses actions in terms of "utility" or wellbeing (de Lazari-Radek & Singer, 2017). Utilitarianism has a strong appeal to rationalists, in part because it is more explicitly mathematical than consequentialism more generally, with its focus on calculating utility, and because it can appear, in theory, to promise precise results if the calculations are carried out correctly. But it is also widely rejected by others, because the prescriptions can seem so strange and deeply conflict with our intuitions—moral and other. This raises essential questions about our intuitions themselves: how much respect do we give intuitions that seem central to leading meaningful lives, and yet prevent us from having as much impact as we could?

Most discussions and arguments about ethics and morality are from the "inside" perspective, seeing morality as being about human relations and acting "correctly" towards one another, and not from the broader perspective of humans as de facto gods on a suffering-filled planet. The former perspective can cause some people to express outrage at utilitarian arguments that seem to lower the dignity of human beings, even though the objective is actually to best improve our situation on this planet. I do discuss issues with what I call "obsessive" utilitarianism in a later chapter.

There are several different varieties of utilitarianism, not all of them incompatible with one another. The classical utilitarianism of Jeremy Bentham and his successor John Stuart Mill is a hedonistic utilitarianism, which considers utility solely in terms of pleasure and pain. More recent twentieth-century variations include preference utilitarianism, which considers utility as the satisfaction of personal interests or preferences, which may encompass more than just pleasure and pain; and negative utilitarianism, which, at least in its strictest form, considers only pain or suffering to be ethically relevant (one of the key subjects of this book and discussed in much greater detail later). Most (some would argue all; MacAskill et al., n.d.) forms of utilitarianism are aggregative, in that they sum up positive and negative utility across a range of individuals. There is also a dichotomy between act utilitarianism, which classical utilitarianism generally falls under and which considers an action to be "right" if it maximises utility, and the more recently proposed rule utilitarianism, which considers an action to be "right" if it conforms to a rule that maximises utility.

Although evaluating concrete impact in terms of things that matter is essential to any useful theory of ethics meant to guide actions, I see most of these theories as being based on dubious assumptions about what matters and about the meaningfulness of aggregation. Much of this book will explore these problems, because they have such great repercussions for how we apply ethics to our world and how we set our priorities. But I would like to address act vs. rule utilitarianism here, because it reflects a general issue with ethical thinking.

The distinction between act utilitarianism and rule utilitarianism is in my view often a distraction caused by a framing issue—again, the perceived need to assign the label of "rightness" or "wrongness" to acts. The real question is whether better outcomes can be achieved by evaluating each individual potential act or by more systematically applying simple rules that facilitate decision-making. In practice, if we had to choose one approach or the other, it seems clear that better outcomes would be achieved if everyone followed agreed-upon rules or heuristics (modifiable if given a reason to update them), rather than everyone attempting to evaluate all the evidence in every case to determine the best action— including whether it represents a valid exception to any putative rule. Many of the actions most likely to have greater impact on wellbeing are likely indirect, such as systematically spreading compassionate values in society, rather than taking direct action to relieve suffering. But when people do break established rules for utilitarian reasons, the meaningful question is not whether it is "right" or "wrong". More meaningful questions are whether some rule-breaking generally leads to better outcomes, and whether tolerating some rule-breaking can lead to the collapse of a rule-based system. In a sense, it's a question of how much ethical autonomy society is prepared to delegate to individuals or to condone, and for which kinds of issues. From a consequentialist perspective, the answer lies in the results.

English philosopher R.M. Hare (1973) distinguished between a specific kind of rule utilitarianism, which is logically equivalent to act utilitarianism when the rules are sufficiently detailed to specify what to do in increasingly specific situations, and a general kind of rule utilitarianism. Describing what he has referred to as "two-level utilitarianism", he wrote that "the two kinds of utilitarianism that I have been speaking of can quite happily cohabit. We have simply to realise that they have epistemological statuses which are entirely different... When we are playing God or the ideal observer, we can legitimately employ the specific kind of rule-utilitarianism. The highly specific principles which we shall then adopt will be the utmost that we can achieve by all the detailed and careful thought that we can command, within the limitations of our knowledge and time available."

In other words, when we have the freedom to choose an approach, the one that will give the best results will depend on the amount of information we have. This is very far from labelling actions as morally "right" or "wrong", and really about how to make good decisions.

A separate ethical theory called prioritarianism is very similar to utilitarianism in that it also assesses overall "utility" or wellbeing, but it gives higher weighting to those who are worse off in determining whom to benefit with an action.

Deontology: follow the rules

Deontology, most closely associated with the philosopher Immanuel Kant and his categorical imperative—that one "should" only act according to principles that one would want to be universal laws—is the ethical view that whether an action is "right" or "wrong" depends on whether it conforms to certain rules. Again, let's strip away the notion of "right" and "wrong" and simply ask, why would we want people to follow rules? In religious societies, rules are often seen as being of divine origin, and therefore the question of why to obey them is not even to be posed. The ancient religious notion of moral duty has probably persisted even in non-religious contexts and found its way into other moral theories that are not explicitly rule-based.

Creating rules can also be a simple way of achieving desired outcomes. This use of rules is very similar to rule utilitarianism (and potentially even indistinguishable from it if it focuses just on hedonics), since it is ultimately the consequences that matter, and following the rules will generally give the best consequences in the absence of more specific information. Societies' thick books of statutes and laws are generally aimed at promoting desired consequences, even if there usually isn't a coherent, logical ethical framework on which these are based. And one of the oldest, simplest and most widespread ethical principles, The Golden Rule, discussed in greater detail further on, can be understood as aiming for a gentler, more harmonious society by asking people to consider whether they would want others to do things to them that they are contemplating doing to others. It is, in fact, closely related to the categorical imperative and the principle of generalising one's actions to others.

The other way that rules are used, by individuals as well as encoded in legislation, is to ensure that people respect widely shared moral intuitions. This usage is more complicated, because it frequently appears to contradict, rather than support, consequentialist reasoning. For example, our moral intuitions would tell us not to kill an innocent person, even if we believed we could save more lives by doing so. The most pragmatic purpose of these rules is to avoid offending, frightening or angering many members of society. From a consequentialist perspective, offending people might not always be the worst possible outcome, although doing so repeatedly in the pursuit of the best outcomes would generate tension and outrage, and probably be counterproductive.

Ignoring people's intuitions would also risk creating a very strange world that few people would want to actually live in. Finding a way to reconcile impact-focused consequentialism with intuition-respecting deontology is one of the big open questions in ethics, and again, one of the key themes I am addressing here.

Virtue ethics: be good

Virtue ethics, most commonly associated in the West with Aristotle, places the emphasis somewhere else entirely: it is about judging people's character traits rather than actions. To the extent that the focus is on labelling people, it can seem an antiquated concept as far as ethics is concerned (though still a contemporary one when it comes to tabloid journalism and the endless assaults on people's characters). From a more modern ethical perspective focused on improving the world, "virtue" only matters in the sense of whether people care or not about having positive impact on the wellbeing of others. Otherwise it is a rather hollow concept focused on ultimately superficial features.

However, spreading compassion to inspire people to care more, and promoting rationality as a way to discover the truth and be more effective, are a means of achieving impact by changing people's values. If scaled up, this may prove to be one of the most useful ways of achieving positive change. In that respect, the spirit of virtue ethics may hold the key, provided it is recognised as a means to an end rather than an end in itself.

Can any one theory be correct?

The three main categories of ethical theories described above are often seen as competing with one another because their respective proponents have usually tried to provide distinct, unambiguous answers to the question "what is morally right?", based on what I have argued is the false assumption that the question is objectively meaningful. But from a consequentialist, impact-based perspective, the different approaches can also be seen as providing answers to different questions:

- What outcomes do we want for our actions when we look at the world objectively?
- What rules can we follow to get there effectively? And what other rules do we need to follow for other, indirect reasons, such as not generating huge tensions and opposition that would ultimately undermine the ethical objectives?
- What character and ways of thinking do we want to instil in people so as to achieve the desired outcomes?

Since what matters is, arguably, ultimately related to wellbeing, some form of utilitarianism is most suitable for keeping tabs on what matters and adapting ourselves and our actions to it. Other theories can feed into utilitarianism by providing the right conditions for improving wellbeing. Adopting a form of utilitarianism as a way of making decisions doesn't require moral realism. Just as you can follow Buddhist principles without believing in supernatural phenomena and dogma (Batchelor, 1997), you can adhere to some form of utilitarianism without believing in the objective meaning of a concept like moral obligation or duty.

Nonetheless, when actions aimed at improving wellbeing conflict with strong moral intuitions and any rules that encode them, there is inherent uncertainty about how to proceed. Some philosophers, such as William MacAskill (Muehlhauser, 2014; MacAskill et al., 2020) and Nick Bostrom (2009) have proposed approaches on how to act when several different ethical theories are each accorded some probability of being "correct". MacAskill's approach is to maximise expected value (value x probability) across the different theories, while Bostrom suggested a "Parliamentary" model where each theory is represented by virtual delegates, in proportion to the probability of the theory being correct, that get to vote on specific issues. A pragmatic solution applied to real-life medical settings — perhaps not coincidentally, being used, among other places, in Switzerland, known for its consensual approach to decision-making — is to "satisfice": resolving medical ethical issues by choosing solutions that achieve an acceptable degree of alignment with each of the ethical frameworks simultaneously (Samia Hurst-Majno, personal communication).

Do any of these approaches actually help with the uncertainty I just mentioned? There's an important distinction between different kinds of ethical uncertainty. There's uncertainty that arises when there's a "correct" or rational answer but we don't know (yet) what it is, and there's uncertainty that is inherent — because there is simply no rational way to resolve an ethical question without resorting to intuitions, or because the rational solution itself runs up against our deepest moral intuitions.

The expected value and Parliamentary approaches, as described by their proponents, explicitly apply to the first kind of uncertainty. To the extent that one theory may be fundamentally "correct", I think this uncertainty can arise because we haven't dug deeply enough in trying to understand the basis for a conflict between different theories, or we need to take a different approach to thinking about ethics, as I am trying to do here. And, even if we have dug deeply, there can still be a persistent disagreement among philosophers about which theory to endorse, and some of these approaches can offer a negotiated, though imperfect, solution.

It's worth noting that the approach based on maximising expected value, mentioned above, is already rooted in consequentialist thinking, though it leaves individual theories to specify how value is to be measured and impact to be determined. It is therefore more applicable to handling uncertainty about several competing consequentialist theories than about consequentialism vs. deontology (a similar point was made by philosopher Simon Beard, 2018).

But the conflict between utilitarianism and deontology is not simply one between two theories that each has some likelihood of being the "correct" one. The need for impact—for having an effect on the world through one's actions—already implies incorporating some form of utilitarianism into the ethical framework. It is, rather, a conflict between two different perspectives, arising from two different levels or modes of being.

It's worth briefly contrasting this notion of levels with Hare's two-level utilitarianism, mentioned earlier, which he also referred to in terms of a critical level and an intuitive level (Price, 2019; Two-level utilitarianism, n.d.). Within Hare's framework, the intuitive level still explicitly aims for the best utilitarian outcomes, using simpler rules that take into account constraints including moral intuitions, whereas the intuitive level I am referring to is about strong intuitions themselves that may conflict with utilitarian reasoning.

We could still try to resolve this conflict using a utilitarian approach, one that focuses on achieving the best outcomes, and that regards the opposition of moral intuitions as an important factor that needs to be taken into account—both as a negative outcome in itself, because a world that defies all our moral intuitions would be a dystopia, and for instrumental reasons, because it could interfere with achieving desired outcomes. The rational, utilitarian approach would therefore still be leading this tango, in the pursuit of the best outcomes, but it will get nowhere without the consent of the intuitions with which it is dancing.

As an alternative approach, we could imagine starting from our moral intuitions and seeing how far we can go in a utilitarian direction before reaching a breaking point in what we find acceptable. This approach is inherently less outcome-focused and therefore, one might argue, less rational. However, it's a humanistic and probably more sustainable perspective that regards people as humans first and agents second, and it therefore needs to be taken into account as well as we search for compromises. In a sense, it adds another variation to the tango, with intuition taking the lead.

The satisficing approach appears to be a pragmatic real-word solution, with some similarities to the Parliamentary model, that goes as far as it can in satisfying the constraints of different theories, including seeking optimal outcomes while avoiding strongly counterintuitive decisions. It may be more applicable to a narrow hospital setting than to big decisions about the fate of the world, but the principle of compromise between rationality and intuitions is obviously highly relevant to larger-scale decisions as well.

Furthermore, as discussed later, in most real-life situations with their complicated combinations of hedonic states, the utilitarian approach to prioritising outcomes simply runs up against the limits of what rationality can do. In these cases, there really seems to be no other choice but to turn to our intuitions to find solutions.

Four
Ethics and Subjective Experience

Subjective experience is what makes anything matter. Feelings, thoughts, perceptions and emotions matter for their own sake, and the only reason that anything *else* matters is for its effect on them. Without subjective experience, there is nothing for anything to matter *to*!

The reference point for understanding others' subjective experience is one's own: we draw on our own experiences, real or imagined, and use them to extrapolate to what others' experiences might be like. Since these experiences are what ultimately matters, ethical decision-making needs to be based on a thorough understanding of the effects of actions or policy on subjective experience, whether in the present or distant future. It means conscious beings taking into account all other possible loci of consciousness, including ones that they do not experience as viscerally.

Note that the fact that an experience is "subjective" does not mean it is less important. We use the word "subjective" in distinct ways and this can lead to confusion. For example, when we talk about a work of art's beauty as being subjective, we mean that there is no absolute way of evaluating its beauty because beauty is relative to the person making the judgement. But when we talk about "subjective experience", we just mean that it is only viscerally knowable by the one experiencing, not that it is less real or has less objective importance. Even though different people may experience different degrees of suffering when exposed to the same circumstances—and in that respect the analogy with beauty holds—what matters intrinsically is the experience of suffering itself, not the cause of it. In this important respect, subjective experience is very real, and subjective experiences of equivalent quality and intensity matter equally.

Hedonic states and wellbeing

Hedonistic (or hedonic) utilitarians, probably the majority of utilitarian philosophers, see hedonic states as the only things that matter ethically.

There is pain or suffering, which people try to avoid, and there is pleasure or happiness, which people seek. This perspective may seem simplistic, but it corresponds to the basic attraction and avoidance behaviours that characterise so much of the natural living world and seem to have a primary quality to them. Setting aside other contributing factors of behaviour, states of being that we try to avoid must be "bad" in some way, and those we seek must be "good" in some way. This obviously doesn't mean that different states are all equally "good" or "bad", much less that ethical evaluations themselves are binary or that it is useful to apply black-and-white ethical labels to actions, as discussed earlier.

Other qualities such as justice, fairness and equality, which consequentialist theories other than hedonistic utilitarianism might also consider important to society, arguably matter for their *effect* on wellbeing—and also, less directly, because they are characteristics of the kind of world most people intuitively want to live in—but not in and of themselves. When there is a lack of justice or fairness, there may be suffering as a direct consequence, and it may cause outrage among those who see these qualities as important. These are two distinct and important consequences, but even the second consequence does not mean that justice or fairness are inherently valuable for their own sake. Hedonistic utilitarianism is, in a sense, a purer ethical philosophy, stripped of secondary elements, because it focuses on actual subjective experience, rather than on more abstract concepts that can influence it. This ethical philosophy therefore has obvious close affinity to the field of study of subjective wellbeing, a concept that integrates momentary positive and negative hedonic states (or "affect") and the more cognitive self-assessment of life satisfaction (Oishi et al., 2014). I will discuss shortly the extent to which ethics and psychology converge, and what I see as flaws or omissions in both fields.

Similarly, at a more individual level, it's sometimes argued that people want more than just pleasure and an absence of pain—that they also want so-called goods like knowledge or freedom. But the acquisition of knowledge by someone who seeks it, or a sense of freedom by just about anyone, invariably contributes to happiness or life satisfaction. If freedom didn't make people happier—if only through the feeling that their lives had more meaning—there would be no value in acquiring it for its own sake. We value freedom precisely because it increases our happiness about being alive.

A well-known thought experiment in modern philosophy, Robert Nozick's (1974) experience machine, is meant to put pure hedonism as an ethical theory into question. "People on this machine *believe* they are spending time with their friends, winning Olympic gold medals and

Nobel prizes, having sex with their favorite lovers, or doing whatever gives them the greatest balance of pleasure over pain. Although they have no real friends or lovers and actually accomplish nothing, people on the experience machine get just as much pleasure as if their beliefs were true… Since it does *not* seem irrational to refuse to hook oneself up to this machine, hedonism seems inadequate" (Sinnott-Armstrong, 2021).

My response to this puzzle is complex, though the reasoning should become even clearer later on as the ethical framework I am proposing takes shape and some of the points I make here are explained in more detail. But basically:

a. If you have chosen to enter the experience machine and then leave it later on, there could be a profound sense of unhappiness in realising that all the experiences were imaginary, like dreams, and there were no real interactions with others. Alternatively, you might find yourself filled with blissful memories that continue to infuse your life with a dreamy happiness.

b. On the other hand, if you enter the machine and never leave, whether or not your instances of pleasure correspond to real-world events is in some sense irrelevant, because you will never know that they weren't—or in any case, even if you were initially aware, you might never think about it. In a similar way, being mistakenly told about the torture and death of a loved one creates just as much suffering in the person being told, even if it did not actually happen.

c. Entering the machine guarantees never experiencing pain or suffering, and most importantly, extreme or unbearable suffering. This alone makes the choice a rational one, at least in terms of your own wellbeing.

d. The actual decision whether or not to enter the machine would usually be carried out with an illusory belief in continuous personal identity and the desire to maintain sources of meaning that are relevant to this identity, at the risk (under ordinary conditions) of otherwise feeling sadness. In other words, it is based on a very strong intuition towards survival in the real world and continuity. A decision not to enter the machine is therefore understandable, but only rational with respect to the goals of this mindset. The decisions that people actually make are not a clear, absolute guide to what matters in a larger sense.

e. A very different consideration that is ethically relevant: entering the machine turns you entirely into a locus of subjective experience and deprives you of any possibility to have net positive impact on the rest of the world, other than to eliminate your own suffering.

Preference satisfaction

As mentioned earlier, there is a version of utilitarianism that nominally focuses on something other than hedonics, namely preferences. The assumption, again, is that there are other things that people or other sentient beings can want that are ethically relevant besides pleasure or the avoidance of pain.

But what ultimately matters is still subjective experience, mental states — including the state of frustration, and more generally, how we feel — and not whether a preference, whether explicitly expressed or revealed through behaviour, is materially satisfied at some later point in time. Satisfying a preference may sometimes relieve frustration and generate a less negative hedonic state, in which case the value of doing so is readily apparent. But it's hard to justify there being any objective value if there is never any effect on hedonic wellbeing. Furthermore, preferences in the more abstract, cognitive sense are a description of the desires of higher organisms, but many sentient beings surely feel pain and seek to avoid it, without having preferences in that higher-level sense. This version of utilitarianism cannot directly address their need to avoid pain except as an implied preference.

Preference satisfaction thus seems an indirect and imprecise way of getting at the underlying, more fundamental phenomenon of wellbeing, including lack of frustration. Its ethical relevance depends on changes in a hedonic state it will achieve. This is true both for the immediate satisfaction of a preference and for delayed gratification — any future moment of happiness or a longer-term increase in wellbeing or life satisfaction that satisfying the preference is expected to achieve. The satisfaction of a preference to avoid momentary suffering or frustration is essentially the same as eliminating negative hedonic states. In fact, at the level of neuronal circuitry, negative hedonic states might even be understandable as thwarted implied preferences (Metzinger, 2003). But these are very different from cognitively held preferences. The eventual satisfaction of such longer-term preferences that were previously expressed arguably has no ethical value unless there is an increase in wellbeing associated with fulfilling them. In fact, the *act* of fulfilling them rather than their fulfilment itself may have a greater influence on wellbeing (Diener, 1984).

And many preferences are fleeting, associated with momentary states of mind rather than a stable strategy for increasing wellbeing. There is therefore even less objective necessity to expend resources trying to fulfil them.

When we respect people's preferences even though we know that fulfilling them won't make them happier, it's because we respect their autonomy to make decisions for themselves. Of course, it becomes much more complicated when their preferences impinge on others' preferences, though the same can be said for wellbeing. In general, when we prioritise preferences over hedonics, we are actually prioritising giving people what they *want* over what they *need*. Scaled up to the level of tribes and countries, this perspective on what matters is often the basis for wars and an obstacle to conflict resolution. Practical strategies for shaping a more peaceful world therefore also argue in favour of addressing people's hedonic wellbeing rather than desires they express that are largely disconnected from it — provided people are shown that this approach is in their interest.

For many of the situations that are most ethically important, preference satisfaction might better coincide with the hedonic framework, because the most urgent cases for preference satisfaction are those of extreme suffering. Yet even here, people's revealed preferences — those that become apparent through their decisions and actions — are poorly attuned to preventing the worst things from happening to them. For a wide range of other, less urgent situations, including those that involve addictive behaviour, there can be a constant tension between satisfying preferences and improving wellbeing. The divergence between preference satisfaction and wellbeing, and, in particular, the prevention of intense suffering, becomes especially important when it comes to the values we would want embedded in a future AGI. I will discuss some of these issues in more detail in the following sections that address suffering and happiness.

Interests

The concept of "interests", used by many philosophers including Peter Singer, captures the idea that sentient beings have desires and needs. Respecting their interests means respecting the specificity of their needs, whatever species they happen to belong to.

The core of a sentient being's interests is its wellbeing, in particular as it concerns pain and pleasure. I actually prefer the term "wellbeing" to "interests" as a descriptor of the fundamental concern that can be more accurately applied to all sentient beings. For example, based on their physiology, I don't believe oysters can feel pain. If they could, they would still, undoubtedly, have no mechanism for thinking about it, and be as remote from personhood as any clump of neurons can be. But any suffering they experienced would still matter. If you wanted to talk about the interests of an oyster, you could similarly talk about the interests of any system, biological or non-biological, that can potentially create a negative experience—including the interests of the universe. At the most basic level, I think it is more precise to simply think of negative and positive hedonic states that can exist, and that wellbeing is a function of these.

In practice, of course, we try to meet the needs of each individual and prevent as much suffering as possible. In this limited sense we try to meet their interests.

The notion of interests can also be extended to include other dimensions, such as the right to have one's autonomy respected, which can also be seen as a contributor to wellbeing—not having one's autonomy respected leads to frustration—but also the right to continue existing. When it includes these aspects, interests is actually a more complicated, higher-level concept than wellbeing, respecting continuous personal identity as an ethical consideration and also explicitly valuing existence. The distinction between these two components of interests is a central facet of the ethical tango, and I will address this second component in more detail later on, including in the chapters on value and especially on existence.

Suffering

There is perhaps nothing so universal and tangible as suffering. All suffering has in common subjective unpleasantness and some degree of aversiveness—the tendency or desire to avoid or escape it. This applies to both raw physical pain and psychological suffering, which may also have a strong physical component, and intensities ranging from minor to extreme. It also includes the frustration of unmet needs or wants.

There is perhaps also nothing so widely mischaracterised or ignored. Suffering is not simply suffering. The term is used to encompass a very wide range of experiences that may have very little in common, and the opacity of others' experience may prevent a full, visceral understanding. These facts make it particularly difficult to communicate through this single word the reality of experiences at the extreme end of the scale. Furthermore, studies of human wellbeing within and across societies tend to look at suffering as a low level of wellbeing, rather than as a phenomenon to be studied separately (Ortiz-Ospina & Roser, 2017; Helliwell et al., 2017). Such a framing shifts the focus away from extreme suffering, away from the phenomenon with the greatest ethical relevance.

The hot–cold empathy gap is a concept in psychology that describes how people underestimate the influence of visceral factors on their attitudes and actions. These factors can include any range of situations and experiences, such as the use of alcohol, or situations that create frustration and anger. How we feel and act is very much state-dependent, and we are very bad at empathising with states we are not currently experiencing. Most significantly here, people have trouble imagining what intense pain is like and how they would actually act if experiencing it.

Yet to carry out rational ethical thinking, we need to overcome any cognitive biases that impede our evaluation and analysis. The hot–cold empathy gap is perhaps the most essential cognitive bias to overcome because it interferes with our understanding of the most ethically relevant parameters. We must be willing to properly acquaint ourselves with the subjective reality of extreme experiences. Not just the objective reality of rare, catastrophic events we want to avoid, like an asteroid collision, but the experience of sentient beings, human and non-human, who endure excruciating suffering. Only complete knowledge, including concrete and not merely abstract awareness of these subjective experiences, can allow appropriate decisions and prioritisation.

Note that intense pain is not identical to intense suffering, though it can directly cause it. The distinction is especially clear in someone with powerful mental coping mechanisms who is able to shift their focus away from the pain. Thomas Metzinger (2017b) wrote, referencing neurophilosopher Sascha Fink, "…the sensation of pain and the emotional *affect* of unpleasantness are as distinct as hue and saturation in colour experience, and pain and suffering are clearly metaphysically independent mental phenomena…" Suffering is a state of distress that can be caused by very different phenomena that may have very little in common. But because these states are all experienced as unpleasant, we can, in principle, group them together as sharing a common ethical dimension. I address this issue in a little more detail in a later section on comparing physical pain and psychological suffering.

There is an unconscionable amount of suffering out there in the world, in the privacy of homes, in hospitals, in prisons and secret detention centres, in the streets, in industrial concentration camps and slaughterhouses that turn animals into food, and also in fields, forests and aquatic environments, where animals are ravaged by the elements, disease and predators. Much of the suffering in the world—though the proportion of total suffering remains uncertain—is caused by humans, often very directly, or ignored by them. It would be impossible to continuously take stock of just a tiny fraction of all the suffering occurring at any given instant and still manage to carry on normally with our lives, pursuing our daily pleasures within our bubbles. It would not just be overwhelming—it would be paralysing. And yet, if we want to live ethically—to think about our priorities in this world and act upon them—we need to be fully aware of it. We need to face up to all of this horrible suffering and confront it. It is not only part of the relevant reality out there, it is the most important part of reality.

The notion of urgency

The term "urgency" isn't that commonly used in writings about ethics these days. And yet, when we are looking at how to prioritise actions, there seems hardly to be a more useful concept.

There is obvious urgency in a situation where not acting quickly means that it will be too late, such as saving a child who fell into a pond from drowning (a go-to example used in ethics, popularised by Peter Singer). In other words, there is a limited time frame for useful action. Some such situations need not be ethically important, and not responding in time might be relatively inconsequential.

But there is also urgency in a situation where suffering is intense, and not acting quickly prolongs a highly distressing or intolerable situation. Someone with a mild skin irritation would obviously prefer it to be treated sooner rather than later, but it's not terribly urgent. Someone screaming in pain from terminal cancer needs pain relief urgently. The urgency is actually inherent to the suffering—a property intimately associated with it. With intense suffering there is literally an "urgent need".

To extend the above example into a metaphor, if a new hospital is being built in a region without medical facilities, the highest priority is to ensure a functioning emergency ward. But the misplaced priorities of our society, often divorced from the notion of urgency, are like a hospital expanding an already large dermatology ward to treat patients with mild skin conditions, even painting the hallways with fresh coats of bright paint, while the emergency ward has limited capacity and has to turn away victims of life-threatening trauma wounds, and the morphine stocks are allowed to run out.

One might ask whether the concept of urgency actually adds anything new to the intensity parameter that is not already there. But the point is not that urgency is a quality separate from intensity, but that it is a *facet* of intensity with an inherent call to action or change. Referring to urgency is a way of bringing attention to the fact that when there is a high intensity of suffering, there is also an inherently great need to do something about it—the intensity is not simply a neutral parameter. Without ceding to the urge to use moral language by trying to bridge "is" to "ought",[1] the concept of urgency creates a factual bridge between the passive—and incomplete—observation of a phenomenon and the associated need for active engagement. It is this need for action that makes urgency so relevant to ethics. If there's no urgency whatsoever—present or foreseeable—there's no need to change things.

An essential aspect of urgency in this sense is that it only relates to suffering—not to states of happiness or to neutral states. As philosopher H.B. Acton wrote, "…when we are moved by someone's suffering we feel called upon to help, whereas when we are moved by someone's joy there is generally no such practical urgency" (Acton & Watkins, 1963). But there is no urgency to *create* such states of joy either (Vinding, 2020a, section 1.4). It is precisely the unique urgency of relieving suffering that argues for it being the essential focus of ethics, often formalised as some variation of "negative utilitarianism", discussed later.

We can therefore reframe the description of situations as ethically "better" or "worse" in terms of how much of this kind of urgency they contain—the intensity of distress as well as the number of instances of it—though the urgency itself is a function of intensity, while the number of instances of it represents the *scale* of the problem. And in the same way that it is inherently good when suffering and the state of urgency it contains are relieved, it is inherently bad when new urgency arises. This is why not causing unnecessary harm and taking actions that will prevent future suffering from arising are inherently as important as relieving existing suffering.

Even though we think of happiness or bliss as good, it isn't inherently *ethically* good in the sense of there being an urgency to create it. This doesn't mean that it can't still lead to less suffering and be ethically good for that instrumental reason. This is often the case. It also doesn't mean that we can't *think* of it as good or that we need to stop striving for it. But this seemingly subtle distinction in the use of the word "good" shows again how important it is that we not transfer common intuitions about

---

[1] For example, Jamie Mayerfeld (1999, p. 112) wrote (italics added), "One might say: it is better if we prevent suffering. But that would be incomplete. The moral charge is missing. We need to say: we *should* prevent suffering. In the same way, it is incomplete to say that it is better if suffering does not occur. Once more the moral charge is missing. To supply it, we must say that suffering *ought* not to occur…" While I strongly share the stance that there is a fundamental need to prevent suffering, the use of moral realist language to convey this need, other than informally for the purpose of persuasion, is a point where I differ with Mayerfeld and others, for reasons I provided earlier.

words into ethical thinking without ensuring we understand precisely what we mean. Just because we have positive associations with a state-of-being doesn't imply that *creating* such states has any ethical urgency or priority.

We can see how easy it is for this flaw to have slipped into ethical thinking. The strongly intuitive notion of happiness as "good" is automatically and unquestioningly translated into an ethical notion of "good", with the implication that more good is better, and finally that there is an ethical obligation to create a better situation containing more happiness. This whole line of implicit ethical reasoning leads from an intuition about a state to an alleged duty. Nowhere along the way is the question usually posed about the hidden assumptions that caused an implied urgency to arise where there actually was none. I discuss this point in greater detail in the chapter on value.

Suffering can also coincide with happiness in "mixed states" where the nature of the urgency is less straightforward. There is always a feeling of relief when suffering disappears, and in that respect there was an underlying need or urgency. But a person experiencing such a state may still prefer it to its absence. This is not an abstract preference regarding the future, but the momentary desire to continue experiencing this mixed state rather than nothing or a state with less intense happiness. In such cases one cannot talk about the overall "badness" of the state and directly compare it with simpler states. There is ethical complexity that cannot be reduced to a single number.

The significance of extreme and unbearable suffering

There is nothing that we seek so hard to escape from as extreme suffering. We know about suffering from our own personal experiences, from extrapolation from our own experiences to imagined worse experiences, and from the observations and accounts of others. Because extreme suffering is so widespread in our world it becomes normalised, and we easily downplay its significance and deem it somehow tolerable, rather than express horror at its scale. Yet no experience cries out so powerfully for action to stop it as extreme suffering. And as Jamie Mayerfeld (1999, p. 16) wrote, "…when suffering becomes extreme, our desire for unconsciousness may enlarge into a plea for non-existence, as in Job's unforgettable appeal…"

Extreme suffering is of course not limited to torture chambers or devastating terminal illnesses. There are many causes, some of them unfortunately common, like kidney stones—which at least are limited to physical pain and not usually accompanied by a fear of dying as a consequence, although dying is in some cases seen as a relief from severe suffering.

Consciousness researcher Andrés Gómez Emilsson (2017b) wrote, "Someone described the experience of having a kidney stone as 'indistinguishable from being stabbed with a white-hot-glowing knife that's twisted into your insides non-stop for hours'." He also suggested that likely reasons why we do not hear about this are "(1) trauma often leads to suppressed memories, (2) people don't like sharing their most vulnerable moments, and (3) memory is state-dependent... you've lost a tether/handle/trigger for it, as it is an alien state-space on a wholly different scale of intensity than everyday life."

The last reason he gives echoes a point I made in *The Battle for Compassion*: "Survivors of torture or other terrible suffering are like first-hand observers, trying to communicate vivid memories that continue to haunt them... the actual victims somehow reside in the past, and the intensity of the subjective experience can be next to impossible for the survivors themselves to adequately relate" (Leighton, 2011, p. 86). It also suggests that we can experience a hot–cold empathy gap with our past selves.

Animal advocate Vincent Berraud similarly described to me his bout with kidney stones, a few hours after leaving the hospital: "10/10 pain with no hesitation. There was nothing else in the world that mattered except having the pain go away as soon as possible." He told me that he would have hit a button to stop it, without giving weight to other considerations, "unless of course I was told one of my daughters would be affected negatively if I hit the button; in this case I would have rather killed myself."

Comparing kidney stones to torture might mistakenly be seen as trivialising or relativising the seriousness of torture itself. What it does, though, is illustrate what extreme suffering feels like—even without a pronounced psychological component—how desperately and urgently people want it to stop at all costs, and how many people actually have first-hand knowledge of the severity of that kind of suffering. Imagine imposing such suffering on a vulnerable animal, or maintaining legislation that prevents a patient with terminal cancer or another condition causing excruciating pain from accessing effective medication to relieve it.

It's important to point out the issue of calibration. Some patients may consider a pain to be 10/10 if it's the worst pain they have experienced or can imagine experiencing, but it could be significantly less painful than the very worst pains that *can* actually be experienced. For this reason, what one patient might call a 10/10 pain may not represent what literally unbearable pain is like.

There are things that countless human and non-human animals have experienced in the past—over millennia, over eons—and continue to experience today, that are horrible beyond one's imagination. The worst suffering probably combines several different elements, which can include excruciating physical pain, perhaps at multiple bodily locations simultaneously; the anticipation of severe pain and bodily mutilation or harm of a potentially permanent character; the threat of imminent death; the loss of loved ones; the loss of highly cherished belongings; penetrating fear; and a feeling of lack of control. Seeing someone whom one is emotionally close to experiencing this kind of suffering may create another, particularly profound suffering.

Some suffering is so extreme as to be literally unbearable, and those experiencing it may attempt to end their lives rather than continue to endure it. A poignant example were the tragic victims of the 9/11 attacks on the World Trade Center, who leaped to their deaths to escape the flames and heat engulfing them. A less known phenomenon that plagues about 0.1% of the world's human population are cluster headaches, an excruciatingly painful medical condition—significantly worse than childbirth, migraines or kidney stones—also known as "suicide headaches" because many patients who cannot find adequate relief see no other option to escape the pain (Organisation for the Prevention of Intense Suffering, 2022).

The distinction between unbearable and extreme yet bearable suffering is somewhat nuanced. It is less a question of absolute intensity but of reaching a point where the will to survive is overtaken by the desire to end the pain or distress. For example, although the physical pain of cluster headaches is often rated 10/10 by patients, most of the time they are (fortunately) borne without an attempt to commit suicide, and the patient aims to get through it. In principle they may therefore often appear to be "bearable". Yet this apparent bearableness is also often thanks to the lack of an immediate means to do otherwise. A friend who has cluster headaches told me that if she had had a gun available, she would have killed herself a hundred times over.

There is something unique about suffering so extreme that you would do anything to stop it, even give up your own life.[2] By extension, suffering so extreme might in that instant have someone momentarily choose to end life in the universe to make it stop, if that were an option. While

---

[2] If one has the stomach for it, I recommend watching a video posted by Brian Tomasik (2016b). See also the corresponding slide presentation (Tomasik, 2016c).

someone suffering at a lower intensity — severe but still bearable — might still find some satisfaction in being alive, and the urgency to relieve the suffering would not demand non-existence, unbearable suffering is by definition a state that is worse than non-existence, and whose being brought into existence cannot be objectively justified. The qualitatively distinct nature of such experiences logically puts them in a separate category of suffering.

John Stuart Mill recognised the importance of the quality of a pleasure and not just the quantity (Macleod, 2020). This distinction is all the more relevant when it applies to suffering and the fact that extreme suffering has a different quality — its ability to entirely monopolise one's attention with agony and make existence itself impossible to endure.

A preference to die is not an absolute determining factor as to whether a state of suffering belongs in a distinctly hellish category, just a strong indicator. Someone with a lower attachment to existence, especially if they are already depressed or just generally apathetic, might well choose to end their life at a much lower level of suffering. They might still, in principle, be able to define a higher threshold of bearableness, beyond which it would be simply physically impossible for them not to opt out of existence, no matter how many benefits they were given to make staying alive attractive. Conversely, even in cases where someone in great pain clings to life — for example, if they know the pain will end soon, or they suddenly experience a simultaneous flash of joy that suppresses the suffering — relief of the suffering can still feel extremely urgent. Whether or not one prefers to die in a given situation may depend on the strength of one's underlying, baseline desire to live, which can still drain out if the suffering persists. Furthermore, most animals probably cannot explicitly contemplate suicide in response to extreme suffering, and animal suicide seems relatively rare,[3] but the experience of the suffering may be very similar to that of humans and belong in the same ethical category.

We know that the continuation of life on our planet entails the certainty of more unbearable suffering of the worst kind occurring. This does not mean that the existence of unbearable suffering is inherently justifiable. On the contrary, its existence poses the question as to whether anything else, including extreme bliss, love, meaning and the continuity of consciousness, is justifiable. By influencing technology and policies that may have long-term effects on the future, we are essentially playing God.

---

[3] But it isn't unheard of, as in the case of a terrified bull whose horns were set on fire at a Spanish festival and who killed himself by running directly into a post (Mortimer, 2017).

And if we are playing God, we need to deeply question the "value" or "obligation" of bringing into existence beings who may suffer at this level.

Understanding the reality of this kind of suffering is a critical reference point in establishing an ethical framework. It reminds us not to distract ourselves with numbers—even if it is psychologically more comfortable—to the point that we lose sight of what matters, and to keep minor suffering in perspective.

Buddhism and craving

Buddhism, which at its essence is about suffering and its alleviation, teaches that craving is one of the main sources of suffering, and that a key remedy is acceptance of what is, including contentedness with what one has. Psychological studies also show that people tend to have relatively stable hedonic set points over time that do not usually change dramatically in response to life events, and while there are strategies that work for boosting our happiness levels, continually seeking to satisfy cravings is not a recipe for long-term wellbeing (Lyubomirsky et al., 2005). The Buddhist philosophy also identifies craving as the upstream source of much of the suffering that humans inflict upon one another or permit to happen.

But much suffering has external causes that are largely independent of craving, in particular physical suffering due to disease or the elements. Animals in nature obviously do not suffer because they cannot let go of their ego. Neither does a human suffering from bone cancer. While there are effective psychological strategies for managing even extreme pain, there are limits to what inner contentedness and mindfulness can achieve, and much of the severe suffering in the world can only realistically be alleviated through actual physical intervention. Even people with drug dependence who experience intense cravings may need more than a book on Buddhism to overcome the powerful physiological mechanisms at work in their brains (though meditation can be helpful in reducing the strength of these cravings).

Furthermore, not everything we seek with intensity is a destructive escape from the present or represents a cause of future suffering. There is sometimes a fine line between craving and strong motivation. Goals are often what give meaning and happiness to our lives. The journey is often the destination, and seeking can lead to a state of flow.

Voluntary suffering

Voluntarily experienced suffering belongs in a separate category from suffering that is imposed or experienced involuntarily, because there is a subjective sense of freedom to avert it. This applies most clearly when we can exit the situation whenever we like. But even irreversible situations that we have entered voluntarily and knowingly may give us a sense of control that overrides the subjective feeling of suffering. Furthermore, sacrifices we decide to make for our own future benefit may be experienced differently from sacrifices we make for others, because we continue to anticipate experiencing future pleasure. Our sense of personal identity has a strong influence on how we interpret present suffering in the context of delayed gratification.

This sense of control is vital to how pain and other forms of suffering are subjectively perceived. Objectively equivalent painful stimuli may be experienced differently — not just quantitatively, but in some way *qualitatively* — depending on whether or not the subject could cause them to stop. Experiments have shown that subjects will endure painful stimuli for longer when they feel they have control over the situation (Litt, 1988), although at some point a threshold of unbearableness is reached.

The travails of early twentieth-century Antarctic explorers battling bitter cold and frostbite, storms, hunger, exhaustion, madness and the deaths of their team members, evoke masochism as much as steely determination (see, for example, Dash, 2012). People who have attended week-long ayahuasca retreats in South America sometimes describe hellish experiences, which they nonetheless do not regret afterwards for the beauty and profound insights gained (see, for example, the account of Zembrzuski, 2015). Adventures with their share of self-imposed misery are something we can choose to partake in or observe from the sidelines.

From a more detached perspective than one that views an individual as a unitary decision-making authority, one could understand the voluntary decision to undergo suffering as the result of different decision-making modules or patterns within an individual's brain interacting and fighting for control, and that the self-imposed suffering, even though fundamentally reduced or altered by its voluntary nature, is still perceived as unpleasant, as is the case with mixed states, mentioned earlier. So from the point of view of the universe, humans feel compelled to put themselves in very unpleasant situations in order to satisfy urges they just happen to have developed. We are prisoners of our own minds. The Antarctic explorer braving a miserable windstorm might not be particularly happy at that moment. We might still see these situations as one part of the brain tricking another part into suffering, and even consider whether it would be compassionate to protect people from themselves.

But the integrated experience is still something very different from torture, precisely because it is perceived as self-imposed. This is the difference between the Antarctic explorer and a slave labourer in a concentration camp. While it would be reasonable to protect people from entering situations where they end up crying out for relief, and government regulations and programmes can help nudge people in the direction of making better decisions for themselves (Thaler & Sunstein, 2009), voluntary suffering is inseparable from human freedom and autonomy and therefore not a primary target of ethical concern.

However, the more the suffering that is experienced is considered necessary for survival, the less "voluntary" it is and the more it resembles real suffering. This applies not only to humans. For example, crustaceans probably experience pain, but, like humans, may put up with it if the rewards are great enough (Stelling, 2014). This pain therefore represents a degree of unpleasantness that an organism feels compelled to undergo for its own longer-term wellbeing. Under the influence of a challenging environment, brains can still be lured into causing themselves to have pretty miserable experiences they entered "voluntarily" — constrained not directly by the force of other creatures, but by their own nominally autonomous decision-making in response to a life situation. The lesson is that reducing suffering in the world also means reducing the necessity for organisms, humans and non-humans, to do things that reduce their wellbeing just for the sake of survival.

Happiness and wellbeing

We all want to be happy. If not permanently blissful, at least generally content, with a sense of purpose and meaning that gives us a feeling of satisfaction with our lives, with regular moments of joy as well. This seems relatively indisputable, and a reasonable theory of ethics would accommodate these facts.

But where does happiness stand in relation to suffering? In writings and discussions about ethics, it is common to refer to happiness and suffering as if they are polar opposites. They are typically represented by the + and – ends of a single one-dimensional axis, with people in hypothetical situations allocated different numerical positions on this scale (e.g. Mayerfeld, 1999, p. 29). Degrees of happiness are talked about as if lower ones (e.g. +1 on a scale of –10 to +10) are, paradoxically, both devoid of suffering and not really very happy, and as if true happiness in the ethically most relevant sense lies at the far end of the scale.

However, it's not clear that this simple representation captures the reality of experience very well, and it doesn't fully integrate the widely accepted concept of subjective wellbeing, with its three separate elements (negative emotions or moods, positive emotions or moods, and overall life satisfaction). How it's interpreted and then plays out in ethical prescriptions has profound implications. We need to think about it all more precisely so that the way we represent wellbeing in ethics captures reality better than some of the dominant ethical paradigms, and so that we can incorporate various aspects of happiness into a coherent ethical framework that allocates priority appropriately.

I think there are several causes for confusion, including:

- There is a tendency to associate happiness with blissful emotion, rather than with the quiet contentedness that comes from having one's needs met and one's frustrations relieved.
- People are often described in ethical texts as being at some specific place on a scale of happiness and suffering, when they are often experiencing combinations of the two states — either simultaneously or sequentially.
- It often isn't clear whether happiness is meant in the sense of momentary happiness or overall life satisfaction.

My goal here is not to explore the whole science of subjective wellbeing and the contributions and interactions of various external and internal factors. What I want to explore is what it measures, how suffering is reflected in it, and how an ethical framework can take into account this model of reality.

Although subjective wellbeing has been intensively studied over the past years, many of the concepts and basic features were laid out decades ago, described in Ed Diener's 1984 review, and appear to have withstood the test of time. Here are a few key features that seem most relevant to this exploration:

- Momentary experiences can be hedonically neutral, or with various intensities of negative affect (suffering) and positive affect (happiness or bliss). Life satisfaction reflects the feeling we have when we think *about* our life — a cognitive assessment that is also coupled to emotions.
- Positive and negative affect are distinct phenomena — positive affect is not simply the absence of negative affect. However, one kind tends to suppress the other at any moment in time. Therefore, increasing happiness can itself be an effective, instrumental way of decreasing suffering — though not the worst suffering that consumes one's entire being. Similarly, reduced suffering can be perceived as an increase in happiness. The two kinds of affect can be experienced simultaneously, though it is claimed that they are rarely, if ever, both experienced at high levels (Diener & Iran-Nejad, 1986). And intensity of negative affect tends to correlate with intensity of positive affect in the same person, because of individual differences in how strongly emotions in

general are felt (Diener et al., 1985). (Of course this may not be the case, such as with a person suffering from unipolar depression.)
- Happiness is often considered as being "a preponderance of positive affect over negative affect" (Diener, 1984, p. 543). This can apply both to a single moment and to an extended period of time. But such mixed states still contain an ethically relevant aversive component.
- There are various factors that can contribute to happiness, including the satisfaction of needs; positive comparisons with others, with one's own past or with one's ideals; genetic and personality predispositions; and activities that produce the pleasurable state that psychologist Mihaly Csikszentmihalyi termed "flow", "when a person is involved in an activity that demands intense concentration and in which the person's skills and the challenge of the task are roughly equal" (Diener, 1984, p. 564).
- For those who optimistically believe that humans are fundamentally cooperative rather than competitive by nature: "Wills (1981) showed that downward comparison with less fortunate persons can increase SWB [subjective wellbeing]. Kearl (1981-1982) found that believing others live in poor circumstances can enhance one's life satisfaction. Easterlin (1974) argued persuasively that the amount of income that will satisfy people depends on the income of others in their society... Emmons et al. (1983) found that social comparison was the strongest predictor of satisfaction in most domains" (Diener, 1984, p. 567).

Daniel Kahneman concurs that life satisfaction is largely about comparisons—not just with others, but with our goals and expectations for ourselves—and that, as he said in an interview, people "actually want to maximise their satisfaction with themselves and with their lives. And that leads in completely different directions than the maximisation of happiness... Happiness feels good in the moment. But it's in the moment. What you're left with are your memories. And that's a very striking thing—that memories stay with you, and the reality of life is gone in an instant" (Stillman, 2019). It's actually the stories people tell themselves about their lives that matter to their sense of life satisfaction.

Meaning is a more complex feeling that can arise intuitively or come from reflection, in which case it is also closely tied to life satisfaction—a feeling of happiness that occurs when one thinks about one's life. Meaning can also give humans a desire to live even when they are otherwise suffering. It thus contributes both to emotional happiness and to the valuing of existence itself—a topic I will address later on.

Although life satisfaction and affect are measured answering different questions, there is clearly a close connection. If someone were in a constant state of bliss (maximum positive affect, no negative affect), the question of life satisfaction would be largely redundant: it would certainly be close to the maximum. It's not quite as clear-cut as that, as the very act of asking someone to reflect on their life might create some dissatisfaction or happiness, depending on various objective circumstances and where they turned their thoughts. In theory, one might judge one's life as objectively perfect when asked, even if one actually feels a constant discontent; or one might judge one's life as objectively average, yet still feel very happy most of the time. But generally, very high life satisfaction probably implies minimal frustration. The same applies if someone were in a constant state of extreme suffering (maximum negative affect, no positive affect): life satisfaction would be close to zero.

For all the situations in between, the measurement of life satisfaction may partly reflect the overall average level of positive and negative moments, but also the balance of positivity and negativity one feels when one turns one's attention to one's life as something to be analysed on the basis of a range of other factors. In fact, that moment of assessment of life satisfaction could *itself* be considered just another hedonic moment. If one regularly thinks about one's life in this way, then such hedonic moments may occupy much of one's time and be especially relevant. If not, then answering survey questions about life satisfaction may artificially force someone to think about their life in a way that is radically different from simply being present and living in the moment.

In any case, if life satisfaction is not maximised, which it almost never is, this usually implies at least some degree of suffering—a lingering discontent with some aspects of life that may be continuously present, or occasional bouts of more intense suffering.

So the two concepts, momentary emotion (positive or negative affect) and life satisfaction, are closely related. But which measure is more ethically relevant? The question then, according to the paradigm of urgency that I am arguing for, is, which measures best reflect suffering or its absence?

All suffering would, in principle, show up as negative affect if this were measured continuously, which of course it normally isn't. Exceptions are patients in palliative care or being treated for chronic pain or mental illness, who may be monitored specifically for intensity of pain and suffering over time.

In measures of life satisfaction, chronic or regular suffering of high intensity can be expected to show up as very low life satisfaction, but isolated acute episodes (such as kidney stones) would not. The World Happiness Report 2017 defined "misery" as life satisfaction below a certain arbitrary cut-off (Helliwell et al., 2017, chapter 5). But those suffering the most intensely are unlikely to be properly represented in country surveys of life satisfaction—neither when the data are collected, nor in the way the data are displayed. This includes people who are homeless, hospitalised for severe illnesses or imprisoned (including, for example, the 374,000 people incarcerated in the US for nonviolent drug offences on any given day; Sawyer & Wagner, 2022), and probably people in too much physical or emotional distress to fill out life satisfaction surveys. And as mentioned, general frustrations—low-level suffering—may show up as anything less than maximum life satisfaction.

So we need to measure or evaluate suffering directly to get an accurate, ethically relevant pulse reading, and especially to identify the most intense, most urgent situations. Life satisfaction doesn't do this. However, it has become a permanent fixture in the study of wellbeing, it's a more stable measure in that it depends on life circumstances that might not change that easily, and it does still give some useful information about suffering.

While there is no inherent urgency to create highly positive hedonic states for their own sake—at a theoretical, pure "hedonic zero" there is momentarily no frustration or other suffering, and just above it there is already a feeling of contentedness—such states can suppress any simultaneous suffering and also reduce any frustration or sadness that occur when one *thinks* about one's life. These positive hedonic states are therefore ethically relevant in a somewhat indirect, instrumental way. This means that characterising increasing happiness and decreasing suffering as entirely distinct interventions is, in reality, also creating a false dichotomy. But from an ethical perspective, the common denominator—the state that ultimately matters—is still suffering.

Since much of the suffering in the world is experienced by non-human animals, how does all the above relate to their happiness and suffering? It seems fair to say that most non-human animals don't cognitively evaluate their lives, but most experience positive and negative affect like humans do. Although many animals can plan ahead (building shelters, storing food, etc.), they live more in the moment without thinking about how good their lives are overall. They are also probably generally unable to mitigate their suffering through higher-level thoughts. Just as for humans, the ethically most relevant parameter is the degree of suffering they experience, and this is in principle what we would want to be able to track.

Capturing the dynamics of hedonic states

Although extreme bliss and extreme suffering are relatively pure states that are unlikely to be accompanied by their opposites, it might be the rule more than the exception that most of our everyday moods and states of being reflect a mixture of positive and negative emotions, feelings or sensations — the mixed states I mentioned above. For example, one might be in moderate pain but be very pleased to receive the company of a friend. An attempted summation of the two states might appear to yield a net affect of zero, but, in fact, the person would probably say that they are suffering *and* that they are happy. The positive and negative components retain their individual character. This feels very different from the neutral void of hedonic zero, and there is still a desire to see the suffering alleviated.

As I said above, the ethical paradigm whereby momentary wellbeing can be represented by a single positive or negative number and plotted on a simple one-dimensional axis thus seems to oversimplify a more complex phenomenon, and it potentially hides the ethically relevant parameter, suffering. Furthermore, the tendency in the ethical literature to attribute single wellbeing values to individuals (e.g. Alice is at –42 and Bob is as +12) not only oversimplifies in this way but also often blurs the distinction between life satisfaction and momentary wellbeing, and also fails to account for the dynamic quality of such measurements over time. And if such numbers are simply meant to reflect an average level of wellbeing, then they fail to capture the most intense suffering experienced, unless the suffering remains at a stable level over time.

To have graphs that fully capture reality as well as information that may be ethically relevant, we need to have two curves in parallel tracking both positive and negative affect over time. Negative affect or suffering could still be plotted on the negative part of the same vertical axis to contrast it with the curve of positive affect or happiness. The ethically important parameter remains suffering, *as actually experienced* in the presence of any simultaneous happiness that could mitigate it. And the deep troughs would represent the most ethically relevant intense suffering.

Absence of suffering: from hedonic zero to bliss

I'd like to explore a little further the idea of happiness as the absence of suffering. On the surface this idea contradicts the observation that positive and negative affect are distinct phenomena. But if there is already some degree of positive affect, the elimination of any suffering would leave just pure, low-intensity happiness in the form of contentedness. And in the absence of suffering, a momentary lack of positive affect is not in itself ethically problematic. We don't need to be blissful most of the time. It might only become problematic upon reflection and comparison with a more blissful life one could imagine having, or that one sees others having. In that case, one might well suffer from frustration and a feeling that one's own life is not worthwhile. This problem lies in large part with our deep-rooted instinct to compare ourselves with others.

Indeed, people are rarely content, especially in a world where social media flood us with enticements for social comparison, and where discontent is carefully nurtured to stimulate consumption. The gaining of happiness and the relief of discontent are actually two ways of framing what is often a similar phenomenon, which may have aspects of both — the disappearance of a frustration accompanied by a momentary release of neurotransmitters and the feeling of pleasure. Although "hedonic zero" — in the pure sense of no positive or negative affect — is a hedonically and also ethically neutral state (there is no inherent urgency to change it), it doesn't take much happiness above hedonic zero to yield a feeling of contentedness. In reality, as suggested above, a pure state of "hedonic zero" with no suffering or happiness is probably rare. There is probably always some degree of neural activity associated with happiness in the brain, and if any trace of suffering could actually be abolished, the brain would probably not be in a state of hedonic zero but in a pleasant, at least mildly positive state.

For this reason, eliminating frustration may be one of the surest ways to feel happy. Much of what we mean when we talk about people becoming happier is not actually that they are having more peak hedonic experiences, but that they are being relieved of a chronic form of suffering. It becomes even clearer, then, that determining ethical priorities is not about comparing pluses with minuses — creating happiness vs. relieving suffering — but about comparing the relief of different levels of suffering.

In an essay defending the concept of "tranquilism", Lukas Gloor (2017), a researcher at the Center on Long-Term Risk, wrote, "What matters according to tranquilism is the prevention of cravings: conscious needs to change something about the current experience. According to tranquilism, cravings are what constitutes suffering." Tranquil states, lacking tension or frustration, may seem hedonically neutral but are actually what many of us would like to achieve.

These tranquil states are equivalent to the katastematic pleasures of Epicurean philosophy, which include absence of pain ("aponia") and freedom from distress ("ataraxia"). In his Letter to Menoeceus, Epicurus (n.d.) wrote, "When we say, then, that pleasure is the end and aim, we do not mean the pleasures of the prodigal or the pleasures of sensuality, as we are understood to do by some through ignorance, prejudice, or willful misrepresentation. By pleasure we mean the absence of pain in the body and of trouble in the soul."

In the absence of any frustration or even minor discontent, there is no urgency whatsoever to change things. Since a tranquil state implies no frustration or suffering, it could translate to as much as a maximum of 10 on the life satisfaction scale and, more dynamically, potentially anywhere from 0 (that is, hedonic zero) to 10 on the positive affect scale.

Again, this is not to say that there is nothing more to happiness than non-suffering, as there is a clear distinction between non-suffering and bliss, with its associated rush of dopamine, serotonin, oxytocin and endorphins. States of bliss still feel pleasurable in a way that the mere absence of suffering doesn't. And the feeling that you would like to stay in a state forever might contain the least amount of hidden frustration or potential desire for change. But it doesn't take extreme bliss to yield a feeling of calm contentedness.

Also, the fact that there is no craving, suffering or inherent need to change when in a state of hedonic zero does not mean that this is a stable state. As just mentioned, a desire for bliss could arise from reflection and some form of fear of missing out (FOMO), especially if one is aware of others having more interesting lives, leading to a departure from hedonic zero to a state of suffering. Aiming for hedonic zero or even minor positive affect is not necessarily a good *strategy* in itself.

Similarly, the state of flow mentioned earlier is clearly more than hedonic zero, as there is a certain real pleasure in involving oneself deeply in an activity and creating meaning. And of course, there is a heightened sense of life satisfaction derived from creating meaning, although the full sense of meaning may only arise when one thinks about it and not necessarily when one is in the actual state of flow.

Mike Johnson (2016) proposed a theory of valence (hedonic tone, or intrinsic attractiveness or aversiveness) based on symmetry, further developed by his colleague Andrés Gómez Emilsson (2018, 2020). According to this theory, positive states, which they posit involve symmetrical patterns of brain activity, can be higher energy (excitement, anticipation) or lower energy (serenity, peacefulness). Although people may have an interest in experiencing the higher energy states, this model also supports the argument that there is no intrinsic urgency or need to invest energy in putting people who are in a lower-energy positive state into a higher-energy positive state, because the lower-energy state is not associated with any suffering.

The moment one compares oneself with others who appear happier, or imagines more blissful states possible, there is the risk of frustration and discontent. There is therefore, in practice, a need to either improve one's objective circumstances compared to others or learn to stop carrying out (or caring about) such comparisons. These are two very different approaches which, if scaled up, have dramatically different implications for the world we live in. In a more equal society, we might be less tempted to make social comparisons and find it easier to simply be happy with what we have.

Five

Evaluating Value

The confusion about value
and the compulsion to create it

The concept of "value" is almost as closely associated with ethics as the concepts of "right" and "wrong". Much of ethical inquiry over the millennia has been into the basis of values and a determination of what things have value or, formulated differently, what things are good. It might seem almost inconceivable to build up an ethical framework in which the concept of value is not central.

Yet if we follow the line of thinking I am suggesting and stick to ethically relevant phenomena—facts about subjective experience and especially negative hedonic states—the usefulness and even meaningfulness of the concept of "value" becomes much more limited. Some of the common uses in ethics then seem to point to something that doesn't even exist as such. And as discussed earlier in the section on urgency, when you add to this the widespread beliefs that more value is better, and that ethics is therefore about increasing value—that there is even an "ethical obligation" to do so—the resulting ethical framework appears to lack a rational grounding.

Part of the problem is due to the persistence of old ethical paradigms whose premises are not put into question. The *Stanford Encyclopedia of Philosophy*'s entry on "Intrinsic vs. Extrinsic Value" makes this point: "The question 'What is intrinsic value?' is more fundamental than the question 'What has intrinsic value?', but historically these have been treated in reverse order. For a long time, philosophers appear to have thought that the notion of intrinsic value is itself sufficiently clear to allow them to go straight to the question of what should be said to have intrinsic value" (Zimmerman & Bradley, 2019).

Another major factor, in my opinion, is the fact that the word "value" can be used in various different ways, and there can be confusion about the actual meaning intended. For example, value can mean:

1. The number attributed to a parameter ("she estimated her pain level to have a value of 6 on a scale of 0–10" or "the 2017 value of Bolivia's Gini coefficient was 44.6").
2. Something an individual or a larger group, such as a society, cares about, considers important or prioritises ("two cultures can have very different sets of values").
3. A benefit ("having a new clinic was of huge value to the community" or "algae provide value to their ecosystem").
4. To appreciate something ("they valued the initiative to combat climate change" or "the rescue chicken valued her new caregiver").
5. That something is important for its own sake ("her life has value").
6. In an economic sense, the maximum amount someone would be willing and able to pay for something ("the land was estimated to have a value of $10 million").

All of these uses, including variations of the last one, can be found in writings about ethics. Perhaps it is not surprising to see a kind of semantic drift from one meaning towards another.

It is obvious that some things can be beneficial for specific purposes. They can be considered to have *instrumental* value (or extrinsic value) in relation to that purpose. Increasing the quantities of things that are of instrumental value to wellbeing, such as a limited supply of essential medicines, is obviously ethically important, because it can help respond to the urgency of suffering. If there is no ultimate impact on the wellbeing of sentient beings, instrumental value can be seen as having no ethical relevance—it is limited to a description of usefulness for some other purpose.

A more fundamental question is what has *intrinsic* value from an ethical perspective, and what we mean by that. In the same way that nothing matters without a sentient being to perceive it or feel something about it (Leighton, 2011, 2015), we can say that nothing external to a sentient being can be said to have intrinsic value—only potential instrumental value for the wellbeing of a sentient being.

To give a common example, people widely believe that nature or the environment is intrinsically valuable. But a world made entirely of plants and microorganisms, without any sentient beings, would have value to no one—neither to itself, nor to others. It would just be molecules in space, arranged in complex patterns but without any subjective experience, and not perceived or appreciated by anyone. Complexity itself is not valuable, nor disvaluable, without there being *someone* there! And in that case, the value is instrumental for its impact on wellbeing. It's the person or animal thinking about it or experiencing it who ascribes the value—even if just implicitly—but such value disappears without an observer.

Many aspects of objective reality are known to be influenced by the very act of being observed, including in the fundamental realm of quantum mechanics. It seems ironic that some philosophers persist in believing that concepts such as beauty and meaning—experiences that so obviously arise in the mind of the observer, even if generated by external objects—might exist in some independent sense, and thereby have value that is dissociated from sentient beings.

Other concepts like knowledge, caring, diversity and justice, which individual people care about and might consider to have intrinsic value for them—as just one example of this kind of usage, a survey conducted by Spencer Greenberg, mathematician and founder of ClearerThinking.org, used the definition of something that you value *for its own sake* and not only for the effects it has (Wiblin & Harris, 2018)—can be seen as ultimately being valuable for their effect on wellbeing, or for the feeling that existence is worthwhile, and therefore actually being of instrumental value. If knowledge invariably made people unhappy, it wouldn't generally be considered valuable. In the same way that I argued earlier that gauging preferences is an indirect stand-in for measuring wellbeing, the things that people value are similarly indirect and potentially even fleeting contributors to something more fundamental.

In *The Battle for Compassion* I proposed what I called four "universal humanitarian values"—freedom, solidarity, diversity and continuity—that I suggested to be the elements of a society that meets people's needs and would be perceived as worth living in. But even then, according to the framework I am proposing here, these values would still be instrumental for their effect on wellbeing.

There's an essential distinction between a person's own feelings *about* the world around them—the importance they attribute to certain things in the world—and the nature of the actual feelings and experiences that exist *in* that world. Ethics is fundamentally about the latter. A person's feelings only matter in the sense of being one set of experiences among many in the world. Their intuitions about the intrinsic value of the world, the environment, abstract ideas, etc. matter because of how it makes them feel as individuals. What are called intrinsic values are often simply what the thinker or philosopher *personally* values.

A sentient being could be said to intrinsically value their happiness and intrinsically disvalue their suffering, because these are the basic common denominators of wellbeing. These were the basic intrinsic values proposed by Plato (n.d.), who had Socrates defend the position (depending on one's interpretation of the text) that pleasure is good and pain is bad. One might also be said to intrinsically value one's own existence, even if one is suffering, because the desire to continue existing also has a fundamental quality about it that can't obviously be reduced to something else. But we need to be very careful not to translate this formulation into a local measure of value, and then use it to perform simplistic calculations of net value, at the service of "increasing value" in the world. In fact, when you add the concept of urgency discussed earlier, it transpires that the only kind of intrinsic value that there is a *need* to create is actually the elimination of disvalue.

To claim, for example, not only that positive hedonic states have intrinsic value, but that we have a "moral obligation" to bring them into existence—by bringing new people into the world who are happy and value their own existence—because morality is about increasing value, is, I believe, unfounded. This is similar to the point I made earlier about the lack of urgency to create states we might intuitively think of as "good".

Although I cannot prove that it is the case, I have a strong suspicion that the compulsion among many rationalists and effective altruists to create value in the universe stems partly from the infiltration into ethics of mainstream economic thinking—the imperative to endlessly increase GDP and shareholder value, regardless of the consequences for suffering—because we are so inclined to think that value, however defined, is something that is fundamentally worth increasing. And classical utilitarianism provides an apparent ethical endorsement of this thinking by characterising more of a good thing as inherently better—without any obvious limits.

There's been a growing realisation in recent years that economic indicators per se are poor gauges of the overall welfare of a population—and this holds especially for the amount of intense suffering—regardless of the happiness of a rich elite. It would be especially ironic for the field of ethics, which is much more intimately concerned with wellbeing than most of economics, to persist in referring to "value" in ways that reflect the philosophy of a deeply flawed economic paradigm, rather than the actual welfare of individual, suffering beings.

So it seems that the concept of intrinsic value is actually of much more limited use than that of instrumental value. As it applies to ethics and the inherent need to change things in the world, the concept of urgency seems much more useful. We could subject the idea of creating or increasing intrinsic value to a few strong caveats:

1. Value in any meaningful ethical sense is ultimately dependent on sentient beings. This contradicts the belief that certain things are worth maintaining or increasing even in the absence of sentient beings who normally depend on them for their wellbeing.
2. Only subjective states of wellbeing or the state of existing per se can have intrinsic value *via a sentient being experiencing them*. Other values are instrumental—higher-order, one could say—for their contribution to these states.
3. Where there is no urgency, there is no need to create so-called intrinsic value. And only suffering has an inherent urgency about it. (This doesn't concern urgency in the somewhat different sense of having a limited time frame in which to act.) Decreasing disvalue—suffering—is the only strictly ethical *need* there is (subject to mitigating factors, such as respect for autonomy). I would argue that any other urges to create value stem from intuitions rooted in existence bias (the strong, widespread desire to preserve our existence, which can override other considerations) and closed individualism (the intuitive view of personal identity, discussed later) which can conflict with the core ethical need to reduce suffering. And to be clear, I am not suggesting that these strong intuitions that we all share are delusions, provided we recognise them as desires rather than true inherent *needs*.

In summary, then, the concept of urgency seems more essential to ethics, with its guidance on where and how to act on the world, than the concept of intrinsic value. I believe we need to separate the concept of intrinsic value from any need to create more of it, or else refrain from using the term altogether.

The fundamental ethical asymmetry between suffering and happiness

Some of those with a classical utilitarian inclination—who believe that suffering and happiness are both ethically relevant in similar ways and can be added up to determine overall wellbeing—will concede that happiness might be morally much less significant than suffering and carry less weight in the overall ethical calculation. Yet the idea that happiness and an "equivalent amount" of suffering differ ethically only in quantitative terms also seems nonsensical. I don't believe that you can reasonably take something powerful like intense bliss and suggest that it simply has much less weight than suffering. This approach is an attempt to arrive at a coherent ethical framework by tweaking numbers, rather than by rethinking the starting assumptions. As I suggested in the previous section, I believe that a more meaningful way of looking at things is that happiness has a *different kind* of value. It is a state of being that people may deeply value or appreciate when they are experiencing it, but it does not "demand" to be created—other than as a way of relieving a craving and preventing any suffering that might be experienced by not fulfilling this desire. Even things that we personally value do not *need* to be brought into existence (Gloor, 2016a).

Furthermore, intense suffering that exists continues to cry out for relief, even if one has chosen instead to devote resources to increasing the number of blissful people. If you acknowledge the need for us to all drop what we are doing to help a child who has fallen down a well, then you tacitly acknowledge that when there are urgent situations there is also a need to put bliss on hold. The urgent problem doesn't go away because one has chosen to attend to something else. In principle, any future situation that contains extreme suffering would place a demand on our resources until it is being dealt with effectively. A decision to turn one's attention elsewhere, away from the suffering and towards the creation of bliss, would not be due to any urgency external to oneself, but due to the rationalisation of one's own personal choices—of one's own personal desire to see more bliss in the universe, regardless of the inherent urgency to relieve suffering.

As I stated earlier in the section on urgency, suffering is a state of being that inherently demands action to alleviate it. Non-existence— emptiness—has no inherent urgency to be "alleviated" by replacing it with something else. Tranquillity, flow and bliss are all states of being that demand nothing once they exist. There is no urgency contained in the state of bliss itself. The only possible concern is any suffering that might occur afterwards once the state ends, including any sense of frustration that comes from self-reflection and a comparison with what could be—in which case one is no longer in a state of tranquillity or flow. Any minor suffering that occurs due to the bliss ending needs to be evaluated on its own terms for the degree of urgency it contains. Yet when a state of bliss ends, while it may generate some disappointment, it is rarely a cause of intense suffering. Frequently it persists in pleasant memories. Certainly there is no strong need to act during the state of bliss in order to maintain it indefinitely.

If someone were undergoing horrific torture and you gave them the choice of creating more bliss in the world or relieving their suffering, they could honestly say that their case has much higher urgency. But someone in a state of bliss could not honestly make a similar claim and demand that their bliss be maintained even if it meant not relieving extreme suffering elsewhere. Magnus Vinding (2020a, p. 87) wrote, "...one can experience extreme happiness without being tempted in the least to claim that one's experiential state warrants overriding moral priority."

Some have argued that we simply might not be aware of the possibilities for extreme bliss, either because we have not personally had the opportunity to experience it, or because we need new technology to make it possible. There is also the observation from chemically-induced states of ecstasy and altered consciousness that the happiness we normally experience may be just the tip of the iceberg. But the suggestion that some not-yet-realised degree of bliss that we aren't currently capable of imagining can compensate for even extreme suffering and tip the balance in our priorities misses the point (see also Vinding, 2020a, p. 161). Empathising with or imagining an experience in order to fully understand it is only one part of determining whether it matters—this can apply to both extreme suffering and extreme bliss. There is also the other essential part of the reflection: is there *urgency* to make it happen? Is there *urgency* to make it disappear?

There's never an urgency to create bliss out of nothing. This doesn't change with its magnitude. Again, the only apparent urgency is in the mind of the individual who is personally attracted to the idea of it. I am, too. I think we can pursue it part of the time. But there's no ethical need to create blissful sentient life, to turn stardust into pleasure. This point is all the more crucial when others are screaming for help.

Philosopher David Pearce wrote in a comment on the now-defunct Accelerating Future blog (2008), "Ultimately [the classical utilitarian's] moral commitments extend beyond a cruelty-free world to maximising bliss across the accessible universe. As it happens, I cautiously predict we will do so—probably in the guise of superintelligent bliss rather than cosmic orgasms. Yet are we morally *obliged* to convert, say, asteroids into pleasure centres as soon as nanotech allows? It's [a] cool idea; but I can't see how it's a moral obligation. Intuitively at any rate, there's nothing wrong with being a rock. Does 'obliged' here really carry the same meaning as our self-intimating obligation to abolish suffering? Or are we instead conflating two different phenomena, one morally urgent, the other motivationally inert?" I explained earlier why I choose not to use terms like "moral obligation". But Pearce hits the nail on the head with his comparison of two situations, only one of which contains urgency.

Mike Johnson has posited, "Re: the relative importance of happiness vs. suffering... I'd expect that if we can move valence research to a more formal basis, there will be an implicit answer to this embedded in the mathematics" (Ford, 2018). However, understanding the physical basis of consciousness doesn't necessarily imply a clear theory of ethics, even if we observe symmetry in the mechanisms of valence (hedonics). According to the model of valence proposed by Johnson and Gómez Emilsson, consonance in brain activity may be the signature of happiness, and dissonance the signature of suffering (Gómez Emilsson, 2017a). Conceptually and perhaps even aesthetically, we can see symmetry in the "balance" between these two signatures. But this balance or symmetry need not extend to ethics, where we actually see a necessity to strive very hard for *imbalance* in the amounts of these two kinds of conscious states through the abolition of the worst states of suffering.

If we think that an acceptable balance must exist between suffering and happiness, I believe this is in large part because our brains are strongly biased towards survival and existence, and that bias is reflected in ethical theories and the acceptance of suffering, even among the most die-hard rationalists. As Thomas Metzinger (2017b) has written, "Our deepest cognitive bias is 'existence bias', which means that we will simply do almost anything to prolong our own existence."

In practice, a life without bliss might still be a life of suffering because it could lead to a sense of emptiness and even depression. Why exist just for the sake of being content, when we know that blissful states are possible? Bliss can feel intrinsically important, it inspires, it can make life feel worth living, and we may miss it if we don't experience it regularly. This means that there can still be an ethical justification for creating it. But again, it isn't an ethical "imperative" in its own right in the sense of having inherent urgency; rather, it can matter instrumentally in preventing the suffering of sentient beings who already exist. While this might, on the surface, seem to be a nuanced distinction, it actually has huge implications for where we set our priorities, because it denies any intrinsic ethical importance—again, in the sense of urgency—to creating new happy sentient beings.

Negative utilitarianism

Negative utilitarianism is a form of utilitarianism that recognises a fundamental ethical asymmetry between reducing suffering and creating happiness, and proposes that our sole (or, depending on the version, main) ethical focus be on reducing suffering—a state of being that has inherent urgency to be relieved. The idea is most closely associated with the philosopher Karl Popper, although it appears that the term itself was proposed by the writer and educator R.N. Smart (Acton & Watkins, 1963). As some have remarked, including Brian Tomasik (2018a), an influential thinker and researcher who has written many essays exploring topics related to suffering, the term is somewhat unfortunate, potentially suggesting that it is the opposite of utilitarianism rather than a narrower form of it, and inherently not sounding very attractive as a core philosophy. But it remains the best-known technical term for a utilitarian framework focused on suffering.

It seems somehow astounding that an ethical framework that focuses on relieving misery has been largely sidelined in philosophy, rather than acclaimed. For example, philosopher Toby Ord (2013) asserted in an essay that negative utilitarianism is treated as a "non-starter" in mainstream philosophical circles, even though it appears to have been taken seriously when it was first proposed early in the second half of the twentieth century and was even the subject of a symposium.

But those who identify with negative utilitarianism or related views—who agree with placing the emphasis of ethics on reducing suffering—neither are weird, nor have strange, irrational views. On the contrary, in my own experience, self-described negative utilitarians tend invariably to be sensitive and compassionate, but also willing to bite certain rational bullets.

The standard objections are that, in its strictest form, negative utilitarianism would seem to dictate that we prioritise reducing trivial degrees of suffering over creating massive amounts of happiness, and that we seek to destroy the world as a way of eliminating all suffering. Objections like these have caused philosophers to overlook the essence of the framework, which is that there is an urgency to relieve suffering whereas there is no urgency to create bliss in people who are not suffering, or to create bliss out of nothing.

Small pains don't have the ethical relevance of intense suffering, and although absolutist, uncharitable interpretations of negative utilitarianism claim it would give priority to avoiding isolated pinpricks over making people blissful, a reasonable, practical theory of ethics based on negative utilitarianism would essentially ignore such trivial degrees of suffering. It's the urgency of relieving intense suffering that gives ethics such a dramatically important role to play in society, and that argues for a negative utilitarian-based approach. Furthermore, as long as there was intense suffering, pinpricks could be ignored even if they did have some minor ethical relevance. And if all non-trivial suffering were ever actually wiped out, it's likely that most people would actually be quite blissful, and attending to pinpricks could be seen as mopping up the final bits of residual suffering. That sounds more like a utopia.

There is also nothing particularly radical about taking stock of the vast amount of horrible suffering in the world and firmly believing that it would be better if nothing existed. Countless thoughtful, ordinary people have this sentiment. An ethical framework that focuses on what really matters can hardly be discarded because it forces some of us to confront uncomfortable truths.

It's also important to note, as philosopher Simon Knutsson (2019) has written, that even classical utilitarianism would—in theory—view the destruction of the world favourably, or prefer non-existence to existence, if the amount of suffering were viewed as outweighing the amount of happiness, or alternatively, if the world could be destroyed and rebuilt to create more happiness. The classical utilitarian inclusion of happiness as a relevant ethical factor appears to its proponents to shield it from the argument that has been unfairly levied against negative utilitarianism. But in fact, the rush by many classical utilitarians to reject negative utilitarianism based on the false belief that it—and uniquely it—implies a need for world destruction would imply, if they were logically consistent, that we need to accept the world being "net good" *as a starting point* and, on that basis, calculate in reverse the acceptable balance of happiness and suffering, rather than first try to estimate the acceptable balance and then add up all the pluses and minuses to decide if the world is actually "net good" and worth preserving. This is motivated reasoning driven by existence bias, by the intuition that existence is always good, whatever the consequences may be. An honest appraisal of the amount of suffering occurring among animals in the wild alone might be enough to tip the classical utilitarian assessment of the world towards net negative. The negative utilitarian assertion that nothing justifies all the horror contained in the world seems a lot more honest than the classical utilitarian claim, perhaps offered with a wink, that it all actually balances out.

To be fair, a classical utilitarian might accept that there isn't *currently* an acceptable balance of happiness and suffering in the world, yet claim that the net overall balance might well tip towards happiness in the future, provided we avoid going extinct and manage to create enough bliss. In fact, this argument seems to be the one most commonly heard, especially among those focused on preventing existential risks, for whom the potential of the future dwarfs suffering in the present. Of course, the argument is still based on the notion that *any* amount of extreme suffering is worth tolerating if you can eventually obtain enough future bliss, and would theoretically justify wars, genocides, torture and rape if the rewards were great enough—an argument directly contradicted by the fundamental ethical asymmetry of happiness and suffering. Even then, there doesn't appear to be any specific amount or proportion of bliss that would be claimed to justify the suffering and make existence inherently worthwhile. It seems, rather, to be taken as an article of faith that the promise of the future and the realisation of humanity's "potential" inherently justify preserving existence.

But if we return to negative utilitarianism and the world destruction argument against it: it's actually the framing of ethics itself in terms of moral realism, combined with strict utilitarianism, that can create the perception of a "moral obligation" or "duty" to bring about situations that are objectively better—that contain less urgency—regardless of any strongly counterintuitive means they might entail. Dropping the "ought" and the notion of obligation, and incorporating intuitions, makes for a more truthful and realistic framework. It allows us to assess our situation honestly and look for practical solutions without the fear of being somehow morally compelled by the God of rationality to carry out acts of destruction. In other words, the fact that strictly following negative utilitarianism might seem to lead to the conclusion that we *must* destroy the world is another refutation of moral realism, not of negative utilitarianism itself.

As I mentioned earlier, in *The Battle for Compassion*, as an answer to the world destruction criticism, I proposed a variation of negative utilitarianism that I called "negative utilitarianism *plus*", in which we simply assert our desire for continuity and refuse to destroy the planet and everything we care about in the process. This is a fundamentally different approach than pretending that all the happiness makes the suffering worthwhile. Rather, it's a pragmatic concession to one of our deepest intuitions.

I have since adopted the shorthand xNU+, with the added "x" placing particular emphasis on intense or extreme suffering, and the "+" now signifying a broader acknowledgement of deep human intuitions, including the desire to exist and to thrive, without putting the creation of happiness on the same ethical level as the reduction of suffering (Leighton, 2019b). I will discuss xNU+ in greater detail further on, including how it serves as the basis for a more holistic and pragmatic ethical framework that accommodates our intuitions, and how it avoids some of the problems of other ethical theories, including classical utilitarianism as well as traditional negative utilitarianism.

Prioritising the alleviation of suffering is hardly an unusual or counterintuitive idea. Most charities aim to relieve misery rather than build theme parks. But few mainstream thinkers or politicians have been willing to propose that we apply this principle consistently. However, in his bestselling book *Homo Deus*, historian and philosopher Yuval Noah Harari (2016) wrote, "One could argue that as long as there is a single child dying from malnutrition or a single adult killed in drug-lord warfare, humankind should focus all its efforts on combating these woes. Only once the last sword is beaten into a ploughshare should we turn our minds to the next big thing." This is essentially negative utilitarian thinking framed in a way that sounds entirely reasonable.

Negative utilitarianism can be difficult to persuade people of, in part because it demands more effort of them—to rethink strongly intuitive notions like "good" and "bad" in terms of actual necessity, and to really try to imagine what torture is like. It's not just a brief physical pain you endure knowing that in 30 seconds everything's back to normal. It's the extreme fear that horrible things may and will probably be done to you or others you care about, and enduring them, knowing that you are at the mercy of sadists, and there is no one there to help you. Surely we don't want a society where things like that are ever allowed to happen to sentient beings. But you have to be prepared to learn about such experiences, in particular the most relevant ones—those you would want to know about if they risked happening to you. Negative utilitarianism can then be seen as applying the precautionary principle, reducing as much as possible the risk of such things actually happening.

Many mainstream ethical frameworks also accord great importance to preventing or alleviating suffering, as convincingly argued by Magnus Vinding (2020a). The term "suffering-focused ethics" has gained ground as a way of placing emphasis on suffering while avoiding the potentially counterintuitive implications of negative utilitarianism and the negative connotations associated with it among some philosophers, and as a way of persuading proponents of other ethical theories to recognise the importance of preventing suffering. Yet as I have argued, negative utilitarianism appears to be the most rational starting point for an ethical framework that prioritises having maximal impact on what intrinsically matters most, based on phenomenal experience and urgency.

There's a common misconception that negative utilitarianism means that pursuing happiness has no value. It's more subtle than that. As mentioned in the previous section, happiness can still be needed for its instrumental value in preventing suffering, including the suffering that comes from feeling that life is not worth living. Negative utilitarianism stems from the inherent asymmetry in the raw states of suffering and happiness, rather than the psychology of actual human beings. Some of its most significant policy implications challenge any supposed necessity to bring new beings into existence in order that they may experience happiness, and the supposed justifiability of allowing extreme suffering to occur if accompanied by sufficient bliss, rather than the usefulness of helping people to be happier as a way to reduce the suffering in their lives.

Six

The Map and the Territory

Since ethics is, as I have argued, most fundamentally about reducing and preventing suffering, what we ultimately care about are, of course, instances of the actual phenomenon of suffering, not abstractions such as numbers. Numbers are merely a tool, though an essential one, to keep track of the suffering and all the relevant parameters associated with it (e.g. intensity, duration, number of instances), towards the goal of actually reducing it. Mathematics can be used to model our ethical thinking and apply it, but it is not mathematics that takes the lead in terms of what matters.

Because much of our thinking and argumentation is done using numbers to represent reality, it is critical that the numbers represent it accurately in every aspect that is ethically relevant. Once we have converted an experience into a number or a series of numbers, we risk overlooking any additional information about the experience that was not taken into account. It's an extremely significant step, transposing the territory onto a map, and it cannot be done lightly—especially if all our subsequent reflections are going to be based on the map, rather than continuing to remain intimately connected with the territory.

Neither can we forget that the map is only a guide, not the territory itself. As we discuss and manipulate numbers, we can fall into the trap of overlooking what the numbers represent, including the reality of extreme suffering. Numbers are abstract. Extreme suffering is as real as it gets.

As I will discuss shortly, the way numbers are sometimes actually used in ethics to represent hedonic states suggests that rather than starting from the territory itself—the actual experiences of sentient beings who feel varying degrees of suffering and happiness, often in combination—the numbers are often rooted in abstract concepts that are almost as simplistic as sad- and happy-faced emojis, replicated as many times as necessary to supposedly represent all that is ethically relevant. Before we start creating maps, we had better ensure that we really know the territory.

The mathematics of suffering

There are few things we can be as certain about in ethics as that two individuals suffering is worse than one individual suffering (the same experience at the same intensity). This principle must have axiomatic status, as it is very strongly intuitive to the level of self-evidence, and without it there is no basis for ethics through a comparison of different situations. Nick Bostrom (2006) has addressed this point through the argument that a physical copy of a brain represents a numerically distinct experience. As Brian Tomasik said in an online discussion, distilling out one of the key messages from Bostrom's paper, "if you don't think two copies matter more than one, then probably nothing we do matters." And it is not just that two instances of suffering is worse than one instance of the same suffering, but that there is a precise mathematical relationship between the two cases. The scale of one of the situations is precisely twice that of the other.

Similarly, we can be just as sure that a longer duration of suffering is worse than a shorter duration of suffering at the same intensity. It involves a greater number of moments or instances of suffering, just as two people suffering involves a greater number of instances of suffering than one person suffering. It is similarly axiomatic, on the same grounds. In practice, the actual experience of suffering taking place within a single brain may change significantly over time due to adaptation or sensitisation, so the equivalence of suffering-moments at different time points refers more to a theoretical situation, and we can't necessarily perform the same precise mathematical operations as we can with different instances of the same exact suffering.

That higher-intensity suffering is worse than lower-intensity suffering is also self-evident and axiomatic, though not in the same way. Here we are considering how the very nature of a subjective experience changes as a function of complicated summation processes in the brain, both in the qualitative nature of the experience and the perceived intensity. Even if we can, in principle, count the number of neurons firing, the relationship between the underlying neurological processes and the associated emergent experience does not lend itself to as clear a mathematical relationship between lower and higher intensities of suffering. And, most importantly, higher-intensity suffering is not simply equivalent to a multiple of lower-intensity suffering.

Reducing the suffering of the familiar, the specific and the present may always be much more intuitive, but the number of individuals spared suffering is objectively equivalent in importance, whether it is here or there. Once you accept this as axiomatically true, you logically have to accept the same conclusion for a whole range of comparisons, even if they seem much less intuitively compelling than the case of two vs. one. We could say that there is a formal equivalence between taking an action that prevents a specific individual's suffering and taking an action that will reduce the total number of individuals suffering in a group by one.

This reasoning can extend to situations where we are considering probabilities rather than certainties (discussed later in a section on "expected value"), future situations rather than present ones, and combinations of all these different scenarios, where the rational answer may seem highly counterintuitive. From a utilitarian or simply an impartial perspective, two actions with the same impact are essentially equivalent. This principle is widely used within the effective altruism community to compare possible interventions. Although slightly increasing the probability of reducing the future number of individuals suffering intensely by a small percentage but large absolute number might seem like an abstract intervention, hard logic obliges you to trust this approach as much as preventing the intense suffering of a defined individual, especially when this strategy is used consistently. The less tangible the impact of an intervention, the greater we need to rely on our trust in rationality to avoid the most harm.

When we state that two people suffering is worse than one, we might be inclined to think that it is not only the absolute difference but the percentage difference that is relevant. Is it really the same as saying that 100,000 suffering is worse than 99,999? Is the higher number in this second scenario "just as much" worse? Again, each instance of equivalent suffering matters equally, and reducing it matters equally, regardless of the background level of suffering. In this respect, the impact of reducing the amount of suffering from 100,000 individuals to 99,999 individuals is the same as reducing it from two individuals to one individual, even though, psychologically, the impact of such an intervention might feel trivial if we just look at the overall numbers.

Nonetheless, the background level of suffering against which our interventions take place reveals how effective or not we are in addressing the overall scale of the problem. For example, every animal spared a life of suffering or a horrible death matters. But a single diseased stray dog or cat rescued from the streets yields a sense of joy, whereas the rescue of a sick animal from a factory farm on which tens of thousands of others are left behind in squalor may also produce a sense of despair or futility and deepen our awareness of the extent of suffering we are up against. So even though each individual matters equally, residual suffering that we cannot reduce can appear overwhelming and affect our sense of agency and effectiveness.

Furthermore, the seemingly powerful axiomatic principles being discussed here reveal their limitations in the real world, where all other things are not equal and we are often comparing situations with different intensities and qualities of suffering and numbers of individuals. In these cases, we may find ourselves left clinging to weaker intuitions to guide us, as I will discuss in detail shortly. In fact, this is part of what makes ethics so frustrating and uncertain: that despite some solid starting assumptions, there aren't enough other axioms on which to build up a logically coherent theory that can tell us conclusively how to prioritise in any given situation—even if our explicit goal is only to reduce suffering. This is one of the main limits to rationality in ethics.[1]

To summarise, then, differences in the numbers of instances of equivalent suffering, and differences in intensities of suffering, allow comparisons between otherwise equivalent situations, sometimes in mathematically precise ways, regardless of the background level of suffering or the identifiability of specific individuals affected. Yet most situations are not otherwise equivalent, and there is usually no purely rational way of determining priorities.

Measuring suffering

Suffering is typically measured in a clinical setting through self-evaluation, often with reference to a numerical scale. This is the case for physical pain, where a numerical scale of 0–10 may be used (for example, the Mankoski pain scale, created by a patient; Mankoski, 2000), with the numbers associated with pain descriptors or visual images depicting different degrees of pain. Similar scales are used for measuring a range of other parameters associated with suffering, such as the Palliative care Outcome Scale (POS) questionnaires. Negative affect is typically measured using a scale such as the PANAS (Positive and Negative Affect Schedule) and its variations (Watson et al., 1988).

Not every measurement will be an equally good measure of suffering, and this may apply especially to some measures of negative affect, which includes such terms as "distressed", "hostile" and "irritable", but the parameters will correlate with suffering to varying degrees. Although the more sophisticated scales and questionnaires identify different

---

[1] I made a similar point in *The Battle for Compassion* (p. 138), where I discussed how easily intuitions take over in cases where we can no longer easily compare two situations.

components of suffering and are therefore useful in determining specific solutions, from a purely ethical perspective, the one feature that matters most is *how unpleasant or aversive* a state is. It is this aspect that, in principle, allows a comparison between different states and individuals, and can help us decide which states are most urgent to alleviate. But there is currently no single scale that aims to capture a unified sense of suffering across all dimensions.

Both in theory and in practice, it can be difficult to ensure that different individuals mean the same thing by the same number, as mentioned earlier. A person who has experienced extreme pain may rate lower intensity pain with a lower number than someone who has not experienced such extreme pain. Qualitative descriptors can help to standardise measurements between people.

An essential and frequently ignored or even contested feature of these scales of pain and suffering is that they are technically ordinal scales, not ratio scales based on cardinal units. That is to say, different points on a scale represent greater or lesser degrees or intensities of suffering, but the numbers are not based on a defined unit and the different points are not clear multiples of one another. One cannot say that someone suffering at level 6 on a scale of 0 to 10 (or –6 on a scale of 0 to –10) is suffering twice as much as someone at level 3, or that someone suffering at level 10 (in theory, if the scale were properly calibrated, this might represent the maximum possible suffering one can experience) is merely suffering twice as much as someone at level 5. There may be numerical trade-offs a person would be willing to make between different intensities and durations of suffering, as I will discuss later, but these cannot be determined simply by reading the positions on a scale of suffering, and trade-offs are, in any case, not a direct measure of actual intensity.

The hedonic delusion

Despite what I just wrote about pain and suffering scales being ordinal, one of the most pervasive flaws in utilitarian ethics is the notion that pleasure and pain can be represented by individual units such as "hedons" and "negative hedons" (or "dolors"), respectively, and that any degree or amount of suffering or happiness can be represented by a certain number of negative or positive hedons that could also be distributed in countless other ways among a population while maintaining an equivalent ethical significance.

This is not an accurate representation of the phenomena of pleasure (or happiness) and pain (or suffering), which are not made up of discrete units that can be added up and shifted around like apples or jellybeans. Using hedons to represent pain and pleasure is like navigating with a hugely inaccurate map of the territory, one that confuses a high mountain with many little hills. This paradigm also ignores the reality of what makes the relief of suffering ethically relevant. If a degree of pain is inconsequential to one subject, it is equally inconsequential to any number of other subjects enduring the same experience. You can run up thousands of little hills but you will never get the altitude sickness you can get on a single Himalayan mountain trek.

It is certainly true that the brain of someone in extreme pain shows much greater quantities of certain basic neurological phenomena than someone in minor pain, and there will be some mathematical relationship between the physiology and the subjective intensity. In theory, we might be able to establish some kind of underlying measure or formula based on these phenomena that closely correlates with subjective experience. The hierarchical organisation of the brain means that suffering intensity may correspond to more than just the sum total of a single basic level of neuronal firing, and reflect more complex phenomena, including increased activation of certain brain areas and groups of neurons once certain thresholds of neuronal firing are reached. There's also evidence for a logarithmic relationship between actual pain intensity (which will correlate to some degree with the number of neurons firing) and pain intensity as represented on a 0–10 pain scale (Gómez Emilsson, 2019; I make a similar point about pain scales compressing actual values in *The Battle for Compassion*, p. 85), and the quality of the pain may also change beyond certain thresholds.

In fact, when someone claims that one kind of suffering is "twice as intense" as another kind of suffering, the numerical value "two" is imprecisely pointing at an underlying physiological phenomenon. Jamie Mayerfeld (1999, p. 64) refers to this assessment of suffering intensity as a "vague cardinal measurement". A numerical comparison of two intensities of suffering is not devoid of any meaning — the higher intensity of suffering is caused by a phenomenon that is neither trivially nor orders of magnitude greater than that of the lower intensity of suffering. But because the assessment is vague, it doesn't have the typical properties of a true cardinal measurement.

But even if we used the term "hedon" to refer to this metric of an underlying physiological phenomenon, it would only have some properties of a unit, regardless of its relationship — linear, logarithmic or otherwise — with subjective experience. It would be closer to a Kelvin unit of temperature, which has a minimum value of zero and measures the average kinetic energy of a system, than to a unit of mass. We could establish a mathematical relationship between different measurements on this scale. But any given value of the metric would not create the same experience if divided up and distributed in different ways. A summation across different brains would be entirely meaningless, as neuronal firings in distinct brains don't create the experiential equivalent of the same number of neurons firing together in one single brain, through the phenomenon of "phenomenal binding" (Pearce, 2014).

When philosophers and others discussing ethics use false or at least distorted abstractions like hedons, or try to represent pleasure and pain as additive quantities on linear scales, they are disconnecting themselves from the reality of the phenomena, and from research on wellbeing and the methodology and tools that are actually used. To be useful, ethics has either to refer to the current tools, or to propose and argue for better ones — as I believe is needed in the case of suffering metrics. But it must remain closely attuned to the phenomena it points to.

Furthermore, descriptions of utilitarian ethical theories and hypothetical scenarios typically involve adding units of wellbeing (essentially hedons) to people at different existing levels of wellbeing and determining what the best outcome is. The most rigid utilitarian theories would suggest that it doesn't matter where the units are added, as the overall wellbeing increases regardless. To continue with an example I used earlier, giving 10 units of wellbeing to Alice, who is at −42 (I assume this means that she is suffering considerably) is considered ethically equivalent to giving 10 units of wellbeing to Bob, who is at +12 (presumably meaning he is not doing too badly). This is another example of the questionable approach to measuring wellbeing that I described above. Translate it to the real world of happiness psychology and worldwide life satisfaction charts and you get nonsensical policy recommendations that equate sparing the most miserable from the worst suffering with making those who are already very happy a little happier. The flawed concept of units of wellbeing or happiness thereby also conflicts with the whole notion of urgency, which I have argued is the most ethically relevant parameter.

This kind of reasoning is hardly limited to abstract ethical examples. It has infiltrated wellbeing economics, where same-sized increases in "units" of life satisfaction are sometimes considered equivalent in importance, regardless of their position on the scale, thereby disregarding the disparities in intensity of suffering. This isn't to suggest that life satisfaction isn't a valuable metric, or that interventions can't be compared in various ways, including across countries and population segments, for their impact on it—just that increasing the life satisfaction of someone at the bottom of the scale has far greater importance than a similarly large increment for someone closer to the top. Similarly problematic analyses are performed in health economics, as discussed towards the end in a section on developing a new metric for suffering.

There is a glaring contradiction in the utilitarian belief that one must trust the numbers even if the conclusion is counterintuitive — as is often the case for physics, for example, with the weird predictions of relativity theory and quantum mechanics — and the lack of rigour with which some of the ethical fundamentals have been argued for, namely, how to use numbers to represent the things that matter.

Lost in aggregation

Let me take the above reflections a little further. In utilitarian ethics, as well as in similar ethical systems such as prioritarianism, aggregation is the summing up of pleasure and pain in a population or across various situations to yield a total measure of wellbeing. This approach is widely used among classical utilitarians, not just in theory but for actual cause prioritisation, to assess the net impact of an action and compare it with alternatives.

Yet in all but the simplest cases, aggregation just doesn't stand the test of rationality. Whether it is stated explicitly or not, aggregation relies on the flawed concept of hedons or units of wellbeing, and on the idea that these units can then legitimately be simply added up or interchanged between individuals. As discussed in the last section, even if we could develop more precise metrics for suffering that allowed it to be represented with well-defined cardinal units, we still wouldn't be able to take independent, qualitatively and quantitatively distinct experiences and simply add them up or redistribute them in different ways with equivalent effect.

Aggregation drastically reduces the amount of ethically useful information by trying to sum up a complex situation made of many individuals, each with a different profile of wellbeing and experiencing a potentially diverse range of hedonic experiences, with a single number meant to represent overall "utility". For example, the Wikipedia page on prioritarianism has referred to a scenario where "Jim's well-being level is 110 (blissful); Pam's is −73 (hellish); overall well-being is 37" (Prioritarianism, 2020). This operation of assessing overall utility is not only irrational but particularly harmful when it is used to "balance out" suffering with happiness, as if they are no more than real numbers to which such operations naturally apply, rather than distinct subjective states represented *by convention* by positive and negative numbers. If taken seriously, it would mean (with a little dramatic licence) that you could take a person in severe pain, and by placing another person in the same room and giving them a bliss pill, you could ethically neutralise the situation — as if the room were empty. If the second person were blissful enough or were joined by some blissful friends, the overall situation would be considered good. And this would be despite the urgent need for action—a concept that is generally absent in most classical utilitarian thinking.

You can quantify the number of individuals experiencing any specific intensity of suffering, and you can, in principle, assign a number to the intensity if you are clear what it is the number actually represents and its limitations. You can also quantify the duration of suffering over time. But these numbers cannot all be multiplied together to yield a single meaningful number. Suffering cannot be assigned a single value like the unit of work "man-hours" (or "person-hours"), which can have the same value through different combinations of numbers of people working numbers of hours. As soon as an ethical framework turns suffering into an abstraction and disconnects the numbers from the underlying phenomena, it becomes meaningless.

Building up a science of suffering or an ethical framework based on these false assumptions is to build a house of cards, creating an illusion of rationality. And to perform calculations and make decisions on the basis of this false assumption is a huge error that can lead to enormously harmful decisions, because the highest-priority causes or situations can be overlooked or downgraded.

The belief in the ability and justifiability of aggregation stems from a deeper belief that all phenomena can be neatly quantified. Of course, at the level of physical matter as well as that of biological processes, everything that is precisely defined can, in principle, be measured and counted. The same applies to people's self-evaluations of their own subjective states. But there can be confusion in interpreting what the actual phenomenon is that we are counting. This is certainly reinforced by the way expressions such as "amount of suffering" are used.

It's been argued that negative utilitarianism can fall into the same trap of aggregation as classical utilitarianism. For example, Animal Ethics, an important advocacy organisation that produces high-quality texts about animal welfare, has written that "negative utilitarianism operates in a similar manner to standard utilitarianism because it only considers a total amount and not its distribution" (Animal Ethics, 2020).

But this need not at all be the case. Despite the common belief to the contrary, utilitarianism does not necessarily require aggregation. The chapter on consequentialism in the *Stanford Encyclopedia of Philosophy* states, "By dropping one or more of those [original] claims, descendants of utilitarianism can construct a wide variety of moral theories. Advocates of these theories often call them consequentialism rather than utilitarianism so that their theories will not be subject to refutation by association with the classic utilitarian theory" (Sinnott-Armstrong, 2021). In other words, some forms of hedonistic consequentialism could also be considered as non-classical utilitarianism.

To properly represent a situation without losing the minimal ethically relevant information, you need a graph that shows the number of individuals suffering at each intensity, and also a way of showing the evolution of that graph over a given duration of time. This contains far more information than summing up each situation with a single number, but it offers the possibility to compare different situations in meaningful ways. In principle, even a few statistical values that provided information about the shape of a population's hedonic curve could be useful as an approximation of the overall complexity from which key information could be estimated. Even without such statistical tools at our disposal, we can retain the essence of negative utilitarianism but constrain the calculus to comparing like with like, focusing especially on the most intense suffering and not aggregating instances of suffering into a single number.

Seven

Determining Priorities

Intensity vs. instances:
the essence of uncertainty

I have argued above that the total suffering in a situation cannot simply be aggregated to yield a single number, and we need a more complex representation that retains all the relevant information. But is there any rational way to determine our priorities when we compare situations with different numbers of individuals suffering at different intensities for different durations?

I believe that this is one of the biggest dilemmas in ethics. As I suggested earlier, we find that the usefulness of our axioms—in particular, that two instances of suffering is worse than one equivalent instance of suffering, and that higher-intensity suffering is worse than lower-intensity suffering—hits its limits, because most situations and choices involve often complex mixtures of numbers of instances and intensities.

If we could interconvert intensity of suffering and instances or duration of suffering, we could solve the problem. But there is no *objective* way to make such a conversion. We can only make subjectively acceptable personal trade-offs for ourselves, and reasonably presume that similar voluntary trade-offs would be made by most other people for themselves. The impossibility of an objective conversion is perhaps the very essence of ethical uncertainty. The problem is not solvable with pure rationality! Whenever we make such a conversion, we are trying to satisfy our intuitions. Derek Parfit made a similar observation: "When two painful ordeals differ greatly in both their length and their intensity, there are no precise truths about whether, and by how much, one of these pains would be worse" (Parfit, 2016).

Importantly, as I briefly mentioned earlier, while urgency is a function of the intensity of suffering, it is not a function of the number of individuals suffering. One single person with terminal cancer does not have any less of an urgent need for morphine than 10 such people. The more individuals, the greater the *size* or the *scale* of the problem—not the urgency. How we *feel* about a situation and how motivated we actually are to act are different from the urgency of the situation as experienced by each individual who is suffering.

Although similar intensities of suffering might be ethically equivalent, at significantly different intensities there can also be qualitative differences that reflect how consuming the suffering is and how much it distracts from being able to focus on other things, function and enjoy life. The Mankoski pain scale illustrates how different intensities of pain impact life quality. As actually experienced, they are not simply multiples of each other.

Yet given a choice between two very different situations that need intervention, our intuitions might kick in and tell us to favour a large number of individuals suffering more moderately, rather than a small number suffering more intensely (e.g. Mayerfeld, 1999, p. 182). Or we might be unsure what to do.

For example, given a choice between providing relief to someone suffering from pain at the level 7/10 and someone suffering from pain at the level 5/10, it is clear that attending to the first person has priority. But what do we do if there are 100 people suffering from pain at the level 5/10 that we could help? There is a significant difference between these levels: according to the Mankoski scale, at 5/10 the pain is strong and cannot be ignored for long, but at 7/10 it is difficult to even concentrate or sleep. The former can be treated with a strong non-prescription drug, whereas the latter requires morphine. So if forced by circumstances to make a choice about how to use resources, do we acquire paracetamol for 100 people or morphine for one person?

One way of thinking about the problem is to ask, do these two situations belong to the same category of suffering or to different categories of suffering? It seems clear that 7/10 pain that interferes with the ability to concentrate or sleep is in a qualitatively distinct category from 5/10 pain. There are aspects to this level of suffering that the lower level of suffering does not have and that are directly associated with its severity.

So what could cause our internal ethical scale to tip and favour those suffering less intensely? It's a somewhat nebulous intuition based on our sensitivities to two distinct variables—intensity and number of individuals—and what "feels right", perhaps similar to an abstract image of suffering as a quantity that grows the more individuals are affected. And the decision might *feel* perfectly rational.

In the tango between rationality and intuition, it seems that in these complex situations it is intuition that is confidently leading the dance, though observers may fail to notice the actual dynamics, believing that rationality is still doing the leading. The satisfaction of carrying out precise utilitarian calculations in a seemingly purely rational fashion is actually something of a self-delusion.

This doesn't mean that such decisions are actually *irrational* either. We tend to assume that any decision can be made rationally, and if it isn't, that the decision is irrational. But if we are making decisions that don't have a clear rational process available, we can only claim that they aren't (fully) rational — that they are at least partly "arational" — not that they are irrational. They can remain reasonable decisions, as we are dependent mainly on our intuitions to guide us.

However, if the differences in intensity are great enough to clearly represent qualitatively very disparate, barely overlapping categories of suffering with very different levels of urgency, the notion of suffering may not properly apply in the same way to both situations, and an intuition to favour a greater number of individuals suffering at the lower intensity can seem *rationally unjustifiable*. That is, when the natures of the phenomena are sufficiently different, accepting a trade-off may actually appear to *conflict* with rationality.

Brian Tomasik, who has an admirable willingness to defend controversial ethical positions in the name of consistency, has similarly suggested, on the basis of pure numbers of organisms and several assumptions, that zooplankton might have a higher amount of total suffering than fish and whales ($-2.5*10^{17}$ vs. $-2.6*10^{16}$; Tomasik, 2016a). This assertion depends on aggregating potentially very different intensities and categories of suffering to yield single numbers. Used as a tool to determine priorities, it would suggest that the scale of the problem of zooplankton suffering is an order of magnitude greater than that of fish suffering. But as I have just explained, I strongly disagree with the meaningfulness of this approach.

At the level of the individual, given the choice, someone might choose to personally experience more intense (though still bearable) suffering for a short period of time rather than less intense suffering for a longer period of time. If they have experienced two different intensities of suffering, they could even attempt to establish some kind of numerical ratio between intensity and duration. And duration is closely related to number of instances, as the two are interchangeable in contributing to an overall measure of consciousness-moments over time. Does this mean that there may actually also be some way of interconverting intensity and number of instances?

Two scenarios that we would voluntarily trade off against each other are fundamentally different from metaphysically equivalent situations. Such decisions do *not* make the experiences "equivalent" or mean that they contain "the same amount of suffering". They are just decisions that someone may make at a given point in time, based on their subjective evaluation of two scenarios and, perhaps, the story they tell themselves about the suffering they are enduring. They are based in part on conflicting desires to be free of more intense suffering and to be free of any suffering altogether. For example, an intense *but bearable* and relatively short pain may produce the thought, "This really sucks, I hope it stops soon." A less intense pain that goes on for a long time may produce the initial thought, "This is unpleasant", but eventually yield the thought, "This is seriously impeding my quality of life—I would rather get it over and done with, even if the pain is worse." On reflection, especially if one had repeated exposure to the two situations as a basis for comparison, one might clearly prefer one situation over the other.

The trade-off an individual might make for themselves could well extend to others with a similar perspective on intensity and time. If there were two specific scenarios involving duration and intensity of suffering where most people were indifferent as to which one they experienced, this could even become a reference for policy-making. This does *not* mean that two such situations are formally equivalent in terms of "amount" of suffering: they are simply equally acceptable to people under defined conditions.

An additional factor that comes into play, briefly mentioned earlier, is that there might also be changes in the subjective perception of intensity over time. When suffering is experienced for a long time, two things can happen in practice. There may be adaptation, where the individual learns strategies to cope with the suffering and lessen its perceived intensity, as some people do with chronic pain. Or there may be sensitisation, where the suffering builds up, even causing people to lose their mind, as can happen to prisoners placed for long periods in solitary confinement. So a longer period of suffering can potentially lead to either increased or decreased intensity. Successive moments in the life of a human being are not independent consciousness-moments, and suffering that persists can be experienced very differently over time. The hypothetical condition of constant suffering intensity cannot be met in the real world, as we are not one-dimensional experience machines, and we evaluate our suffering with respect to our lives and existence.

For this reason, slicing up a duration of suffering into moments of constant intensity that can be formally redistributed among other brains as separate instances of suffering is only possible in an imaginary world of simplified, unreflective human beings with no memories. Of course, such fictitious human beings wouldn't be able to make trade-offs to begin with, either. And the same applies to the reverse operation, that is, concentrating suffering in one brain.

In practice, a given duration of suffering could indeed be distributed among a greater number of people for shorter periods of time in a way that was generally viewed as acceptable, because it would be seen as distributing a fixed burden of suffering more fairly (again, with the caveat that one person's experience of suffering may evolve over time, complicating this thought experiment). The reverse operation, concentrating suffering in one person, would mostly not be viewed as acceptable, because it would be seen as grossly unfair (I discuss this more later on). It logically follows from the two previous operations—the personally acceptable trade-off between intensity and duration, and the acceptable attempt to distribute the suffering more evenly among more people for shorter durations—that it would be viewed as equally acceptable for many people to experience low-intensity suffering instead of one person experiencing intense suffering for a similar period of time—again, as a way of distributing the burden of suffering rather than concentrating it. But this conversion between intensity and number of instances is based on intuitions, including the desire not to concentrate suffering, and not on any formal equivalence.

It goes without saying that the long-term consequences of any experience that causes suffering need to be factored in as well, as they would reduce the willingness of anyone to undergo such experiences. The hypothetical torture found in many thought experiments that leaves no trace and only causes suffering while carried out is very different from actual torture and rape that can leave lifelong physical and emotional scars.

Comparing physical pain and psychological suffering

The suffering caused by severe physical pain has an inherent psychological component—a feeling of distress that would be captured in a measurement of negative affect—and there is also evidence for a shared affective component with psychological suffering that relies on the same underlying neural circuitry (Eisenberger, 2012). But it is still qualitatively very different from forms of suffering that are primarily psychological, such as deep depression or severe personality disorders. How then can we compare two qualitatively very different kinds of suffering if we are forced to prioritise resources? Can we plot them on a single scale of suffering? What is the common ethical dimension on which we can compare them?

Striving to answer a question like this that might at first seem unanswerable obliges us to return again to the concept of urgency. The raw intensity of the experience, its domination of one's existence and the inherent urge to be free of it—its aversiveness—remain the most relevant ethical considerations, whether the suffering is of physical origin or psychological.

Someone who experiences two sources of suffering, one physical and one psychological, might be able to express which one they would prefer to be rid of, and thereby help establish a ranking. This is similar to how people who have suffered different kinds of physical pain can rank them in intensity and thereby provide a more absolute assessment of intensity (see Burish et al., 2021, Figure 1).

But it's not clear that people can always give meaningful answers as to what is worse when the experiences are so different. The clearest ethical overlap between physical and psychological suffering is probably at the extreme end of the intensity scale, where the suffering in the moment overwhelms the desire to live. While the actual experiences of extreme physical pain and extreme psychological suffering still cannot be equated, there is probably a similar mechanism in operation when they override the survival instinct, in which case both might be considered unbearable.

Lower levels of suffering, which can include depression and loss but also chronic physical pain, might also yield existential thoughts over the longer term about whether life itself feels worthwhile, and therefore also be more readily comparable on this dimension. Other qualitative dimensions, such as the ability to function, could also help to normalise suffering ratings across different experiences.

On the other hand, there are situations that seem almost impossible to compare, especially when they pit the momentary unbearableness of an experience with a general sense of life being unbearable. For example, how can you compare the horrible pain of a cluster headache with the devastating loss of a child? In theory, virtually any parent would choose to endure the pain of cluster headaches over losing their own child. This is surely based not only on an implicit comparison of the momentary intensities of their own suffering, but on the long-term feeling of emptiness and hopelessness that can arise when one loses a child, and probably even more so, on the deeply rooted and powerful intuition to prioritise the wellbeing of one's child above all else. Yet some cluster headache patients choose to end their lives over continuing to live with the pain. These situations are therefore on the verge of unbearableness in different ways.

The actual decisions made by society about where to prioritise resources do not currently reflect the degree of tolerability of various experiences. But while thought experiments such as the one above may seem to depict unlikely scenarios, reflective policymakers may well be forced into making difficult decisions as they grapple with different aspects of badness, including extreme physical pain and the anguish of profound loss and hopelessness.

Unbearable suffering as an ethical tipping point

I have referred repeatedly to extreme or unbearable suffering, arguing that it can be considered a different category of suffering, in an even more fundamental way than distinct levels of less intense suffering. Although the notion that unbearable suffering cannot be "outweighed" doesn't quite seem to have the strength of a self-evident ethical axiom, there is something uniquely "bad" about bringing into existence an inherently unbearable state.

Some thinkers are uncomfortable with applying a threshold in ethics — of treating differently two similar situations, such as two degrees of what might seem to be the same basic phenomenon, rather than applying a continuous function. The argument is sometimes made, including in Toby Ord's essay on negative utilitarianism, that defining such a threshold is both arbitrary and irrational, because the difference between the two sides of the threshold may be imperceptible.

But that argument is clearly flawed. Two adjacent levels might be imperceptibly different, but two that are slightly further removed from one another might be perceptibly so, in which case the threshold could be considered to encompass a zone. It doesn't matter if you can't consistently identify a precise point where you notice a difference in intensity — the change can occur over the zone. And two situations that are quantitatively far enough apart on one parameter can warrant different treatment. One could imagine a function that slowly changes the treatment as a function of the level of that parameter, or instead apply a seemingly arbitrary but practical threshold, as is done in defining acceptably safe speed limits for road traffic, for example.

Two situations that differ quantitatively may also differ qualitatively in a profound way. This applies in countless situations outside of ethics. For example, adding enough CO_2 to the atmosphere can result in a climactic tipping point — even if we can't identify a single CO_2 molecule that causes such a point to be crossed. On a smaller scale, if I drink a few glasses of water I may feel rehydrated, whereas if I drink 10 litres in a short space of time I may die of water toxicity (Ballantyne, 2007). Somewhere between those two quantities there is an approximate threshold beyond which I risk dying. There may be a zone between healthy and lethal in which the risk of dying steadily climbs, and to be safe we can set the safety threshold at the lower level or below.

In fact, the existence of a qualitative difference—in the last example, actually dying; in the case of unbearable suffering, it could be defined as *choosing* to die—means that there really is a tipping point that defines a hugely perceptible difference.

Magnus Vinding, who similarly believes in classifying extreme suffering separately, has also argued that sometimes you actually can identify that "one molecule", so to speak, that causes the tipping point to be reached: "One might argue that such a discrete jump seems 'weird' and counterintuitive, yet I would argue that it shouldn't. We see many such jumps in nature, from the energy levels of atoms to the breaking point of Hooke's law: you can keep on stretching a spring, and the force with which it pulls will approximately be proportional to how far you stretch it—up to a point, the point where the spring snaps. I do not find it counterintuitive to say that gradually making the degree of suffering worse is like gradually stretching a spring: at some point, continuity breaks down, your otherwise reasonably valid framework of description and measurement no longer applies" (Vinding, 2016).

As I suggested earlier, what is considered unbearable may depend on the individual, the circumstances and competing motivations, though beyond some intensity probably everyone would hit a button to make the suffering stop, even if it meant ending their life.

The basic things that matter in ethics are often simple, and they get diluted or lost through abstractions. Minor pain and suffering are unfortunate but we often can and want to put up with them in small doses. Truly unbearable suffering is not something that anyone can voluntarily put up with.

If there are trade-offs between intensity of suffering and numbers of individuals that might still seem intuitively reasonable for lower degrees of suffering, such trade-offs seem intuitively much harder to justify when they include a situation involving unbearable suffering. And they certainly have even less claim to rationality because of the greater qualitative distinction between the experiences. Yet some people persist in asserting the contrary, based on the same flawed assumptions.

For example, there's a certain now-classic scenario referred to occasionally in rationalist circles discussing ethics, called "torture vs. dust specks". The original question posed by Eliezer Yudkowsky (2007) was whether you would prefer one person to be tortured for 50 years, or an extremely large number of people to receive a just noticeable irritation in the form of a speck of dust in the eye. (The large number was 3^^^3, which looks not that impressive, but the notation actually means something inconceivably large, dwarfing by far the number of atoms in the universe; see the reference for details.) A surprisingly large minority of rationalists surveyed (including Yudkowsky himself) preferred to have the person tortured (Alexander, 2012). The argument is that 3^^^3 is such a large number that even though the dust speck is a very minor degree of suffering, in sufficient quantities it adds up to the equivalent of a long period of torture.

I find this scenario a perfect example of much that is wrong—in the rational sense—in the way many rationalists think about suffering, how they use numbers to represent experiences, and how they argue about ethics. The experiences of a dust speck in the eye and torture are entirely different animals. Not one of the 3^^^3 people with dust specks would feel any of the urgent need for help or relief that a person being tortured would feel. And if it's not that bad for one individual, it's not that bad for many individuals. One could even imagine all of them agreeing, shouting out in deafening unison, that the potential victim must not be tortured.

Of course, if a single person had a huge number of dust specks in their eye, the experience might be torturous, or at least highly unpleasant. But that is not the scenario.

I suspect that the reason many would make the choice mentioned is partly due to a linguistic convention obscuring differences in semantics: that by using the word "suffering" to encompass a wide range of experiences, we can be misled into thinking that they are all just different amounts of an identical thing, when there are clearly fundamental ways in which they differ, in terms of areas of the brain that are activated, distinct neurological phenomena, and the raw nature of the experience. There is a qualitative difference between unbearable and bearable suffering, and also between suffering that dramatically affects one's quality of life and minor suffering that is inconsequential because it is just a discomfort. The fact that we might label them all "suffering" because they have some degree of aversiveness is not a basis for regarding them as fundamentally interchangeable.

I think that a scenario I suggested above may be useful to extend: that whenever there is a large group of people suffering in different ways, we simulate—and ideally, actually carry out, if possible—a dialogue among all of them, where each one is made aware of the intensity of the suffering of all the others, and a conclusion is reached about whose suffering is attended to in the most rational and caring way possible. It can be seen as a form of collaborative negotiation where the intuitive view of personal identity cedes some space to the metaphysically accurate view that sees continuous, distinct personal identity as an illusion (these views can be termed "closed individualism" and "empty individualism", respectively, and are discussed shortly in a section on personal identity). Those suffering unbearably would probably always be attended to as urgently as possible, whereas for different intensities of bearable suffering that were qualitatively more similar to one another, an arrangement would be reached that all could agree to. This arrangement isn't to be mistaken as revealing a rock-solid, objective ethical truth about how to prioritise, but it suggests how shared awareness of subjective reality can lead to acceptable practical solutions.

Of course, it's possible that someone suffering significantly though bearably might have difficulty agreeing to persist with their own suffering just because others were suffering much more intensely. There is always potential tension between people's capacity to take a fully objective perspective on their identity that puts aside their own ego, and the natural tendency not to want to feel like a martyr or scapegoat. But even given these constraints, it wouldn't be reasonable to prioritise lower intensities of suffering when those suffering at that level would *themselves* acknowledge the higher priority of someone suffering unbearably.

Some rationalists would say that if you wouldn't choose a single instance of torture over a huge number of dust specks, then you are refusing to bite the bullet of rationality through a supposed failure of the imagination—an inability to understand how large a number 3^^^3 is. But they are missing the point! Those who would choose torture are the ones who refuse to bite a more rational bullet because the focus on numbers is obscuring a basic difference in *category* of phenomenon. A thousand musicians playing individually during rehearsal will never recreate the phenomenon of the harmonious sound of an orchestra unless you bring them together in one concert hall. While both belong to the category of music, they are different in the category of effect they create.

Now, if the intensity of the more minor suffering were to become much more significant than a dust speck, the distinction might appear less obvious. To extend the last analogy, we might then be comparing an orchestra with a small chamber ensemble. But a major qualitative difference persists, and bearableness remains a significant threshold.

If we consider extreme and, in particular, unbearable suffering to belong in an ethically distinct category, would this justify putting all our resources into preventing a single case of unbearable suffering (let's say, 10/10 where 10 was calibrated to be truly unbearable) rather than a very large number of cases of moderate or even severe suffering (let's say 6/10 or 8/10)? For example, would we prefer to save one person from being horribly tortured, perhaps by carrying out a successful campaign to petition a repressive foreign government, or treat 1,000 people with a very painful though still bearable form of bone cancer by securing them morphine? The unique "badness" of unbearable suffering might argue for the former. Jamie Mayerfeld (1999, p. 183) concurs, at least when the difference in intensity is large enough, writing, "The severe torture of one person seems worse than the painful frustration of *any* number of people." But at some point, the amount of resources needed and the number of others left suffering would make it highly counterintuitive, to the point of seeming absurd. Peter Singer (2002) has argued that it would, in fact, be an absurdity for a society to spend all its resources on bringing one member above the minimum entitlement level before it spends anything at all on raising the welfare level of anyone else, no matter how big a difference the resources could make to everyone else in society. Although he was not explicitly comparing unbearable with less intense suffering, one can see how his intuition could extend even to more extreme cases. Huge numbers of people experiencing suffering close to the limit of bearableness would represent a very strong competing call to action.

But as is the case where we are comparing less extreme intensities of suffering, any such decision to shift a society's priorities is not inherently rational. It is simply an intuition that, at some point, a large enough number of individuals suffering at a lower but still severe level warrant our attention instead. This thought experiment illustrates how our decision-making, even when explicitly intended to be as rational and ethical as possible, finds itself seeking to minimise the tension that arises from counterintuitive outcomes, especially when even pure rationality fails to yield definitive answers.

The very fact that we are forced to take decisions that could involve tolerating the intolerable is a reflection of the quagmire we find ourselves in on this planet, not an argument that the intolerable *is* ever actually tolerable.

Ironically, one of the arguments thrown at people who view ethics as being most essentially about reducing suffering, and who therefore naturally gravitate towards negative utilitarianism, is that they might theoretically commit all kinds of horrible actions if the numbers dictated it, such as torturing people to avoid a sufficiently large number of minor pains elsewhere (see comments in Stafforini, 2013). Not only would this kind of reasoning be deeply flawed, as I have just discussed, but it seems much more prevalent among classical utilitarians, who are prone to counting everything and throwing it into a single pot, and who are more willing to overlook suffering in order to create bliss. Negative utilitarians, on the other hand, are drawn to the philosophy precisely because of how horrifying they consider extreme suffering such as torture, and not because of a strict theoretical belief that even pinpricks and minor pains are a relevant ethical concern.

7. Determining Priorities

Expected value and cause prioritisation

Expected value is a basic formula—at its core: value x probability—that allows one to calculate the net value one can expect to achieve, on average, over multiple, independent occurrences of an event. Under these circumstances, maximising expected value will tend to yield the biggest returns in terms of value. It is most obviously applicable to cases where the probability is not negligible, and an event with value associated with it has a likelihood of occurring in the real world given enough time. As mentioned earlier, the concept of expected value is widely used within the effective altruism community as a tool for maximising the overall impact of altruistic actions and interventions despite risk and uncertainty.

How does it apply to suffering? If we see our goal as being to prevent as much intense suffering as possible from occurring in the world or even the universe throughout time, then the concept of probability is very relevant. We are mainly focused not on alleviating the suffering of identifiable individuals, but on reducing the total number of individuals suffering, or the number of moments of intense suffering, and we are rationally obliged to compare the probabilities of various events and their impact in terms of suffering. Applying this approach repeatedly will lead to greater impact over time.

Given the argument I made earlier that intrinsic value is a concept with limited usefulness for ethics, that urgency is a more central concept and that only suffering has urgency associated with it, instead of talking about maximising expected value it might be more precise to talk about "minimising expected disvalue". Although I will stick to the more common terminology, this is actually the ethically relevant sense in which I mean it. And even then, as I have made clear earlier, I am not suggesting that we can sum up an entire situation with a single measure of disvalue, nor an intervention with a single measure of expected value. But it is an approach that can help us to compare the impact of different interventions.

Our minds like certainty. If you asked me whether I would rather eliminate 1% of the suffering in the world with 100% certainty, or 100% of the suffering with 1% probability, I would probably go for the first option, even if the impact is equivalent in terms of expected value. That's intuition speaking, in a case where there is no clearly rational basis for a preference. Not only do we like certainty, but it also feels very good to be able to point to concrete impact—to be able to say, my actions helped *these* individuals. But if the amount of suffering being eliminated in the first option were reduced to 0.5%, I would surely switch my preference to the second option, which would have the higher expected value. In fact, for these kinds of decisions, provided we can obtain accurate probability estimates, expected value is the approach that is likely to have the greatest impact in the world if applied consistently, and that is a good reason to promote it.

However, among many effective altruists and others who identify as rationalists, there is often a use of expected value as more than just a tool but as the *key parameter* on which all rational decision-making hinges. I believe that this is conceptually to mistake the means for the end. Maximising expected value isn't an "ethical imperative" of the universe the way $E = mc^2$ is a law of physics. It's a rational heuristic that works in many cases, rather than a goal in itself. Focusing just on suffering, I would therefore suggest that rather than saying that one's goal is to minimise the *expected disvalue* of intense suffering in the universe, one's goal is to minimise the *amount* of intense suffering in the universe, using expected value as a strategic tool.

I'll discuss some other issues around expected value in later sections, especially in a section on the potential suffering of insects and other invertebrates.

Eight

Suffering and the Illusion of Separateness

The true nature of personal identity

Historically, ethics has concerned the way we interact with other people, including through the decisions we make as individuals and as a society. In its focus on "the other", ethics is about mitigating the pure pursuit of self-interest and caring for others' wellbeing as well. This framing is based on a conventional understanding of the nature of our relationship with the other.

But a deep exploration of personal identity puts into question the idea of ethics being about selflessness, because it puts into question the very idea of a "self" altogether and points to the profound metaphysical connection that exists between all moments of consciousness. It suggests that a more comprehensive and universally applicable theory of ethics focus not simply on the welfare of any individual physical being but, more fundamentally, on the quality of subjective experience wherever and whenever it exists. This approach might, in principle, allow us to arrive at a purer theory of ethics based on consciousness-moments that doesn't depend as much on intuitions and illusions.

In *The Battle for Compassion* (pp. 63–73), I devoted a chapter to the topic of personal identity, and to the illusion that it is something distinct, continuous and stable—a highly intuitive view that has been termed "closed individualism" by philosopher Daniel Kolak (2004; see also Gómez Emilsson, 2015, 2018). I discussed the fact that our own personal identities change over time during the course of our lives, and also that we are less distinct from one another than we might think—that we are all actually variations on a single theme, that of consciousness. These reflections dramatically change what it means to think about another sentient being suffering.

One of the questions I asked was, why am I alive now and not in the past? Expressed more generally: why am I here and not there? Why do I wake up in the morning looking at the world through the same pair of eyes, having similar patterns of thoughts, blessed or burdened with the same memories, experiencing the world through the same body and never someone else's, past or present? It might not be possible to offer a simple, straightforward answer to these questions, because they might not be logically meaningful as formulated. But thinking about these questions and why it might be difficult to give a meaningful answer yields a profound insight. If we dismiss the idea of each body literally being given a unique soul and recognise that—from a detached perspective—there is nothing "special" about the consciousness associated with your body or anyone else's, the whole paradigm of separateness disintegrates and we see our attachment to the idea of a self as a kind of deception, a trick performed by the brain.

The flaws of closed individualism as a useful framework for understanding reality become apparent when we do such thought experiments and see that our intuitive view of identity leads to contradictions or absurdities. In particular, we may question our strong bias towards securing the wellbeing of our future self rather than helping others, in the present or future. Two alternative philosophical frameworks have been proposed for thinking about personal identity that are meant to provide metaphysically accurate models of its true nature. One framework, which Kolak termed "empty individualism", says that identity is something fleeting that changes from one moment to the next. Our lives are therefore composed of many slices of consciousness-moments, which we can think of as separate identities, stitched together in space-time through physical continuity, and there is no single stable personal identity. Another framework, which Kolak termed "open individualism", in what may appear to be a contradictory claim, says that there is only one single identity in existence and that we are all—each consciousness-moment that comes into being—manifestations of it (see also Vinding, 2017).

For a long time, even before I came across the term, I have thought that empty individualism best captures the true nature of identity, and that we can see slices of identity as having more or less in common with one another, whether or not they are associated with the same physical body. Empty individualism takes a reductionist approach to understanding identity (as in Derek Parfit, 1984) by breaking the perception or experience of it into its momentary phenomenological components, and thereby pointing at a deeper truth about existence. This doesn't mean that empty individualism is the ideal framework for explaining everything about human behaviour and experience, such as the emergence of meaning, though it is compatible with it—as it is with all of physical reality.

Empty individualism also captures some of the essence of Buddhism: the notions of impermanence and the lack of a self. Or perhaps more correctly, it's Buddhism that captured some essential metaphysical truths thousands of years ago, including the nature of personal identity. Two of the Three Signs of Being have been described as follows: "The first, Change, points out the basic fact that nothing in the world is fixed or permanent. We ourselves are not the same people, either physically, emotionally or mentally, that we were ten years—or even ten minutes ago!... No-I, the third Sign, is a little more difficult. Buddhists do not believe that there is anything everlasting or unchangeable in human beings, no soul or self in which a stable sense of 'I' might anchor itself. The whole idea of 'I' is in fact a basically false one that tries to set itself up in an unstable and temporary collection of elements" (The Buddhist Society, n.d.; see also Siderits, 2015).

Open individualism, on the other hand, feels more sentimental or spiritual, expressing the idea that "we are all one". But open and empty individualism are compatible with and complementary to one another, explaining different aspects of the reality and experience of identity. Open individualism perhaps better accounts for the perspective I mentioned above, where you realise that what you think of as "you" is just one manifestation of consciousness popping up in space-time. It also provides another perspective on the connection of someone else's suffering with your own—that it is not just a different version of you that is experiencing it, but that it actually *is* you—just in another location and/or time. The difference from the perspective of empty individualism is actually subtle, and the choice between the two frameworks seems to depend on the purpose and the philosophical issue one is grappling with.

I still think that empty individualism is a more useful framework for explaining and resolving philosophical paradoxes associated with identity because, by retaining a notion of fleeting personal identity, it more readily shows where closed individualism goes astray. With its use of the paradigm of discrete consciousness-moments, it is also more closely aligned with an ethical framework that aims to reduce instances of suffering through calculation. But open individualism may be a better paradigm for creating a powerful sense of connectedness between sentient beings, one that is also based on metaphysical truth.

Yet closed individualism remains an essential paradigm as well, not as the ultimately correct metaphysical framework for thinking about personal identity, but for reflecting how sentient beings actually function, how they intuitively think about their lives, and also how they think about personal risk. The intuitive view of personal identity is intimately tied to our motivations and happiness. It's the state-of-mind in which most of the meaning we generate occurs, as well as some of the empathy we feel for other creatures. Indeed, one of the greatest sources of meaning and happiness is love, which when focused on another being requires, at least at the subconscious level, an intense belief in distinct, continuous personal identity, rather than seeing the other person as a string of consciousness-moments.

Furthermore, decisions are made within single interconnected masses of neural tissue where suffering is created, and the actual intensity of suffering itself depends partly on the brain's hardwired belief in closed individualism. The philosophical exercise of splitting experience into consciousness-moments is not only potentially psychologically alienating, it can also be misleading if it treats them each as independent, simple moments of hedonic value, rather than extremely rich and complex brain states that intimately refer to one another through stable patterns and the mechanism of memory.

Jaron Lanier, a writer, musician and computer scientist who helped create virtual reality, expressed something about the meaning that comes from seeing ourselves as distinct individuals, rather than as mere strings of physically generated consciousness: "Humanism means we're willing to mystify people a little bit. We're willing to say that there's something we don't understand, something extraordinary, something perhaps even a little supernatural about the way people experience what they're doing… that people are special, that people are central, that everything else becomes absurd if you don't believe in the specialness of people" (Weyl, 2018). In fact, I would argue, only when we adopt something of this perspective does life actually feel worth preserving.

Whether adopting a perspective that reinforces our existence bias is something to promote is another question. But for human beings with a passion for life, negating such feelings seems needlessly destructive. For purely instrumental reasons, it also seems counterproductive to encourage those most concerned with preventing suffering to value their own existence a little less!

The fact that subjective experience (currently) occurs within the context of brains with a deeply hardwired notion of stable, distinct personal identity means that if, for the purposes of ethical reflection, we only considered consciousness-moments in isolation from one another, we would be ignoring all the complicated ways that they actually influence one other and are themselves affected by the belief in stable personal identity. That is, we would lose useful information with explanatory power. This is true even if, all other things being equal, equivalent moments are in principle interchangeable over time and space.

For many if not most practical purposes, closed individualism therefore remains the most useful paradigm for translating ethical ideas into action. But it is the other frameworks that provide a more universal basis for thinking about ethics and that demonstrate the objectively equivalent importance of all similar instances of suffering.

Although the open individualism perspective can open us up to feeling a stronger connection with all sentient beings, accepting the reality of open individualism can actually be terrifying. You imagine the worst torture, rape and violence, and realise that in a genuine sense it actually has happened to you, is happening to you in the present and will continue to happen to you in the future. The problem is magnified when you consider the possibility of an infinite universe with infinite suffering, which you actually experience. It can create a dreadful feeling of vulnerability and impotence. For this reason, closed individualism can protect us, serving as a retreat from this highly disturbing view into the abyss of existence, and allowing us to feel safer within the limits of our own personal identity, however illusory.

The conflict between the perspectives of closed and both empty and open individualism is another manifestation of the tango of ethics, the tension between how things normally feel in the most immediate, intuitive sense, and the understanding of reality that comes from a more detached analysis or introspection. A useful, holistic ethical framework needs to reconcile or at least accommodate these conflicting perspectives.

The Golden Rule

The Golden Rule, sometimes known as the ethic of reciprocity—treat others as you would like to be treated—is the most widespread ethical principle, found with slight variations in many cultures and religions around the world going back millennia. From a purely practical perspective, it provides the basis for a peaceful, cooperative society. But it also reflects a deeper truth that is the essence of ethics: an awareness of the other as a suffering, feeling being who matters as much as oneself. Given that our intuitive view of personal identity is an illusion, and that other sentient beings can be seen as variations of, or even different manifestations of, ourselves, applying the Golden Rule can be more than just a matter of altruism or charity, or even of pragmatic self-interest, but a rational implementation of this deeper understanding of identity.

Even though the Golden Rule is very simple, its alignment with a metaphysical truth, its key message and its deep cultural roots make it very useful as a foundation for ethics that can easily be promoted. As an illustration of this, the sage Rabbi Hillel, using the negative formulation of the Golden Rule (also known as the Silver Rule), said, "That which is hateful to you, do not do to another. That is the whole Torah—the rest is commentary."

To ensure that its scope is universal, we need to explicitly specify that all sentient beings with the capacity to suffer, and not just humans, are included in "others". That is, that all manifestations of consciousness are taken into consideration. Other aspects of a more detailed ethical framework, such as the notion of giving highest priority to the most urgent cases, also fall into place when we consider that we would also want to be treated with high priority if we were suffering severely. Of course, for it to be effective as a basis for ethics, it needs to be applied not just in direct interactions with others, but consistently throughout policy-making and governance, so that all sentient beings affected are taken into account in priority-setting.

The Golden Rule doesn't only mean act towards those with similar power to you the way you would want them to act towards you, but also act towards those with *less* power than you the way you would want those with *more* power than you to act towards you. It actually can be seen as transcending mere reciprocity and cooperation. It means, I'll scratch your back even if you can't scratch mine, and I *won't* make you suffer even though you *can't* make me suffer. This aspect is profoundly important for our interactions, not just with other human beings, but with non-human animals as well, and demands that we treat them the way we would hypothetically want powerful aliens visiting our planet to treat us.

Rawls's veil of ignorance

Philosopher John Rawls proposed that, in the interest of fairness, decisions that will affect society be made from behind a "veil of ignorance"—as if one doesn't know who one would be in a population subjected to these decisions. The principle is closely related to the Golden Rule, and it reaches conclusions similar to the application of a view of personal identity based on empty individualism. It could be seen as another means of applying the Golden Rule and the objectivity of empty individualism to public policy.

The Rawlsian veil of ignorance powerfully imposes more careful negative utilitarian reasoning, because it requires decision-makers to imagine the worst things that happen in the world happening to themselves. It ensures that whatever terrible experiences we would never risk enduring—even if the risk were very low—we ensure that others don't risk enduring as well, and that only things that would be acceptable for us to experience are imposed on others. If we refuse to go behind the veil, then we are irrationally giving our own identity metaphysically unjustified importance, and we are no longer caring for others in society as if we are one of them.

As David Pearce commented on a previously mentioned blog post, "Perhaps one believes that [atrocious] suffering of such enormity is a price worth paying for the blessings of sentient existence elsewhere, notably one's own. Yet this judgement is feasible only because the suffering is borne by others rather than oneself—a weak basis for moral argument."

Although the concept of the veil of ignorance was developed with human members of society in mind, it becomes a universally applicable tool if we imagine the impact of our decisions on all sentient beings—in the same way that the Golden Rule can also only be a universal basis for ethics if it includes all sentient beings.

Anti-speciesism

Suffering is an internal phenomenon whose significance is independent of an organism's other traits, including abilities like intelligence or external appearance such as fur or scales. These other traits have no bearing on the inherent urgency of preventing or relieving an organism's suffering. The only thing that matters is the intensity and duration of the suffering itself. Treating a sentient being's suffering as less important because of its species classification is to devalue the one parameter of overriding ethical importance and to give importance to features that are simply irrelevant.

Anti-speciesist thinking and actions seek to overcome this bias, in the same way that we seek to overcome discrimination based on race, religion, gender identification, sexual orientation, age, ability and other characteristics in attending to people's wellbeing and carrying out actions that affect it. Anti-speciesism does not mean that we treat every sentient being identically. It does not mean that we treat pigs, chickens, lobsters and bees as if they were human beings. Some define anti-speciesism as caring about a sentient being's specific *interests*, which are obviously different for a pig or chicken than for a human being. At its most essential, though, anti-speciesism says that suffering matters regardless of species classification and demands that we treat all equivalent suffering as equally important. Most urgently, it demands that we prevent other sentient beings from experiencing extreme suffering that we could never willingly experience ourselves.

Is this meant to suggest that it is irrational or "unethical" to ever discriminate? We clearly discriminate in some sense whenever we give priority to helping a family member or friend over a stranger or non-human animal, especially when we could have more impact by helping the stranger or animal. But it would be deeply counterintuitive to deprive aid and support to someone we are emotionally close to. In fact, a functioning, compassionate society requires that we be able to count on those closest to us for support. It would be very difficult to care about the potential suffering of a snail or a mouse as much as the suffering of a fellow citizen. Being fully anti-speciesist is a difficult philosophy to abide by in practice.

However, looking at the bigger picture beyond the objects of our greatest spontaneous empathy, the way our institutions prioritise and the laws that encode our ethics need to weed out discriminatory decision-making as much as possible and aim to give the suffering of non-human animals the same importance as that of humans. And certainly we can start by not doing them any harm where it can be avoided.

In fact, one could argue that discrimination itself is never the core issue, but rather, the suffering that discrimination can cause. Many kinds of selection processes in society, such as hiring, and in the personal sphere, such as choice of friends and partners, are a kind of discrimination, and are often justified by specific needs or personal interests. The problem is when discrimination causes needless pain, often due to a lack of empathy for those discriminated against, whether human or non-human.

A broader view of speciesism includes notions like autonomy and the right to life as part of a sentient being's interests. These kinds of interests exist on an entirely different level than freedom from suffering. Compared to the relief of extreme suffering they are of secondary importance, though they have a strongly intuitive component. Autonomy is arguably largely a matter of perception, and a dog or pig who is loved and well cared for by a human is probably happier than an animal suffering from cold and hunger in the wild—although the basis for comparison is, once again, freedom from suffering. And an animal that ceases to exist—whether human or non-human—cannot suffer. Nevertheless, we may still strongly prefer a world where we don't needlessly commit acts of violence against sentient beings. If we feel more strongly about not killing pigs and chickens than we do about not killing insects—under the key theoretical assumption that there is no suffering involved—it's ultimately because of what it feels like for *us*, not for the animals in question. I will return to this later in a section on painlessly killing happy animals.

Awakening awareness

Ethics does not end at one's line of sight, at the walls of factory farms, at international borders, or even at the edge of a thick forest in which countless sentient beings may be suffering. If one isn't taking into account all subjective experiences, and especially all instances of intense suffering, then one isn't applying ethics universally or impartially. And in that case, one is acting as if some are more equal than others—that some loci of intense suffering intrinsically matter more than other loci of intense suffering. Although limiting our exposure to many of the things happening in our world may be a necessary coping mechanism, awakening awareness is essential for putting ethics into practice.

The veil of ignorance mentioned above refers to ignorance of *who* the victims are of a decision, but not ignorance of what their experiences are actually like. It is probably not the ideal metaphor for what we want to achieve, because, in fact, it is not actually *ignorance* that we want to promote, but visceral *awareness* of what intense suffering is actually like, coupled with the realisation that the suffering of others is equivalent to our own. We cannot make rational ethical decisions without maximal awareness of the consequences of our decisions for subjective experience and suffering, wherever they occur.

It is therefore important for us to regularly revisit certain mental states to some degree and reacquaint ourselves with the reality of intense suffering, to ensure that our priorities are properly calibrated. It's a balancing act. Too much and we can become emotionally overwhelmed and depressed by the state of the world. But too little and we might forget what really matters.

Nine

Our Complex Relationship with Suffering

The fleetingness of momentary decisions

In the last chapters I have been discussing the equivalent importance of suffering no matter who experiences it, the inherent limits to rationality when it comes to determining priorities among situations with different numbers of instances and intensities of suffering, and the unique quality of extreme, unbearable suffering. In this chapter I would like to explore the various trade-offs and risks of suffering we are willing to take, or even impose on others, in pursuit of happiness, and what these say about the rationality of our decision-making. Research by psychology pioneers Amos Tversky and Daniel Kahneman (e.g. Tversky & Kahneman, 1981) and books such as psychologist and behavioural economist Dan Ariely's (2008) *Predictably Irrational* illustrate just how irrational our everyday decision-making is, including in assessing probabilities. Here I would like to delve into the very rationality of risk-taking altogether.

We make all kinds of sacrifices in order to survive. Whether seeking to survive is a rational decision is a separate question! (I will address this shortly.) But if survival is your goal, then it is rational to endure some bearable, at least nominally voluntary suffering. And it is certainly rational if the alternative is to endure even greater suffering. So people struggle with stressful jobs and a lack of free time in order to pay their bills and avoid poverty. A poor Indian who spends long days pedalling through heavy traffic and selling scrap metal for a meagre income may see the alternative as literally starving to death.

But we may also be willing to suffer in the present in the hope, not just of surviving and minimising our suffering, but of achieving greater happiness or bliss in the future — or even just contentedness. For example, people decide to endure the sometimes intense pain of a divorce or relationship breakup in order to reach a future stage where they can achieve greater happiness and self-realisation. They may be willing to risk even severe suffering, or to experience it with certainty.

Yet there is nothing sacred or purely rational in a larger sense about decisions we make to experience significant suffering for the sake of future happiness. That is, while the decisions may be rational in the narrow, instrumental sense of helping to achieve the goal of future happiness, the goal itself may not be fully rational. Such decisions are not necessarily *irrational* either, as long as the suffering is experienced voluntarily. But there is no objectively valid trade-off between suffering and happiness that justifies such decisions. They are just decisions our brains are prepared to make—brains that were originally designed through natural selection to increase the likelihood of having offspring that survive to the age of reproduction.

Our preferences are often fleeting, varying as a function of thoughts, momentary cravings, memories and outside influences. For example, Daniel Kahneman and colleagues found that subjects preferred to repeat an experience containing more suffering than another containing less suffering, when the suffering during the *last moments* of the experience was less intense (Kahneman et al., 1993). Furthermore, imagining a potential blissful experience may motivate us to make sacrifices we would never agree to in hindsight, or to take risks of unbearable suffering. Such decisions are really just instantaneous preferences coupled to some degree of personal engagement to act on these preferences. They are rarely made after a careful, objective weighing of *all* relevant information. And even if they were, the actual decisions would still be based on an underlying, momentary motivation. At the moment when decisions are made, some information dominates, and it isn't often the reality of intense or extreme suffering. This applies to decisions we make for ourselves, but also to decisions we make with consequences for others.

These reflections are important for better understanding some of the motivations that could lead one to defend classical utilitarianism, and why a person's willingness to experience a certain amount of pain in order to experience pleasure can be mistakenly seen as representing some objective truth about the relationship between pleasure and pain. While voluntarily putting up with bearable suffering for some future benefit may not be inherently problematic, even in cases where it appears delusional, the situation is very different when we use this reasoning to impose suffering on others, or when the suffering crosses the threshold of bearableness. I explore these ideas further in the next two sections.

Voluntary personal sacrifices don't justify imposing suffering on others

Given that voluntary suffering is experienced very differently from suffering that is imposed, and also that happiness and suffering are not composed of discrete hedons that can be arbitrarily distributed with equivalent effect, one might think it obvious that we can't simply extrapolate from sacrifices we make for ourselves to creating suffering and happiness in other people. Yet the belief that this is possible is also found among advocates of classical utilitarianism, eager to give their framework a more concrete numerical grounding.

Any apparent "balancing out" of suffering with happiness that seems reasonable to someone to endure occurs within one single brain that processes and evaluates these anticipated experiences and remains in a state of perceived control. As suggested earlier in a section on voluntary suffering, the experience of the suffering is interpreted differently as a result of this sense of control, which includes any implicit calculation that the experience is worth undergoing. Even if there may be uncertainty about whether the decision is a good one, and the will itself may be conflicted, there is no conflict between the will as acted upon and the experience—no frustration of one's net preference while experiencing the suffering. And even though such personal decisions may not be inherently rational in a larger sense, and only in the limited sense of trying to achieve a specific form of happiness, they are voluntary. And because they are voluntary, there is not the same experience of suffering.

Imposing suffering on some—that is, harming them or allowing them to be harmed—for the increased happiness of others is totally different. There is no sense of control in those suffering, no feeling of justification. It just creates new urgency.

This fact holds regardless of the validity of empty individualism and of distinct personal identity being an illusion. A consciousness-moment of involuntary suffering is fundamentally different from one of voluntary suffering, where there are different processes going on in the brain. Voluntary trade-offs are specifically and intimately associated with brains embodying a notion of personal identity, and they cannot rationally be applied to the involuntary imposition of similar experiences on others through the fallacious notion of universal exchange rates between pleasure and pain.

As an example of the absurdity of trying to apply intra-personal pleasure–pain exchange rates to society: imagine someone who decides to carry out very hard labour for six months in order to afford a Porsche and considers that a worthwhile sacrifice. Would it be rational on this basis to distribute these experiences around the population, so that some people have to labour for months while others are given Porsches?

To provide a more dramatic scenario: a short story by Ursula Le Guin (1973) called "The Ones Who Walk Away from Omelas", a reference often cited by those focused on the ethics of reducing suffering, describes a utopian city where everyone lives blissful lives in a festival-like atmosphere. But this bliss depends (for unknown reasons) on the suffering of a single child kept in a dark dungeon in a state of perpetual misery. Everyone knows this truth, and most accept it as the condition of their happiness. But from time to time, some quietly decide that this situation is intolerable. These are the ones who walk away from Omelas.

What's noteworthy about this story is not just the degree of suffering but its concentration in one person, and how unacceptable this is seen to be by some—that a single child be made to suffer involuntarily as the price for the bliss of thousands. And of course, if it is shocking when there is just one single child, it would be shocking if there were many such children—hundreds, thousands, millions...

The reality is that we do condone and support the certainty of other sentient beings experiencing often extreme suffering for our pleasure—in both direct ways (e.g. paying for the flesh of tortured, miserable animals confined to small cages or cramped enclosures) and indirect ways (e.g. voting for governments that cut spending on healthcare and other essential services so that the rich can become richer and buy a few more luxurious properties). Planet Earth *is* Omelas—with a dungeon of dramatic proportions.

Tolerating the intolerable

Much of decision-making, especially governmental and institutional, but also less formally in our daily lives, is about risk management, which can include keeping the risk of certain bad things happening below a maximum acceptable level and preparing for such eventualities. But is there any acceptable risk of extreme, unbearable suffering happening? If you are inclined to answer "yes", then rationally, as we have discussed, you would need to be willing to subject yourself to the same risks you would support subjecting others to, once you were fully aware of what the experience entailed. Would you? Keeping in mind that some of the worst forms of suffering cannot even be experienced without irreversible consequences by someone seeking to understand them, such as losing a child, being painfully killed, or having parts of one's body mutilated.

The fact that humans, individually or as a society, *do* take on risks of extreme suffering happening to themselves raises the question whether such decision-making can even be anything *other* than irrational. It is widely assumed that decision-making can be fully rational if it takes into account all relevant information and weighs the expected costs and benefits of the outcomes using appropriate statistical reasoning. But when the relevant information includes subjective experience, our decision-making is severely hampered by the hot–cold empathy gap — whether the decisions concern others or ourselves. There are a wide range of other cognitive biases (List of cognitive biases, n.d.) that limit our capacity to make rational decisions. But it is our failure to fully grasp the reality of extreme suffering that is perhaps the most serious cognitive bias of the entire lot. Can it ever actually be compatible with rationality in the big-picture sense to follow our intuitions and run the risk of bringing unbearable suffering into existence?

In an earlier section, I acknowledged that our intuitions might overwhelm us into preferring to allow a small amount of unbearable suffering to occur to some, in order to spare many others somewhat lower levels of significant suffering, given sufficient numbers. Even then, the decision is not a fully rational one, other than as a considered means of satisfying intuitions and implementing policies that are seen as acceptable. And if the less significant suffering is sufficiently minor, the decision may indeed be considered irrational because it treats essentially non-overlapping categories of suffering as interchangeable (as seen in the torture vs. dust specks scenario). If the unbearable suffering is chosen merely to gain more intense happiness for others, such a decision appears even more clearly to be irrational because it ignores extreme urgency for the sake of something with no urgency at all.

Let's take another scenario as a thought experiment. Imagine you voluntarily decided to endure a sustained period of brutal torture that would not actually kill you, in order to achieve what you saw as a great outcome for humanity — a future full of bliss. You decided that this was a worthwhile trade-off to make and you were prepared to make a benevolent sacrifice. What if, after the torture began, you realised it was literally unbearable, regretted your decision and pleaded for it to end? How rational then was your initial decision in retrospect? Surely you would never have made that decision had you known how intolerable the suffering would be. But if they stopped torturing you, would you ever make the decision again, perhaps after a long delay where you forgot how terrible it was? Or would you take that first-hand knowledge you acquired into your subsequent decision-making?

What if, instead of the certainty of torture, you took a 1% risk of it happening, and in fact it didn't happen. Would the decision have been rational? What if you were unlucky and it did happen, and you pleaded for the torture to stop? Would it only then have been irrational?

9. Our Complex Relationship with Suffering

You could demand, while making the initial decision, that any subsequent pleas of yours to stop the torture be ignored and to just carry on with the deal, because you believed that your decision was rational and you wanted to stick with it. But of course, adding that constraint—a firm commitment to carry through with the decision—does not itself make the decision any more rational. It just makes it irreversible.

So in fact, we couldn't actually voluntarily go through with unbearable suffering (by definition), regardless of any calculation we thought justified it. Any trade-off for happiness would not be voluntarily executable. And the same applies to taking a risk of enduring such suffering. Any such decisions could not actually be voluntarily abided by if it came down to actually experiencing the suffering.

Brian Tomasik (2017c) has written about similar scenarios, defining unbearable suffering as an experience one would not be able to maintain consent to, regardless of any future benefits. He explains the different decisions someone would take before being tortured and during torture as being the result of distinct "utility functions" corresponding to two different person-moments (Tomasik, 2017b). But this more mathematical framing does not imply that both utility functions are inherently rational — it merely illustrates that decision-making is very sensitive to conditions.

If you are not willing to experience a certain degree of horrible suffering for any amount of bliss, that says something important about the nature of that suffering and the rationality of any decision to prevent it from happening, based on facts about subjective experience. On the other hand, even if you claim to be willing to experience it, that doesn't say very much about how rational the decision is unless you would maintain that decision even *during* the actual suffering.

Let's carry out a slightly different thought experiment. Imagine there are 1,000 copies or versions of yourself all together in a large room. Each is offered extreme bliss—whatever that personally means to you, whether an endless sex-, drug- and champagne-fuelled party on a yacht (yes, very clichéd); or spending the rest of your life in tranquillity, surrounded by family, friends and companion animals, bathed in love; or perhaps meditating alone or with your partner in a mountain cave (and yes, why not, with an espresso machine, expensive wine collection and sauna). But in exchange for the bliss, you were also required to accept that one of you would be brutally tortured for a year. We could even allow that after that year they would be set free and taken to the yacht or mountain cave of their choosing. You would all look around, realising that one copy of you — and therefore, you—would actually experience torture. Would you take the risk? We could even change the numbers so that there were actually one billion copies of you, and only a one in one billion risk of any of them being tortured. In other words, a relatively minute risk to any single copy of you, but still certainty that one copy of you would be tortured. Would you accept bliss under those conditions?

If you (and your copies) did agree to the offer, you would indeed be condemning one copy of yourself to horrible suffering—regardless of whether "you" ended up being the copy that experienced it. The large majority of the copies would enjoy the consequences of the decision and probably be pleased, but one copy would undergo an unbearable experience that would cause them to regret their decision with the entire force of their being. Whether "you" considered the decision to be acceptable in retrospect would depend on your preparedness to face the consequences and empathise with the copy of you being tortured. Were you prepared to do that, it's probable that you would regret the decision, considering it irrational for having brought into existence an unbearable state-of-being.

If you were not willing to accept the offer—or if you did but, in retrospect, regretted it—there would be an equally strong argument for you not to accept a similar offer where the others were *less perfect* copies. Just ordinary people, a little different from you but with the same capacity to suffer.

Similarly, if we imagine a variation of the Omelas scenario where anyone who wants to live blissfully in the city takes a small, voluntary risk of being the sacrificial child, the scenario might appear less shocking than the original, where the suffering is involuntarily imposed. Yet the consequences are the same—one person condemned to a life of misery while others live blissful lives. The voluntary nature of the initial risk would quickly become irrelevant, other than as a psychological justification for others to maintain an intolerable status quo. Sharing rather than concentrating a risk does not lessen the urgency of a situation that emerges from it, and the suffering is not perceived as voluntary when it was a risk one was hoping to avoid and one can no longer escape it.

People generally strive to stay alive, even if they are vaguely aware that there is a risk of suffering severely in the future. In fact, even if they were told the size of the risk, most people would probably continue puttering along, considering the risk relatively insignificant or tolerable. Yet, as I've been arguing, there are experiences that no one would willingly endure if they were viscerally aware of what it meant. Carrying on living in spite of the risks of suffering unbearably, and passing on those risks to offspring we intentionally bring into the world, is something we are hardwired to do. The risks we accept in practice are never an objectively rational trade-off.

We may think the implicit decision to try to stay alive is a rational one, but there is, arguably, scarcely any less rational behaviour than the instinctive one that keeps us living and creating offspring, a fraction of whom are condemned to a horrible death, whether being raped and killed by a psychopath, or being eaten alive by an animal, or being tortured and killed by a fascist government, or dying in a terrible accident. And even a low risk multiplied by sufficient time or a sufficient number of sentient beings produces near-certainty. At some point, someone ends up being condemned to experience unbearable suffering. Given a sufficiently long existence, there is also virtual certainty that you — that is, your current physical "self" in its future manifestation — would experience intense suffering of an unbearable nature. My colleague Manu Herrán (2017), a computer engineer who writes extensively about sentience and suffering, has written about this in an essay called "The Big Lie". This framing of the problem, combined with an open individualism perspective that blurs the distinction between you and others, reveals that we are "all" condemned eventually to experience unbearable suffering.

The existence of a moment or a period of truly unbearable suffering during someone's life causes that life to pass through a bottleneck of unbearableness. Whatever they might claim afterwards about the acceptability of that moment, their self during that unbearable moment would plead for that moment not to happen — now or again in the future. A life that contains unbearable suffering can itself be viewed overall as unbearable, as it contains what can be seen as a society of sequential consciousness-moments in which bearableness does not outweigh unbearableness. Similarly, the life of an actual society of sentient beings that contains such lives can also be considered unbearable.

Even a low risk of something happening doesn't detract from the awfulness when it does happen. The whole mathematical concept of risk is something that humans invented, even though it is implied in our intuitive reasoning about situations and the relative dangers they represent. It is powerful and especially helpful in determining rational behaviour where we are trying to optimise outcomes. But any outcome that can include extreme suffering is hardly "optimal" in any absolute sense.

The precautionary principle captures the need to anticipate the possibility of bad things happening and to act cautiously until the risks have been established as acceptably low. If we were to seriously apply the precautionary principle with unbearable suffering in mind, we might conclude that such risks are never really acceptable. Yet as a society, we do collectively take risks that lead to unbearable suffering to some. How then can those risks themselves be considered bearable?

The argument for avoiding even low risks of extreme suffering has an obvious parallel to Pascal's Wager, the classic philosophical argument that states, in part, that it is safer to believe in God in order to avoid a small risk of ending up in an eternal hell. While I question the solidity of Pascal's Wager itself (for example, the actual existence of a vindictive, omniscient God would make beliefs claimed for instrumental reasons a doubtful cause for clemency), there is a strong argument for the avoidance of the earthly hell of extreme suffering, which has nothing to do with supernatural beliefs. Here, the risk is not about whether or not it will happen at all—that it will happen, given the status quo and a long enough period of time, is a certainty—but about specifics such as the times, locations and amounts. In other words: since extreme suffering does happen, there is a compelling argument for reducing as much as possible the risks of it happening.

To illustrate a further point, let's now make a fundamental change to an earlier thought experiment. Let's say that you were prepared to experience unbearable suffering, such as horrible torture, not in order to create bliss for humanity—something that, as discussed earlier, has no inherent urgency to be created—but to prevent much larger amounts of unbearable suffering from happening. In this case, the decision seems objectively rational: you are attempting to reduce the total amount of unbearable suffering that will occur. In fact, it represents pure utilitarian reasoning applied to the most urgent situation—there is no greater ethical certainty than that!

But again, you would not be able to execute this decision voluntarily. You would plead for the experience to stop. There is no way you could sacrifice yourself for others and willingly experience the consequences as an autonomous being.

A similar argument applies if we imagine agreeing to more evenly distribute the burden of unbearable suffering so that, while still unbearable, it isn't concentrated in one person (which would infringe on a deep moral intuition and perhaps also further amplify the intensity), but rather, is experienced for a much shorter time by many people—perhaps for a shorter cumulative duration, ensuring that the utilitarian calculation was solid. Again, we would never be able to voluntarily go through with the decision ourselves.

Of course, most privileged people would never agree, even in theory, to evenly share the risk or length of exposure to torture with the less privileged, even if we were all somehow to accept the metaphysical principle that distinct personal identity is an illusion. A pragmatic ethical framework does have to accommodate our intuitions about separateness and self-interest as part of human nature. But it is precisely this illusion of separateness that allows us to tolerate the intolerable, as objectively irrational as this is.

These thought experiments further illustrate something profound about the nature of unbearable suffering and about ethics. The most urgent ethical call-to-action could never be carried out voluntarily by taking on some of the burden oneself, without the constraint of irreversibility and the associated loss of autonomy. Because of the objective equivalence of one locus of suffering with another, it shows again how intolerable any instance of unbearable suffering actually is. This means that the only rationally tolerable risk of it happening is zero.

Conversely, we see that it's only the segregation of suffering, its concentration in others rather than its equal distribution, that makes existence desirable or even just bearable for some.

So we are left with a paradox. We can stick our heads in the sand and take irrational refuge from it, based on the illusion of separateness, leaving other versions of ourselves to experience what is unbearable, including as the result of decisions we erroneously deem rational. Or we can regard this suffering as our own, and take every measure possible to prevent it from ever happening.

The need for systems that are more rational and compassionate than we are

We respect human beings' right to autonomy and even to take risks for themselves of bad things happening. This is a concession to closed individualism and to the strong intuitive desire for freedom, including the freedom to make mistakes that affect one's own wellbeing. If we used empty and/or open individualism as a stronger guide to ethical policy and action, we might more often justifiably intervene to prevent people from making disastrous decisions that cause themselves great suffering. And even if we choose not to intervene ahead of time, those who make mistakes still deserve compassion. Of course, there is no such concession to autonomy needed when it comes to not imposing risks on others of unbearable things happening to them.

But we do a bad job at protecting our future selves from great suffering, and we are even more inclined to allow others to shoulder such risks. While the desire and need for personal autonomy limits how much we can expect others to protect us from our own bad decisions, we need to be much more rational as a society so as not to impose the consequences of such bad decisions on others. Our systems need to be more ambitious, more rational and more compassionate than we ourselves are. Those making decisions that affect others—designing new governance systems or implementing ethical principles that will guide our future—must aspire to apply ethics more objectively and fairly than we do in our own personal lives.

The intuition towards fairness and against the concentration of suffering

We saw with the Omelas short story that allowing one person to suffer in order to ensure bliss for others is shocking. But a similar intuition persists even if there is no bliss to be obtained, and we are only considering how to distribute unavoidable suffering. As I discussed earlier in the section on the interchangeability of intensity of suffering and number of individuals, the very idea of concentrating suffering feels repulsive, whether in a single individual or group, whereas a more even distribution of the burden of suffering generally feels more acceptable (even though one may doubt how many people would personally volunteer to share the burden).

One could still ask whether a concentration of suffering could be rational from a pure utilitarian perspective. If the intensity hypothetically remains constant over time, one might say that it doesn't matter if the suffering occurs for a short time in several people or for a long time in one person, and that, other things being equal, the two scenarios are actually equivalent in terms of instances of suffering. Even then, the realisation that one has been condemned to suffer so that others can be spared suffering can create an additional layer or dimension of suffering. So it might actually lead to a greater intensity of suffering than if the suffering were spread out among many people.

Although a narrow, purely utilitarian analysis could still argue for the concentration of suffering in some situations, the intuitions against it are very strong. A world where we turn individuals into scapegoats so that others can be spared suffering hardly feels like a world worth living in. Even if others do not actually gain bliss, the scenario bears a similarity to the one in Omelas: one suffers so that many can live relatively suffering-free. It feels inherently cruel, and it goes strongly against our intuitions that aim for some degree of equality and not treating people or other sentient beings as means to the happiness or wellbeing of others.

In fact, if the suffering were more fairly distributed, even if the intensity were slightly greater, it would still be more aligned with the kind of world that feels acceptable to live in than one where the suffering is imposed on a few scapegoats. The more individuals share the burden of suffering, which would have an inherently voluntary nature to it if the arrangement was generally agreed to, the weaker any intuition against the situation. This is why I suggested earlier that we might consider it acceptable to prefer many people suffering a little for short periods of time to one person suffering for a long time, or intensely for a short time.

Note that when I brought up the Omelas short story earlier, I suggested that if there were more scapegoats suffering in dungeons so that others can experience bliss, the situation would be even *worse* because of the greater amount of suffering. However, that was a different scenario: there was no distribution of suffering, simply more scapegoats, there for the benefit of others.

The intuition against concentrating suffering among a few individuals — which might be more or less strong depending on the society and, for example, the degree of collectivism it practices — is very similar to the intuition against causing harm, though the scenarios might appear to be different. In both cases, we are considering situations where the suffering is not experienced voluntarily but is imposed by people in power, such as governments. Causing direct harm to identifiable individuals goes most strongly against our moral intuitions, whereas suffering that is allowed to happen passively (by omission, that is, by not acting), or where the initial risk is shared — even if just a few end up suffering the consequences — goes less strongly against these intuitions.

There have been other attempts to defend concepts like fairness on utilitarian grounds by claiming that it is also a form of human wellbeing. But as I have been arguing all along, wellbeing always relates to hedonic states. In a critique of Sam Harris's views in which the authors refer to a "devastating" review by Whitley Kaufman of his book *The Moral Landscape*, they write that Harris "offers a framework that sounds a lot like classical utilitarianism and suffers from utilitarianism's well-known defects (e.g., its inability to resolve questions of what should happen when the reduction of suffering, or maximization of well-being, runs up against other competing moral instincts like fairness). Then, in order to avoid this problem, Harris defines well-being to include both suffering-reduction and fairness, making the term all but meaningless again" (Massey & Robinson, 2018).

Fairness — like everything else — ultimately only matters because of its *effect* on hedonic states — directly, through its effect on those suffering from unfairness, and indirectly, when unfairness causes tension with our moral intuitions. But this doesn't mean we can always defend fairness on purely utilitarian grounds. As Simon Beard (2018) wrote, "there are good arguments to be made that some non-consequentialist concerns could never be justified on consequentialist grounds." Even a feeling of unfairness may be a lot less bad than significant physical suffering, and therefore potentially acceptable as part of a calculated utilitarian solution. The effect of unfairness on suffering in observers (i.e. those not directly affected by inequality) may be subtle, the main consequences being discontent, a kind of existential malaise with how the world is run. On the other hand, it could lead to extreme frustration, especially among those involuntarily subjected to the unfairness, and completely shift the balance of suffering.

Regardless, the intuition towards fairness is a very strong one—different but perhaps no less relevant than those intuitions needed to make decisions in situations combining different numbers of individuals and intensities of suffering, situations where rationality alone can't help us. It is ultimately their deeply intuitive unacceptability that makes unfair solutions unsustainable, and not necessarily the suffering they cause per se. But since unsustainable solutions for society may ultimately hinder the prevention of suffering through tensions and distractions, there is a strong, indirect argument against unfairness from a utilitarian perspective as well.

Spencer Greenberg (2017) outlined a thought experiment about this kind of scenario that pits utilitarian thinking against intuitions, where we have to decide how often the populations of each of two different-sized villages will experience a high degree of suffering, of different intensities depending on the village, in order to avert a worse fate. A purely utilitarian solution would require only one of the two villages to always experience the suffering, whereas a solution that takes into account fairness would split the burden in some way, even though there would be more suffering experienced overall. (In the example, there is the notion of aggregating suffering across different numbers of individuals and intensities of suffering, but this is not an essential aspect of the thought experiment, since even with equal intensities of suffering, the village with fewer residents would always be chosen according to a utilitarian solution.)

A negotiated solution means trying to find a solution that the vast majority find fair and will therefore agree to, not necessarily a solution that is most effective at preventing as much suffering as possible. Our brains are simply not hardwired to accept solutions based purely on empty individualism, where our own individual identities don't matter. Our moral intuition against doing harm kicks in when the prospect of concentrating suffering arises.

Scenarios such as the preceding one—and, in fact, any such serious ethical dilemmas we face in our world—represent conscious beings trying desperately (within the limits of their awareness) to minimise the worst effects of a system they involuntarily find themselves in, using rational tools that battle it out with the deeper intuitions they serve.

So to summarise, even though there are utilitarian arguments for fairness based on a possible reduction of the most intense suffering, the strongest argument is not usually utilitarian in the direct sense, but lies in the strength of our moral intuitions and the unviability of a world where some suffer for the benefit of others. Unfairness not only creates more suffering, it also undermines the system by creating deep tension with our moral intuitions. It's not sustainable and probably leads to more suffering in the long run as well.

Unfairness and inequality can, of course, include situations where there isn't so much a concentration of suffering as a concentration of benefits or wealth. The widespread intuition against this kind of inequality isn't identical to the intuition against causing harm, but we can also analyse it in terms of the suffering this unfairness causes, due to the failure to allocate resources to those who need them most, and more generally, to the fallout from competition in a world of scarcity where some kinds of goods, especially status, are zero-sum. I won't focus specifically on the intuition against this kind of inequality, partly because it doesn't have as strong a moral character as the intuition against causing harm, and partly because in a world where we sought to relieve suffering and avoid causing or concentrating harm, this kind of inequality and the intuition against it would become less pronounced as well.

Ten

Existence

A life worth living

It is common in the ethics literature and discussions to talk about "a life worth living", and about the conditions or balance between happiness and suffering that make this the case for any individual life. It is applied to humans, perhaps most famously in Derek Parfit's "Repugnant Conclusion" thought experiment (Arrhenius et al., 2017), as well as to non-human animals and calculations to determine when they are worth bringing into existence.

The idea that a life may or may not be worth living is strongly intuitive, and the default belief of many is that it is better to bring humans and other sentient beings into existence, unless there is a preponderance of suffering in their lives. We would all mostly agree that it is better not to bring a creature into existence if its life will be one of torture, but most people would probably also claim that a life full of bliss is one worth living, and that it is better to bring such people into existence. And between these extremes there lies a grey zone where we need to make a determination where to draw the line.

Yet the framing of the question and the phrase itself are based in large part on a few closely related beliefs or assumptions that I have argued are not justified: that existence is *inherently* worth preserving and replicating; that there is an obligation to create positive "value" in the universe; and that even severe suffering can be compensated by sufficient happiness. A determination of whether a life is "net positive" or "net negative", and therefore whether or not it is worthwhile, is closely tied to classical utilitarian reasoning and what I've maintained is its flawed use of aggregation.

I have argued, on the contrary, that there is never an inherent need or obligation to bring new sentient beings into existence. In many cases, particularly when it entails extreme or unbearable suffering, there is a strong rational argument against doing so. This includes not just the suffering of the sentient being in question, but also suffering they cause to other sentient beings through their existence. Only in a narrow range of cases where there is an expected net decrease in extreme suffering as a result, such as bringing into existence a successful activist, is there actually a clearly rational argument for doing so.

If an individual perceives all the suffering they endure during their lifetime as bearable and they never experience a desire to stop living because of the suffering, the issue of suffering may be less problematic. The suffering still brings with it an inherent urgency to be relieved, but the individual also still prefers to live with the suffering than not to live. Their subjective *feeling* may be that their life is worthwhile, even if that is not an objectively meaningful assessment.

But if the individual experiences suffering so intense as to cause them to wish to end their life, their life becomes literally unbearable at that moment, and no number of future instances of bliss can objectively compensate for it. This does not mean that the same individual might not, at some future moment, again claim that their life is worthwhile, having survived the earlier suffering. But that is the assessment or feeling occurring during a separate consciousness-moment without unbearable suffering — not an objectively valid assessment of their entire life. Certainly, there would be a strong argument *not* to create more such lives that would also experience equivalent unbearable suffering.

Let's take a concrete example to illustrate the conflict between how an individual might evaluate their own suffering and the problem with bringing new such lives into existence. Imagine that someone has chronic pain that, even when taking the best medication they can tolerate, they estimate at 7/10 — at the low end of the severe range. Let's also say, for simplicity, that they also rate their degree of negative affect or suffering at 7/10 when experiencing this pain. They learn to live with it and find it bearable, and they prefer to continue living, though they are usually in severe pain. Their degree of positive affect is usually about 2/10. But they also regularly meet good friends and close family, and in those moments they rate their positive affect at 6/10 and their negative affect drops to 5/10. They rate their overall life satisfaction on average at 4/10, though it varies depending on the moment of the day they are asked. What can we say about their situation from an ethical perspective?

There is obviously a high degree of urgency in their suffering most of the time. When they meet friends, the urgency drops because the happiness suppresses the suffering to a degree. If you asked them if they are happy to be alive, they might reply with an ambiguous answer. But if you asked them whether they would choose to bring a new person into the world who would experience their life as they do, they would probably say "no".

So on the one hand, as long as the suffering is bearable and the person explicitly prefers to be alive because they are also experiencing regular happiness, there is not the critical problem there is with extreme or unbearable suffering. On the other hand, not only is there no need or urgency to bring anyone into existence, but by bringing a suffering person into existence we are creating a sometimes urgent need for suffering to be relieved that there was no need to create.

The fact that a human suffering severely might not want to die does not mean that we can apply the same reasoning to hypothetical future lives. The same person might not be prepared to go through their life repeatedly if it meant re-experiencing the same suffering. Similarly, it would not be obviously better to bring into existence many more people suffering greatly but still wanting to live, than not to create more such people altogether. The choice to continue living a life filled with suffering is very different from the choice to create such a life.[1] Intentionally creating new beings who will be burdened with a combination of intense suffering and a hardwired motivation to endure it is objectively perverse.

The above argument largely applies to non-human animals as well: while there is never any urgency or objective need to bring into existence even happy non-human animals, there is a strong argument not to bring into existence animals who will experience severe or unbearable suffering. The whole idea of non-human animal lives being objectively worthwhile is as fallacious as it is for humans.

An animal living a short life filled with pain may intuitively seem much worse than the same animal experiencing the same pain in the context of a much longer life during which it is largely pain-free or experiencing pleasure. I see this partly as a reflection of our very strong existence bias. We think that a short life of pain is not worth living, but that the same pain is a small price to pay for a long, largely pain-free life. This is what we tell ourselves about our own lives, and we extend this reasoning to other animals.

But most non-human animals probably experience pain in the moment without any mitigating thoughts, and without the capacity to evaluate their lives at a meta level, as humans do, and to consider whether or not their lives, on balance, feel subjectively worthwhile. While many animals clearly enjoy being alive, the assertion one sometimes reads that animals

---

[1] Anti-natalist philosopher David Benatar (2017) wrote, "Asking whether it would be better never to have existed is not the same as asking whether it would be better to die. There is no interest in coming into existence. But there is an interest, once one exists, in not ceasing to exist."

"value their lives" is imprecise. Most animals, even if injured and evidently suffering, have a strong will to survive, and it may appear that they are able to bear even very negative experiences, when in fact they are simply suffering. The lack of a cognitive coping mechanism means that there is therefore an even stronger argument against bringing non-human animals into the world who will experience a significant amount of moderate suffering, let alone severe or unbearable suffering.

Escaping the Repugnant Conclusion

The famous "Repugnant Conclusion" of Derek Parfit, according to which a world of many people living lives barely worth living would — problematically — be considered "better" than one with fewer people having happy lives, is based on a view of ethics with several assumptions I have argued are contestable:

1. That the concept of a "life worth living" is objectively meaningful.
2. That positive and negative hedonic states can be aggregated to arrive at a "net value".
3. That it is an inherently "good thing" to bring more beings into existence if their value is calculated to be "net positive".

Although the Repugnant Conclusion appears to be the result of meticulous argumentation, it in fact rests on possibly unacknowledged intuitions about value and life that are not tenable as objective truths. These intuitions continue to pervade much of modern philosophy and, ironically, much of the rationalist community, with dramatic consequences for cause prioritisation.

Here is one explanation offered as to why the Repugnant Conclusion persists: "The suggestions regarding how to avoid the Repugnant Conclusion are diverse… Although these theories often succeed in avoiding the Repugnant Conclusion, they have other counterintuitive consequences. In fact, several impossibility theorems demonstrate that no theory can fulfil a number of intuitively compelling adequacy conditions which, most agree, any reasonable theory of optimal population size must fulfil… — for example, the condition that one population is better than another if everyone is better off in the former than the latter, and the condition that it is better to create people with a higher rather than a lower level of well-being" (Richardson et al., 2016).

Indeed, we will be stuck with the Repugnant Conclusion as long as we stick to certain intuitions and classical paradigms for how to think about ethics. On the other hand, the focus on the urgency of suffering that I have been advancing and a revision of the way we think about the term "better" — thus reframing how we think about population ethics — allows us to avoid the Repugnant Conclusion while constructing a logically coherent ethical framework.

Why non-existence isn't a bad thing

Imagine that everyone on the planet went to sleep at the same time. Imagine that they could sleep for a very long time without being fed and without ageing. A long, dreamless sleep. And during this sleep, no one suffered. Would there be any need or urgency to wake everyone up? Would it matter if they woke up after a day, or a month, or a year? Or even a thousand years? Would it matter if their active lives were delayed, and that there were no thoughts or feelings while they slept? While they would technically be existing, there would be no subjective content to their existence. But imagine that waking them up would mean that some of them would soon experience extreme suffering. Would we still wake them up? Would we wait just a little bit longer? A decision to let everyone continue sleeping would, in practice, be similar to maintaining non-existence, though in a way that wouldn't feel as intuitively disturbing.

The authors of a page on negative utilitarianism wrote, "Isn't it a plausible intuition that non-existence cannot be a problem, because no one is bothered by it?... It is perhaps only when we contemplate the matter from the (heavily biased) perspective of already existing and biologically evolved beings with a strong System 1 drive towards continued life, that we may find the idea abhorrent" (Negative Utilitarianism FAQ, n.d.).

The universe appears to be largely empty of conscious life. That emptiness is not in any way problematic. For example, most of us don't observe a sterile, rocky planet in a distant solar system and feel a desperate need to cover its surface with life. On the other hand, filling even some of that void with extreme suffering would be very much problematic, to say the least. And how many well-meaning actions to preserve life actually cause more intense suffering in the world by perpetuating the Darwinian nightmare?

What matters about non-existence is only phenomenological, in specific ways — the fear itself of non-existence, especially through the anticipation of some kind of Armageddon, and the suffering brought about by any action or event that were to cause non-existence. For this reason, there is a huge difference between a human-caused or natural catastrophe that leads to widespread destruction and misery, such as nuclear war, bioterrorism, severe climate change or a large asteroid impact, and any nonviolent scenarios that might slowly but harmlessly lead to extinction. This doesn't mean we need to choose non-existence, but we do need to distinguish between existential risk itself and any catastrophes that could cause it.

Reducing existential risk: an intuition with conditions

The reduction of existential risk, also known as "x-risk", has become an area of intensified research and also a major philanthropic cause area. Existential risk has been defined by Nick Bostrom (2002) as "one where an adverse outcome would either annihilate Earth-originating intelligent life or permanently and drastically curtail its potential". While averting our own demise, due for example to bioweapons or unfriendly/misguided AGI, is an obvious and natural endeavour to embark on, some of the most explicitly voiced ethical underpinnings of such projects are a *desire*, framed as a need, to create positive expected value, translated more concretely into future sentient beings experiencing happiness or bliss. Once again, we find intuitions such as existence bias seemingly dominating the discourse on priorities. The more rationally compelling *need* to prevent extreme suffering from occurring is usually overlooked.

Imagine a group of engineers with God-like powers in front of a drawing board or computer screen, working out designs for the future of our planet. And imagine that their design was already pretty good—almost perfect!—but they knew that, according to this design, some people would experience extreme suffering, like children being raped, parents losing their children, and countless sentient beings tortured. They would keep working on it until they got it right. Just like a car manufacturer that had produced an amazing model—powerful, responsive, economical, environmentally friendly, comfortable, aesthetically pleasing—that, however, has a defect causing one in every 1,000,000 cars to spontaneously explode, leading to the incineration of its occupants: it would be back to the drawing board until they solved the problem.

We are a conscious manifestation of the universe and, in a very real sense, playing God. If we are trying to influence the future, why would we be any more lax than those engineers in trying to rule out the very worst possible consequences of existence? Affirming a desire for indefinite life on the planet holds you to a very high level of responsibility. Is there any failure rate that is acceptable? Is having a few women raped with an iron rod and left to die (TOI-Online, 2019) acceptable so that we can create happy organisms too, rather than trying to keep the matter of the universe inanimate? Would you yourself accept the fate of experiencing similarly brutal torture, or for someone close to you with whom you deeply empathise to experience it, or is it only acceptable if "others" experience it? Is it possible you would change your mind if you had experienced it? And—again—where does this compulsion to create "value" come from? Is it not the product of Darwinian minds, designed without any overriding ethical constraints except as they are instrumental to survival and reproduction?

The Omelas short story, though revelatory of one of our strongest moral intuitions, is the product of one brilliant woman's mind (inspired by Dostoyevsky's *Brothers Karamazov* and an essay by William James, 1891) and obviously does not provide an absolute prescription for what to do about existence. It is more like a thought experiment that teases out the huge inconsistency between our sensitivities and the consequences of our actual actions, and forces us to rethink our priorities. It's not simply that we are taking the *risk* of a future Omelas scenario. By making decisions today to ensure the survival of humanity even if there is extreme suffering, we are playing a similar role to those who *created* Omelas, even if the child is chosen randomly.

In hopeful talk about a future served by new technology, there often seems to be an almost religious-like hope in a messianic turning point in the nature of the world that will make all the past suffering worthwhile. But those who are horrified by existential risk might want to think more deeply about why they consider risks of the worst suffering to still be acceptable. Furthermore, the flourishing future they seek to ensure is a difficult proposition given what we know about human nature and the hardware of our brains, and more generally, the apathy of competitive, evolutionary processes to the suffering they generate. There seems to be an unjustifiably optimistic view of our capacity to shake off our propensity for self-interest even if it causes great harm to others—at least as long as we retain our current biological form, but perhaps even if we transcend it.

Philosopher Roger Crisp (2021), who does not even identify as a negative utilitarian, wrote, "Perhaps one reason we think extinction would be so bad is that we have failed to recognise just how awful extreme agony is. Nevertheless, we have enough evidence, and imaginative capacity, to say that it is not unreasonable to see the pain of an hour of torture as something that can never be counterbalanced by any amount of positive value. And if this view is correct, then it suggests that the best outcome would be the immediate extinction that follows from allowing an asteroid to hit our planet."

Derek Parfit (2017) wrote a passage about the future in which he expressed the conflicting sentiments of being happy one exists while recognising that the happiness doesn't justify the past suffering (italics added): "Life can be wonderful as well as terrible, and we shall increasingly have the power to make life good. Since human history may be only just beginning, we can expect that future humans, or suprahumans, may achieve some great goods that we cannot now even imagine ... Some of our successors might live lives and create worlds that, *though failing to justify past suffering*, would have given us all, including those who suffered most, reasons to be glad that the Universe exists." I would strongly contest that the future bliss of any successors would make the past victims of the worst torture glad that the universe exists. But the thought expressed in this passage also implies that if the future also contains similar suffering, it does not justify *itself*.

Some thinkers, such as Nick Bostrom (2003), have entertained the idea that our entire world is a simulation on an extremely powerful computer. I think this is highly unlikely to be the case, for several reasons, including that the complexity of the world and the need to maintain smooth internal consistency between everything experienced would make it technically unfeasible; and that it seems an unnecessarily complex explanation for the phenomenon of life and therefore, by Occam's Razor, unlikely to be true. But if we really were in an intended simulation, wouldn't it be extremely cruel for someone to allow this to happen, with all the experienced suffering that the simulated world contains? If so, why would we be more accepting of the same situation just because it is the product of random, "unintelligent" processes?

Yet the absurdity of life seems lost in very serious mathematical calculations about hedonics and value, which I have argued are based on various flawed ideas about the meaning of value in an ethical context. There is an implicit principle that "life must go on", even if terrible things continue to happen, because our imperative is to create value or utility. In these discussions, we seem to have lost the critical, less rosy perspectives and insights of philosophers and writers such as Arthur Schopenhauer (1890, "There is no doubt that life is given us, not to be enjoyed, but to be overcome; to be got over") or Franz Kafka (2004, "One of the first signs of the beginning of understanding is the wish to die. This life appears unbearable, another unattainable"). If we get things wrong, what's the worst that can happen? Which scenario better represents Hades, an actual eternal hell of tortured sentient beings, or the emptiness of another barren planet?

The classical utilitarian perspective that aims to maximise future "value" and uses expected value considerations abhors existential risk but isn't nearly as bothered by catastrophic risk except where it could become existential. The result is a reluctance to focus excessively on the spreading of compassion, and a greater focus on measures to increase expected value, such as space colonisation. There is also an associated tendency to support measures such as life extension, cryonics and mind uploading, which actually have less to do with net value and more with an intuitive desire for self-preservation.

A few quotes from Nick Bostrom's (2013) paper "Existential Risk Prevention as Global Priority" illustrate this perspective: "Many theories of value imply that even relatively small reductions in net existential risk have enormous expected value." "Let us suppose that the lives of persons usually have some significant positive value and that this value is aggregative (in the sense that the value of two similar lives is twice that of one life)." "To calculate the loss associated with an existential catastrophe, we must consider how much value would come to exist in its absence."

A post on the website of 80,000 Hours, which contains high-quality, thoughtful analyses and interviews, states: "The most powerful way we can help future generations is, we think, to prevent a catastrophe that could end advanced civilization, or even prevent any future generations from existing" (Todd, 2017). But future generations do not need help unless they exist, and then the highest priority help would be to prevent them from suffering! Protecting humanity's "long-term potential" needs to be done safely. This means, protecting any future beings from the potential for great harm.

One of the most apparent inconsistencies seen among many self-identifying rationalists is in the degree to which they apply rationality to their core ethics. While ethics is inseparable from some core intuitions—don't cause direct harm, be fair, try to survive—the arguably most rational principle, to prevent extreme suffering that you couldn't voluntarily bear yourself, is the one that is possibly most neglected. The relief of extreme physical pain is currently still an overlooked area of intervention within the effective altruism community, while reducing existential risk is literally a "cause célèbre" that attracts huge attention, though the suffering that would likely be contained in the future is viewed as being of secondary importance.[2] The significance of suffering at the extreme end of the intensity scale is undervalued—the very fact that the scale is logarithmic does not even seem widely appreciated, let alone the existence of tipping points into unbearableness—while the theoretically astronomical number of future potential sentient beings dominates the thinking.

The phrase "suffering is part of life" can be a philosophical acceptance of things one doesn't see a possibility to change, but it can also be an

---

[2] See Phil Torres's (2021a, 2021b) scathing critique of this thinking and subsequent, more comprehensive and philosophical analysis, as well as David Pearce's (2021b) more nuanced reflections.

excuse for continuing with harmful behaviours and the acceptance of structures that serve one's own interests, rather than honestly assessing reality and priorities.

Appeals by rationalists for reducing existential risk would be more compelling or at least appear more genuine if explicitly argued from the perspective of human intuition—that, as human beings, we just don't want to see our entire world go up in flames during our lifetime. The acceptance of potentially astronomical amounts, or even much lower quantities, of torture-level suffering that not one of the proponents of existential risk reduction would personally be able to bear is inherently irrational. Rather than trying to ensure a situation where such scenarios can take place, even if the suffering is an unintended but expected side effect, it would be more rational to focus our energy on ensuring that such experiences are never allowed to happen.[3]

Of course, many of the scenarios that risk causing human extinction would also cause a huge amount of suffering, whether or not they actually led to extinction. And existential risk events that are anything less than total can create a huge amount of short-term suffering with little impact on the long term—for example, the atomic bombs dropped on Hiroshima and Nagasaki. There are also certainly more intuitively appealing approaches to warding off future suffering than to wait in anticipation of a catastrophe that finishes us all off. There are therefore good reasons for collaboration between those who seek to eliminate extreme suffering and those who seek to minimise existential risk (see also Baumann, 2020). But it is essential that a willingness to pursue the former goal be a condition of the latter.

Preserving consciousness

Although it may seem contradictory and therefore fundamentally irrational to value both the eradication of extreme suffering and the preservation of existence, the latter is a concession to the intuitions, desires and striving for meaning of people alive in the present. Although, as I argued above, there is no inherent necessity to preserve the existence of consciousness, we can still aim to do so within the context of a larger ethical framework that prioritises the prevention of suffering.

As a purely speculative and perhaps impractical scenario, we could imagine aiming to preserve blissful consciousness in a protected capsule,

---

[3] Simon Knutsson (2016) made a similar argument, writing, "instead of trying to ensure that humanity survives, we should prioritize making the future less bad, in case it will contain sentient life."

after first slowly and voluntarily scaling down the overall number of sentient beings on the planet, and carefully enhancing life, to be replicated only under conditions that eliminate the possibility of extreme suffering. Neither would there be any rush: after all, what's another million years in the grand scheme of things if it would allow us to get things right? This approach is driven by a radically different motivation than the classical utilitarian argument that creating many instances of bliss is morally "required" even if it entails some extreme suffering.

If most people who value existence would be reluctant even in theory to endorse such an approach because it would push potential flourishing further back into the future, this would at least indicate that the core concern is less about preserving future existence and consciousness, and more about continuity. In other words, that clinging to the idea of blissful future existence is really about satisfying human intuitions rather than about an inherent, supposedly utilitarian need.

Eleven

A Holistic Ethical Framework

One of my main missions for this book was to propose an ethical framework based entirely on phenomenological description and logic, and see how rationality interfaces with and can accommodate our intuitions and their constraints. An ethical framework based on the ideas I have been discussing cannot specify in absolute terms what you "should" do or what specific action is required. It can provide principles based on rationality and intuition, acknowledge the inherent conflict between negative utilitarian reasoning and deep human desires, and the very different perspectives on existence these represent, and suggest means for resolving conflicts between them. In this chapter I will set out some key principles and propose how they can be incorporated into such a framework.

Key principles

The following is a set of principles, axiomatic and otherwise, that I propose as the building blocks of an ethical framework. There is no foolproof means to determine whether an intuitive principle is so self-evident as to merit axiomatic status. In some cases I labelled as "axiomatic" principles that might also be derivable from other axioms but that seemed important enough to merit being stated explicitly. It is perhaps even less obvious to determine how strongly intuitive a principle is. For some people, principles listed here simply as intuitions may feel even more strongly intuitive than others that I consider axioms. And some principles that I labelled as intuitions are actually facts about human psychology, about what humans feel about morality, but the feelings themselves can be seen as contestable intuitions about the objectivity of moral facts. Yet the fact that certain things feel true is itself a relevant fact about human nature and intuitions, and therefore an important part of an ethical framework with practical aspirations.

This list might be longer than needed, or not comprehensive enough. But it is an attempt to state clearly what I think we know with certainty, and what things simply feel true without necessarily being true.

- Things only matter with respect to subjective experience.
  Status: axiomatic.
  Commentary: nothing can matter without someone for it to matter to.

- There is an inherent urgency for suffering to be relieved, and this urgency correlates with the intensity of suffering.
  Status: axiomatic.
  Commentary: this is essential to what suffering is—an aversive feeling that people and animals want to end (except for voluntary suffering, which is perceived differently), and the strength of this desire increases with intensity.

- One instance of suffering (in time and space) is proportionately better (i.e. preferable, less bad) than two instances of suffering (anywhere else in time and space) of the same duration and level of intensity.
  Status: axiomatic.
  Commentary: fundamental intuition.

- An instance of suffering at a lower intensity is better (i.e. preferable, less bad) than an instance of suffering at a higher intensity.
  Status: axiomatic.
  Commentary: fundamental intuition.

- Non-existence or emptiness has no inherent need to be changed.
  Status: logical deduction.
  Commentary: where there is no suffering, there is no urgency.

- Species membership doesn't change the inherent urgency of suffering.
  Status: logical deduction.
  Commentary: suffering is an internal phenomenon that matters intrinsically and doesn't depend on other factors.

- Unbearable suffering is qualitatively distinct from other, bearable levels of suffering in a way that is uniquely significant.
  Status: logical deduction.
  Commentary: a preference to die rather than continue to endure the suffering, in someone with a normal will to live, gives it a different quality, overriding our strongest instinct—existence bias—and unbearable suffering cannot be voluntarily agreed to without the

constraint of irreversibility of the decision and loss of autonomy throughout the experience.

- It feels important to preserve existence and the environment on which existence depends.
  Status: strong intuition.
  Commentary: going against this intuition can create huge cognitive dissonance with our existence bias and our desire to thrive, especially when we experience love, happiness and meaning.

- It feels "wrong" to harm another sentient being or to concentrate suffering among some sentient beings.
  Status: strong intuition.
  Commentary: going against this intuition can create huge cognitive dissonance and lead to a world that doesn't feel worth preserving.

- It can feel as important to help many individuals suffering at a moderate intensity as to help fewer individuals suffering at a higher intensity.
  Status: (strong) intuition.
  Commentary: sensitivity to two distinct variables, especially when there is some qualitative overlap in the suffering.

- It can feel "wrong" to infringe on someone's personal autonomy in order to prevent them from experiencing bearable suffering.
  Status: intuition.
  Commentary: going against this intuition can create cognitive dissonance with our desire for personal freedom and potentially lead to a world that doesn't feel worth preserving.

xNU+

An ethical framework that can provide universal guidance to decision-making needs to be consistent with the truth and remain relevant even as new technologies create new paradigms and ethical challenges. Based on everything I have written above, the obvious starting point is to put the ethical focus on suffering, with overwhelming priority to eradicating unbearable suffering—situations where existence is simply not a voluntary option. This implies some form of negative utilitarianism.

As discussed earlier, negative utilitarianism is still a minority view among philosophers. But the problem is not negative utilitarianism. The problem is reality. And many people are afraid to confront it. So instead of facing the truth about suffering and existence, and then seeing how we can compromise, if necessary, with our other values or intuitions, many philosophers neglect this truth and adhere to a more palatable framework that, I argue, is inherently flawed.

Negative utilitarianism is a logical consequence of simply accepting a metaphysically accurate view of personal identity, and the fact that suffering has a uniquely inherent call to action—with certain degrees of suffering literally unbearable. The implications may be counterintuitive, but they are no less rational in the context of ethics than are special relativity and quantum entanglement in the context of physics. Rather than sweep aside a transparent, rational ethical framework because we don't like the implications, we need to honestly explore why we don't like the implications, and how our own perspectives and beliefs conflict with deeper truths that are central to ethics.

A vision of a sustainable utopia is obviously compelling, as it provides a concrete goal for people to work towards and inspire others to share. But what if the apparent logical extension of an ethical theory is non-existence—that is, non-existence appears a better state-of-affairs than a world that contains extreme suffering? Non-existence is hardly an inspiring goal for most people, even for those who are strongly compassionate, and it has the marketing appeal of a death cult. What do you do? Do you change the starting assumptions of your theory, or your arguments, no matter how rational they appear, in order to arrive at conclusions that better accommodate common intuitions and strivings? Or do you acknowledge the conflict and seek a post hoc compromise that doesn't fault people, including compassionate activists, for wanting to exist, and allows us all to adopt a variation of the framework that we can live with?

This was the original reason why, in *The Battle for Compassion*, I proposed a variation of negative utilitarianism called "negative utilitarianism *plus*" where we accommodate the human desire to exist. The "plus" softens the potentially nihilistic implications of applying hard negative utilitarianism to life, including one's own, and this makes it pragmatic and useful.

David Pearce wrote in a social media comment, "Negative utilitarians are sometimes suspected of plotting Armageddon." Even if this suspicion is false, we can put in a non-Armageddon clause! This is part of what the "plus" achieves. It is disingenuous to discard a whole framework that is based on truth and compassion because we don't like some of its conclusions, and blame the messenger. The reasonable response to negative utilitarianism is not to reject it outright but to decide how far we want to go in applying it. You don't change your views about the overriding urgency of avoiding concentration camps, torture and factory farms because taken to the limit it suggests that life, overall, isn't as inherently wonderful or as worthy of preserving as we would like to believe.

It's also important to emphasise that just because we wouldn't have decided to create a situation doesn't mean that we can simply change it back once it arises. We can evaluate situation B as being much worse than situation A, but this doesn't imply that the path from A to B is reversible, as the current situation constrains which goals we can reasonably seek and which paths are available to us. As Jamie Mayerfeld (1999, p. 159) wrote, "there may be a crucial difference between thinking that it would have been better if the world had never come into existence, and thinking that we may take it upon ourselves to destroy the life that already exists."

As I wrote earlier, I have since expanded the framework to "xNU+" in order to place the appropriate emphasis on extreme suffering. The "x" clarifies that extreme/unbearable suffering is in a separate category altogether and ensures that the framework prioritises what matters most, and that we are not distracted with arguments about minor suffering such as pinpricks. I have also expanded the significance of the "+" to include more broadly the desire to thrive, and to better accommodate our most deep-rooted intuitions, without putting them on the same ethical level as the rationally justified, inherently urgent need to eradicate extreme suffering.

So if we were to summarise xNU+ with a few principles, we could say: prevent as much suffering as possible, especially intense or extreme suffering, while also avoiding excessive conflict with our deepest intuitions, namely, to survive and thrive, and to avoid causing direct harm or concentrating suffering. Again, the point of the framework is not to determine what actions are "right" and "wrong" in a moral sense—I explained why I consider such a framing misleading or meaningless—but rather, to try to align our goals and actions with compassion and rationality while navigating with conflicting moral instruments.

The "+" plays an additional, important role in accommodating our other intuitions. Support for classical utilitarianism seems due in part to a common way of framing ethics, where an ethical theory is often seen as applying to all human activity and allocating a judgement about whether a behaviour is ethical or not. If this were the case, we would have to consider ourselves full-time moral agents, and any behaviour departing from the ethical prescription for a given situation might be considered unethical, rather than simply neutral. In principle, this could even include choosing to alleviate suffering instead of producing a "greater amount" of bliss. Under such an ethical framework, someone who takes pleasure in life but attributes much greater negative ethical weight to suffering than positive weight to bliss might have to pretend that they *personally* really don't value all those earthly pleasures very much, because to admit otherwise might require shifting their activities towards pleasure-seeking in order to maximise utility. But not every action we take, such as those we take in pursuit of pleasure, can be driven by compassion or an attempt to change the world. Ethical thinking is still there in the background, keeping track of our choices and ensuring we don't do unnecessary harm. But we can acknowledge that, as individuals, while we do indeed value bliss, we don't try to bring it under the same utilitarian umbrella. A viable, sustainable ethical framework can simply acknowledge the deep human desire and intuition to thrive and even seek bliss, without labelling it with an ethical stamp of approval, and also without considering it as inherently unethical either.

In this way, xNU+ distinguishes itself from standard negative utilitarianism in how it resolves the meta-ethical question about the meaning of an ethical framework. It more explicitly acknowledges a fair degree of human behaviour as ethically neutral—still fun and perceived as "inherently valuable" when experienced, just lacking in "moral necessity" or urgency.

The xNU+ framework reconciles the ethical need to reduce extreme suffering with the intuitive need to thrive as human beings, by treating them as distinct modes of being. It acknowledges the practical need to maintain a world perceived as worth living in as a concession, while valuing the prevention and ideally the elimination of all extreme suffering as our ethical priority. It respects our desire to remain "romantic" human beings even while we rationally aim for as much impact as possible.

The balance we seek thereby shifts entirely from the actions we prioritise in the world—where the balance represents an attempt, according to classical utilitarianism, to equate reducing suffering and increasing bliss, with just the right exchange coefficient—to our *personal balance* between pursuing bliss and acting as agents aiming to prevent or alleviate suffering in the world. The xNU+ framework acknowledges that we have deep moral intuitions, and also a desire for continuity, and respects them as integral to being human, without placing them on the same level as the urgent elimination of intense suffering. It recasts the debate about the "correct" ethical framework as a search for a practical, sustainable inner balance in the tango between the agent aiming to act on the world and the romantic human with strong drives and intuitions that require attention.

Given that any amount of extreme suffering is inherently intolerable, it would be both rational and compassionate to use as much of our time as we can trying to reduce it, while living a baseline lifestyle that seeks to avoid causing harm. A meaningful "trade ratio" between happiness and suffering is then the amount of time and resources you need to spend to feel an overall sense of thriving compared to the amount of time and resources you can reasonably make available for thoughtfully preventing suffering.

Does this mean the "+" in xNU+ is only there for instrumental reasons? That is, is it only there to make the "NU" part palatable? From the perspective of a rational agent who wants a strict suffering-focused framework to be as acceptable and applicable as possible: yes. From the perspective of a person who is first and foremost a human being before being an agent of change in the world: no. So how do we answer the question definitively? Well, who is leading the tango? I don't think we can really give a clear answer. It always seems to be changing, depending on our mood and that of the "music" that is playing around us—our immediate environment. And we may have no realistic choice but to relent and become the dance.

Another way of looking at it is that the "xNU" part corresponds more closely to empty individualism and the objective equivalence of all extreme suffering, while the "+" better represents closed individualism, a perspective that allows so much of the meaning and happiness people commonly experience (though it is also the source of so much misery, through ego-driven competition). In that respect, the "+" captures much of what classical utilitarianism seeks to include but frames it more accurately in terms of strongly intuitive human aspirations.

I also don't believe we can clearly differentiate between ethics and its implementation. If intuitions were not taken into account because they were seen as irrational or at least arational, an idealised rational ethical framework could simply demand non-existence as the ultimate goal and prescribe that any ethical action move things in that direction. But trying to impose an ethical theory that is rationally grounded but that most people find deeply appalling—rather than, say, simply inconvenient—isn't viable. Especially if it seeks to turn us all into both agents and potential victims of destruction.

Although the focus on improving the world implies consequentialism and specifically some form of negative utilitarianism as the reference ethical framework, the intuitive human being is the reference for thriving and being. We can't separate the two so long as we are trying to maintain a world perceived as worth living in. The detached utilitarian mindset and its more radical implications lose sway when we interact with other human beings, connect with them emotionally and work together for a more peaceful, more empathetic and more cooperative world.

The implementation of a purely utilitarian ethical framework that applies ideal prioritisation, based on rational detachment and the categorisation of extreme, unbearable suffering as uniquely urgent to prevent or alleviate, would run up against a practical barrier. The average person puts their own wellbeing first and doesn't apply the principles of cause neutrality (most commonly meaning, to select causes based on impartial estimates of impact; Schubert, 2017) and empty individualism, where no person (or more correctly, no consciousness-moment) matters more than another, and degree of suffering is the primary determinant of prioritisation. Humans want to be treated in a way that feels fair, even if it seems metaphysically "incorrect". So a viable ethical framework has to allow for compromise and solutions that satisfy people's expectations, even if these are different from what a more objective analysis might prescribe. Ethics, to be practically relevant, has to try to meet some strong wants as well, even when these don't seem readily reducible to the most fundamental needs.

As I mentioned earlier, in *The Battle for Compassion* I proposed four "universal humanitarian values" that capture four key elements of a world that feels worth living in: most importantly, freedom and solidarity; and on a secondary level, diversity and continuity. If I were to draw a correspondence to the xNU+ framework, the "xNU" part represents solidarity, that is, the will and commitment to protect all sentient beings from harm, and especially from extreme suffering; and the "+" represents our strong intuitive desire to be free, and also to survive into the future and enjoy a variety of experiences — in short, to thrive. The deep moral intuitions not to cause direct harm to others or to concentrate suffering can be seen both as aspects of solidarity and of respecting the freedom of others to thrive.

Is there a practical distinction between self-identifying primarily as an ethical change agent who also optimises their wellbeing in order to be most effective, and, conversely, viewing oneself first and foremost as an intuitive human being who thrives but also seeks to reduce as much suffering as possible in the world? That is, do these two distinct starting points yield very different results? In fact, the real-world priorities of these two perspectives might converge in practice. The first perspective might continue to resist existence bias as well as our other deep intuitions when they may lead to more extreme suffering. But we are likely to be much more effective in persuading others to prioritise the prevention of suffering if we serve as relatable role models for how to live (Leighton, 2017). And the real-life tango that inevitably emerges between these two perspectives ends up blurring the distinction between the starting points.

It would be ironic if a classical utilitarian who attributes a high weighting to suffering became a full-time agent aimed at reducing suffering while rejecting the principle of negative utilitarianism that they are de facto practising. Unless they would really be willing to abandon altruistic work in favour of promoting widespread hedonism were the levels of expected bliss sufficiently high, they are a classical utilitarian by identification only. They just might not want life on the planet to end. xNU+ provides a way to accurately capture this vision of the world.

How xNU+ compares to prioritarianism

Prioritarianism says that "benefits to the worse off matter more than benefits to the better off" (Prioritarianism, 2020). The ethical framework I've described seems closely aligned with this view, which would seem to prioritise helping those who are suffering the most and whose situation is most urgent. However, as mentioned earlier, prioritarianism does not reject the classical utilitarian principle that enough pluses can formally outweigh the minuses; it just says that the minuses have extra weight. It does not put extreme/unbearable suffering in a separate category. In addition, the vague term "worst off" could be interpreted either as referring to those suffering the most at a particular instant, or those who tend to be suffering the most overall due to their life circumstances (which is closer to low life satisfaction). Aside from the flaws it shares with classical utilitarianism, it therefore appears to be a less direct means of addressing the core phenomenon of urgency.

A version of prioritarianism that has been termed "negative prioritarianism" (Animal Ethics, 2020) explicitly puts the emphasis on reducing suffering, again with greater weight or priority to those suffering the most, and precludes giving ethical weight to happiness. While there are relatively few mentions of this term in the literature, xNU+ is much more closely aligned with this view than with traditional prioritarianism, and is even closer to it than to negative utilitarianism itself. But both negative utilitarianism and negative prioritarianism — and the latter could also be seen as a variation of the former — formally accept the aggregation of suffering, just with different weightings, whereas xNU+, as I define it, puts extreme/unbearable suffering in a different category, while considering trade-offs between intensities and numbers of individuals to be a question for intuitions and not something for which there are precise rational answers. These are important subtleties that are not readily captured by employing two- or three-word terms that have already been used with somewhat different specific meanings.

How xNU+ responds to common objections to negative utilitarianism

I addressed the main criticisms of negative utilitarianism early on, and later the objection to the use of thresholds. Other objections that have been made (Ord, 2013) are based on a view of ethics that focuses on determining what is "morally permissible" or "morally right", and also what is "plausible" — a vague word frequently used in ethics that seems most meaningfully substituted with the notion of an idea being intuitively acceptable, or a statement being potentially true. I have explained why I don't consider the framing in terms of moral permissibility to be objectively meaningful, and also that an idea that is counterintuitive is not inherently irrational.

I have also discussed how we can incorporate the human desire to thrive within the framework without giving the creation of happiness the ethical importance of reducing suffering; how there is no inherent need for bliss unless its absence causes frustration; and, more generally, why even according to the xNU+ framework, happiness has important instrumental value for the suffering it reduces. I have put into question the relevance in most cases of the term "value" as it is generally used, and I have explained why voluntary trade-offs between happiness and suffering that an individual makes for themselves are not translatable to objectively valid trade-offs imposed on different people.

The xNU+ framework as I have described it is based on actual phenomenal experience, on determining where there is an inherent urgency for action or intervention, and on striving for objectivity, consistency and the incorporation of metaphysical reality. It seeks to avoid imprecision in ethical terminology, while acknowledging the inherent ethical uncertainty in most situations instead of imposing arbitrary ethical prescriptions.

As I discussed early on, the field of ethics is closely associated with certain established framings of the problem of how to make decisions. Ethicists often seek precise answers to vaguely defined questions (e.g. what "ought" we to do?), instead of admitting inherently uncertain answers to more clearly defined questions (e.g. where is there urgency to act?). A paradigm shift in how we think about ethics as I have described above, encapsulated in the xNU+ framework, can provide a more accurate model of the problem and greater clarity in how we think about our priorities.

In the belief that unambiguity is essential for a practically implementable ethical framework, some might argue that the "+" in xNU+ is simply too vague or "intellectually messy" (Pearce, 2005), and that, because it brings conflicting values into the framework, it does not even theoretically allow for unambiguous decision-making, making it unusable for, say, establishing clear programmable values for ethical AGI. But the alternative is an arbitrary resolution to a complex problem, which might also prove ineffective or entirely unacceptable. In cases where we are

11. A Holistic Ethical Framework

forced to provide greater precision or else forfeit any attempt to specify the ethical principles, we can attempt to provide solutions that capture as closely as possible the essence of the conflicting concerns embedded in the framework. I will offer some specific examples in a chapter on resolving ethical conflicts.

Consistency: being truthful and rational

Once you accept a principle or set of principles, failing to apply them consistently suggests that there are other principles governing your behaviour that you are applying, even if only implicitly and subconsciously, that you may not be admitting to. If you accept the initial principles as rational, contradicting them suggests that you are prepared to act irrationally. For example, if you agree that it is uncompassionate and unjustified to torture non-human animals for your pleasure, as you yourself would not want to be treated like that, yet you continue to eat bacon from factory-farmed animals because it tastes good, your actions would be inconsistent with the rational, ethical principles you claimed to agree with. The implied additional "principle", if one can call it that, would be that when you enjoy something, or would otherwise be inconvenienced, you can ignore the ethical principles themselves. But such self-interested rationalisation is precisely what rational ethical thinking seeks to constrain.

On the other hand, the ethical framework may itself harbour conflicting principles, as discussed. That presents a different kind of issue and requires potentially creative solutions to try to resolve it. But causing harm to others as a means to personal pleasure is not an example of conflicting ethical principles in the framework I've described.

On a page about ethical theories, Animal Ethics (n.d.-a) writes, "Some theories may themselves be internally inconsistent, and thus have to be rejected." But a truth-based theory that provides clear, absolute prescriptions or guidance may not be possible, and, in fact, conflicting principles seems to be an inevitable characteristic of an authentic ethical framework. We may not be able to achieve unambiguity, but a holistic framework like xNU+ can provide a pragmatic guide to achieving the best world we can. Seeking unambiguity may itself stem from moral intuitions that want clear codes of conduct in a messy world.

One might ask whether it is meaningful to espouse a utilitarian or consequentialist framework and then, as one self-proclaimed "dyed-in-the-wool consequentialist" phrased it (during an animal rights conference at which, I can't help but mention, wool-dyeing would surely be frowned upon), "just throw in a deontological principle every time one arrives at a consequentialist conclusion one doesn't like." Is there not the risk of diluting away the essential principle of preventing intense suffering by accommodating all manner of preferences as intuitions to be respected?

Aside from existence bias itself and the desire to thrive, the main potentially conflicting principles are the core intuitions against directly causing harm and concentrating suffering, intuitions that we cannot ignore at the risk of undermining our overall ethical project altogether. This means we are not casually "throwing in" deontological principles as they pop up but acknowledging a few very strong ones that already exist in people's minds.

This is not to say that the question of how far to accommodate these intuitions is a minor one. I address some such conflicts in a separate chapter.

How everything is connected by utilitarianism

Once we acknowledge the prevention of intense suffering wherever it occurs as our core goal, and that every instance of equivalent suffering matters equally, rationality compels us to accept comparisons between situations that are formally or practically equivalent, and ultimately to strive to evaluate the impact of our actions on the absolute amount of intense suffering throughout time and space, using expected value as a tool.

This means that the number of steps between our actions and any suffering we can impact is irrelevant, as long as there is a causal chain. It means that any distinction we make between actions with equivalent outcomes in terms of reduced suffering is due to intuitions, including their reflection in societal norms we try to abide by, or a desire for personal purity. It also means that utilitarianism usually provides a poor rationale for choosing between small-scale actions when there are larger, more impactful ones we could be focusing on instead.

How obsessive utilitarianism can be self-defeating

I have been addressing in depth the need to accommodate our intuitions as we strive for impact in preventing suffering. But because utilitarianism remains a reference for measuring impact, in this section I would like to explore in more detail how obsessive (or "naïve", as some say) utilitarianism can be self-defeating. By "obsessive", I mean both an excessive focus on calculating the consequences of small-scale actions, and an overall mindset in which utilitarianism dominates one's daily life.

Utilitarianism is most purely applicable to situations where we have a clear view of the alternative outcomes and there aren't strongly competing intuitions. This can apply, for example, to situations such as spending money most effectively to treat as many individuals as possible suffering from a specific disease, or deciding whether to use money to prevent animals from being tortured or to build a new museum. The clearest cases where it is applicable are often trivially obvious because of a lack of complicating factors, but these cases may also be small-scale and relatively inconsequential because of the low degree of impact, though utilitarianism itself implies shifting our attention away from such small-scale situations altogether and towards ones with greater impact, including large-scale systemic change, where possible. Utilitarianism would be most relevant to any hypothetical situation where one is in a position to "play God" and make decisions that could dramatically change the future of life on our planet and beyond.

When we focus on short-term utilitarian gains, these may be all we can realistically hope to achieve under given circumstances. But it may often be more about having a good conscience, and even a sense of personal moral purity (though in a more rationalist, numbers-focused sense), than about significantly impacting the amount of suffering in the universe.

Pure utilitarian decision-making is, in any case, rarely applicable because "all other things being equal" is rarely the case and there are almost always complicating factors. In most situations, there are downstream flow-through effects of one's actions that severely complicate the calculation, to the point of impracticability.

But aside from the practical difficulties of taking all relevant factors into account in determining impact on suffering, intuitions will play a significant role because we have to live with the consequences. Obsessive utilitarianism can literally blunt our capacity for empathy by leading us to overrule our emotions. The cognitive dissonance would accumulate to make even everyday life feel utterly absurd, a dystopia in supposed service of hedonically-based ethics, turning individuals into disposable appendages of the whole. What then would be left to want to preserve? Applying such a hard utilitarian framework would, ironically, make world destruction a more attractive option, not directly through calculations in the way that people sometimes accuse negative utilitarianism of, but because such a world would be awful to live in for everyone—one where friends might turn disloyal, break commitments in an instant and even harm others if the utility calculations warranted it.

"The ends justify the means" is a poor basis for promoting a more compassionate world, because it requires us to carry out acts that undermine our strongest intuitions about what it means to be compassionate. This is why pure utilitarianism is so limited in its applicability, even though it provides an overall strategic goal. The xNU+ framework is more humanistic and viable than pure utilitarianism of either the negative or classical varieties, because it explicitly accommodates both our ethical priorities and our human needs.

Utilitarianism is intellectually most compelling from a detached, bird's eye perspective, where personal identity doesn't matter. It clashes with brains that value trust, intimacy and commitment, and that are not designed to be happy (and thus more effective) when operating according to utilitarian rules.

In fact, commitment can be seen as a deontological concept that is itself necessary for overall utilitarian outcomes. It translates to an explicit engagement not always to act according to small-scale act utilitarianism—specifically, not to change an agreed-upon decision because of a reassessment of the parameters. You can still break a commitment for utilitarian reasons, but in so doing you reduce the value of your future commitments and the possibilities for cooperation.

In interpersonal relationships, being calculating is often seen as a flaw, not an advantage. People generally want to feel that you are making decisions in a relationship based on a gut feeling of goodwill and not a calculation of cost–benefit based on whatever personal and ethical principles are being applied. People want commitments that won't readily change with circumstances, even if the other person would benefit from breaking the commitment. The whole realm of meaningful existence as most humans experience it is based on such non-analytical, intuitive and emotional experiences as love or a feeling of close connection. To be able to empathise with humans, and to feel that life is rich and meaningful, we have to leave space in our lives to have intuitive, human experiences, and not to operate mostly as pure utilitarian change agents in our relations with those closest to us.

Pure negative utilitarianism is, on the one hand, actually a deeply caring philosophy because it recognises the reality and extent of suffering spawned by the universe, and considers the pursuit of pleasures to be ethically neutral and even a distraction from the urgency we are faced with. On the other hand, by turning us all into full-time methodical change agents, it would risk disconnecting us from our own nature and the ability to lose ourselves in feelings such as love.

An obsessively utilitarian mindset can also kill spirituality—experiences we are capable of when we live in the moment and suspend our impulse to analyse and explain everything at a reductionist level. E.O. Wilson (1998, p. 36), the eminent scientist who founded the field of sociobiology, wrote, "Pure reason is unappealing because it is bloodless. Ceremonies stripped of sacred mystery lose their emotional force…"

The complex knock-on effects of trying to be too rigorously utilitarian in specific situations, effects that can include an erosion of empathy, are often a good reason to fall back on more conventional and even intuitive decision-making, which may give a better long-term outcome from a utilitarian perspective. Ironically, then, it's that capacity to temporarily suspend rational thinking and connect with others at a raw, intuitive level the way non-human animals so readily do that may hold the secret to widespread change. A viable theory of ethics meant to be implemented by and applied to human beings cannot realistically demand that people act against their deepest human intuitions.

Educator and activist Satish Kumar (2002) has expressed similar ideas about the consequences of divorcing rationality from intuition: "Pure Rationalism is in itself violence of the mind. Rationalism by its nature cuts through, separates, divides, isolates. This is not to say that rationality has no place in our lives. It has. But it should be kept in place and not given an exaggerated status in society. Rationality tempered with the feelings and intuition of the heart, the yin-yang balance, can create a culture of non-violence, wholeness and compassion whereas pure Rationalism creates a culture of violence."

Strict utilitarianism based on empty individualism can also potentially destroy one's sense of personal identity and capacity for self-care. For example, if one treats one's future self as of no greater importance than anyone else, one might seek to have maximum impact now, perhaps by taking risks, even if it's destructive to one's long-term future.

Yes, you could view things like respecting personal identity and keeping personal commitments as modes of being that are *instrumentally* useful to fulfil in pursuit of an optimal utilitarianism. This is true. But the *mindset* itself is different when you are attending to some of the needs of the ego and plunging into the complex beauty and meaning of life.

Although this may be a clichéd and inaccurate portrayal, I have sometimes felt that some of those who subscribe to utilitarianism and acknowledge as well the need for personal happiness for instrumental reasons view the latter as a numerical quantity of positive hedonism that needs to be thrown into the equation, potentially devoid of the beauty that comes from immersing oneself in life, guided by the raw senses, feelings and intuition. By enjoying oneself just for the instrumental purpose of being more effective, one is actually closer to an ascetic form of negative utilitarianism than to the "romantic" form of it I have proposed.

Utilitarian reasoning is also far from how we typically evaluate current events and judge the decisions of political leaders. It would appear disturbing, at the least, to suggest that an apparently horrific decision involving suffering and death could be defended on overall utilitarian grounds—even in the highly improbable case that this was how a world leader was actually making decisions. For example, it seems unlikely that drone strikes in Pakistan saved lives overall, but even if this were the case, it would be impossible to accept an American president explicitly justifying them for having saved more innocent American lives than they destroyed innocent Pakistani lives.

Obsessive utilitarianism also risks diverting our attention from longer-term systemic solutions that might lead to far less suffering and therefore ultimately be more utilitarian in the long run. For example, some have suggested that factory farming, due to the clearing of land needed to supply food for the animals, might lead to reduced suffering of wild animals in the long term through a reduction of habitat and hence reduced populations (e.g. Tomasik, 2019b). Aside from it possibly being wrong in the calculation of the amount of extreme suffering spared, this idea, if widely followed, could provide a justification for stabilising a horribly unacceptable situation in which the widespread torture of animals is tolerated, rather than promoting solutions where we eschew the torture of animals while also aiming to reduce the suffering of wild animals. This is one of the ways that narrowly focused utilitarianism risks missing the forest for the trees. It can seem to validate a micro-calculated short-term perspective while devaluing more inspiring visions for the future.

Utilitarianism can also too easily be manipulated by wishful thinking to justify behaviours that would normally be considered "unethical". For example, you might decide to compensate for harm that you cause—for instance, by eating factory-farmed animal products—by spending money to prevent harm elsewhere. This specific reasoning is actually used by some utilitarians. In fact, the approach seems fundamentally flawed. The reasoning only works if you have arbitrarily decided on an upper boundary on how much you are normally willing to spend to relieve suffering in the world, and you dip into your additional reserves to "cancel out" additional suffering you create. But if it's money you had available that you would not otherwise have donated, this raises the question, why not? The same criticism can, incidentally, be levied against carbon compensation: if we have the ability through carbon offsets to negate carbon emissions due to flying and thereby have an impact on climate change and all the likely suffering that arises from it, why don't we do it *without* flying?

In fact, what looks like strict utilitarianism in these last examples seems to be more about personal purity—about wanting to claim that one's personal net contribution to animal cruelty or to climate change is zero—than about maximising one's personal impact in reducing these phenomena. Moral compensation is actually just a more calculated equivalent of moral licensing (Dodgson, 2017; Cascio & Plant, 2015)—an established behavioural effect whereby after having done something "ethical" one feels permitted to act less ethically later on — with the order of events reversed.

Furthermore, unless you're in principle willing to undergo unbearable torture to spare two others similar to you the same (which, as I've discussed, you couldn't do in practice anyways without committing to an irreversible decision you would subsequently regret), or even to share the risk of extreme suffering equally with all other sentient beings, you're not even technically a pure utilitarian, as you're attributing greater importance to your own identity or locus of consciousness than to others'. Although overcoming biases can lead to more rational decisions and be appropriate at the systemic level, it's not realistic to expect people to overcome their own instinct for self-preservation. As writer Rick Coste (2013) asked in a now-defunct blog post, though referring to lives saved rather than suffering averted, "Could you live in a society in which your life, at any moment, could be sacrificed to save the lives of two people, one hundred, or even one thousand? Of course not." No one would feel safe in a utilitarian world where an optimisation of the algorithm could mean their own sudden and possibly painful death.

For all of these reasons, it seems wisest to focus explicitly on relieving as much intense and especially extreme suffering as possible, within the limits of what feels intuitively reasonable or at least feasible, rather than carrying out minor, relatively inconsequential utilitarian decisions. Sticking to general ethical principles — provided they are centred on preventing intense suffering — may lead to better long-term consequences than simplistic, short-term utilitarian calculations.

Twelve

Current and Potential Causes of Intense Suffering

Human suffering

I won't go into detail here in describing the many causes of human suffering. Most of them are well known, often communicated in distressing news stories. I'm listing them for the sake of completeness, as these are some of the specific incidents that we are trying to prevent — the ultimate subject of this book. As mentioned earlier, physical pain and suffering always have a psychological component, and psychological suffering can also have physiological causes or be accompanied by physical symptoms, so the distinction is rarely clear-cut.

Causes of physical pain include diseases and physical conditions, physical attacks and abuse, rape, torture, armed conflict, burns and other accidents, bites and stings, natural disasters, hunger and childbirth.

There are many other forms of physical distress that may not be strictly painful but still cause suffering, including the symptoms of many illnesses.

The causes of psychological suffering are often less precise than for explicitly physical suffering. It can appear as a mental illness, including depression, severe anxiety or schizophrenia, or as agonising phantom noise as in severe tinnitus, or a shorter-term reaction to events, such as grief. Causes can include loss, fear, past trauma, emotional abuse and torture, violence, severe or chronic pain and other health issues, suppressed anger, social isolation, lack of romantic connection, relationship issues, lack of purpose or hope, lack of autonomy or agency, lack of self-esteem, poverty, financial difficulties, chemical imbalances, solitary confinement and others.

Abuse and torture of non-human animals

In terms of sheer scale, the harm that humans inflict on non-human animals represents the greatest moral catastrophe of our times. While humans have been hunting animals since our species first emerged, industrialisation and the commodification of animals have led to unimaginably cruel treatment of billions of animals a year, raised for human consumption or for the use of their skin, or for other purposes that serve our interests. They are often kept in abominable conditions, including tiny cages where they can't turn around, or tightly packed together, deprived of love, comfort, stimulation and freedom. Babies are separated from their mothers and kept in isolation so that humans can eat their flesh and drink their mothers' milk. These animals' lives usually end in terror, watching others being killed before succumbing to the same fate, often neither instantaneously nor painlessly. For example, it's been estimated that about a million chickens and turkeys are boiled alive each year in the US alone (Dockterman, 2013). The comforting narrative that animal products are humane when local is just a fable, and local suffering matters as much as distant suffering. The vast majority of animal products that are sold entailed intense suffering.

Fish are the most abused vertebrates in terms of numbers, and their suffering, unquestionable as it is, is even more commonly ignored. While most people would probably decline to personally drag a pig by a hook caught in its mouth and then suffocate it, replace the pig by a fish and this is considered by many a way of passing a peaceful afternoon. On a commercial scale, fish are hauled up from the depths en masse and similarly left to suffocate. Those raised on fish farms spend their lives tightly packed just like factory-farmed land animals, their existence consisting of stressful monotony.

All this cruelty occurs with the active participation of the majority of the population who pay others to carry it out—somehow still oblivious to the reality, indifferent to it or simply unwilling to change their behaviour. The failure of even much of ethical writings to address the massive torture of non-human animals shows how ethics can serve as a distraction when it fails to focus on what really matters.

Many of the animals we consume for our pleasure are essentially like small children. They may not have complex thoughts, but they feel, they have emotions, they experience joy, they love, they get hurt. And while we consider our own children deserving of the highest protection, we abuse and eat others—often literally, such as calves and lambs, who really are children, or chickens raised for meat, who are killed at an average age of 42 days (World Animal Protection, 2019).

Even companion animals (or "pets") who are not intended for consumption are emotionally abused in ways that would be recognised as such were these human children. For example:

- Dogs left outside, attached to chains their whole lives.
- Dogs left alone indoors the whole day, every day. Many undoubtedly suffer from depression due to solitude and emotional deprivation, kept to fulfil a function in their owner's life.
- Songbirds confined to small cages where they spend their entire existence providing ornamental value, despite their natural urge to fly and explore.
- Fish placed in small tanks or even clear bowls with little or no source of stimulation, kept in a kind of suspended animation for decorative purposes.

In many zoos, depressed animals in small, barren enclosures pace endlessly in displays of madness. Other commercial uses reveal the depravity of human beings, including turtles and fish packaged alive in tiny plastic bags as novelty keyrings (Mikkelson, 2012).

One possible obstacle to getting people to realise the barbarity of eating the products of tortured animals or otherwise contributing to the torture is that, if they are to maintain internal consistency and harmony in their worldview, they have to come to grips with the scale of the crime and the part of their identity that has tacitly accepted and indirectly embraced this torture. The pressure to conform is another, possibly even more powerful force. A shift in perspective has wide ramifications for one's life. It means looking at everything with fresh eyes, including everyday items like restaurant menus and clothing ads. The roots of this ethical quandary go deep, and digging them up may be hard but essential work. On the other hand, sudden changes in behaviour are also possible as the result of a personal epiphany or dawning realisation that one can no longer justify to oneself causing unnecessary suffering to others.

Nature and wild animal suffering

We are all products of nature who emerged through evolutionary processes. The sophisticated civilisations we have built up give us the illusion of separateness from nature and a pretext for categorising the planet's other inhabitants as being largely beyond the scope of our moral concern. Those who belong to civilisation are usually afforded care—including certain classes of non-human animals we consider companion material, and sometimes their stray cousins—while others are left to their own devices because we "mustn't interfere with nature". As a result, we are conditioned to remain detached observers of the drama going on in the wild and not to empathise with the victims.

And a drama it is. Nature is a brutal place, and huge numbers of wild animals suffer in all kinds of horrible ways, including from being eaten alive by predators, but also from hunger, thirst, disease, parasites, injury, stress and the elements (Animal Ethics, n.d.-b).

The suffering of a wild animal doesn't intrinsically matter any less because we don't feel any personal responsibility for them, or because we see them as a functional unit in an ecosystem, rather than as an individual with feelings who was born into a world where they are forced to fend for survival. While compartmentalising suffering that we cause separately from suffering that occurs in the wild is operationally necessary because the problems are distinct and require different solutions, from the perspective of the victim, the cause of the suffering is irrelevant to its urgency.

Most of the suffering in nature is still beyond our current ability to alleviate, but there are many things we can already do to help some animals, as Animal Ethics (n.d.-c) and others advocate, including helping individual animals who are suffering and carrying out vaccinations on a larger scale (Wiblin & Harris, 2019). Longer-term strategies to help many more animals are potentially feasible as well, including applying existing genetic technology that could, for example, prevent wild animals from being infected by parasites (Esvelt, 2019) or reduce their ability to experience pain (Tomasik, 2018b).

Insect and other invertebrate suffering

The huge number of invertebrates on our planet makes the possibility of them suffering a question of correspondingly huge importance. This applies both to invertebrates living in the wild—a subset of the issue of wild animal suffering—and those that are caught or raised for human consumption. It includes insects as well as various other invertebrates such as spiders, worms, crustaceans and molluscs—a diverse phylum comprising animals such as octopuses, known for their intelligence, snails, as well as bivalves such as oysters and mussels, which I specifically discuss in more detail in a later section on food choices.

The charity Rethink Priorities has done a remarkable job of comprehensively exploring the question of invertebrate sentience. They examined 53 features that, based on analogy with humans and other sentient beings, might correlate with sentience, across 18 biological taxa (Rethink Priorities, 2019), written up in a series of research posts (Rethink Priorities, n.d.). Features of potential relevance include anatomical features such as nociceptors (used to detect harmful stimuli) and opioid receptors;

reactions to noxious stimuli such as movement away from them, protective behaviours and vocalisation of distress; learning; navigational skills; cognitive sophistication; motivational trade-offs; behaviours typical of distress, fear and anxiety; and responses to drugs, including certain behaviours and a tendency to self-administer (Schukraft, 2019).

In an overview of this work, Jason Schukraft (2018) wrote, "If invertebrate animals experience morally significant pain, then, given the sheer number of invertebrates, an almost incomprehensible amount of morally significant suffering occurs beyond the ken of normal human attention." Calling attention to the possible significance of invertebrate suffering is crucial. It is worth pointing out, however, that the above framing could be interpreted as falling into the old paradigm of using aggregation to determine the total "amount" of suffering, rather than looking at both the numbers of individuals and the actual intensity of suffering experienced by each. Even a huge number of sentient individuals suffering intermittently at low intensity, such as from minor pain, though still morally significant, would not necessarily represent a moral catastrophe. But the widespread presence of intense suffering would change the picture dramatically.

A critical question for applying ethics is, indeed, which beings are sentient (Animal Ethics, n.d.-d), and more specifically, which ones are capable of experiencing suffering? We have very good—though not definitive—reason to think that plants are not sentient and thus incapable of experiencing suffering, even though they respond in various tangible ways to their environment, including to other plants. Most importantly, plants lack the neural structures required for sentience in organisms that we know are sentient (though it would be imprudent to assert that those structures are the only possible way for sentience to exist). Animals that are similar to us in anatomy and behaviour are undoubtedly sentient. But where is the dividing line between sentience and non-sentience? The boundary between the plant and animal kingdoms is unlikely to represent that line. For example, sponges are technically animals, but they lack neurons and are no more likely to be sentient than plants. What are the minimal characteristics needed to experience pain and other forms of suffering? Many biologists believe that a central nervous system is a requirement, though not necessarily that it is sufficient. Even if this is true, it still leaves a huge number of invertebrates potentially able to suffer.

A hypothesis discussed and evaluated by Brian Tomasik (2019c) is that sentience comes in degrees and correlates with brain size. In one respect, this seems entirely reasonable—a human brain surely has a lot more going on than an insect brain. But one could ask whether a honeybee, with a brain several orders of magnitude smaller than a human brain, really navigates the world in some kind of barely conscious haze of perception. While the nature and richness of insect sentience might be very different from human sentience, it might still have a fully functional awareness of its environment, attuned to its needs. It's not clear exactly what it means to say that it is "less conscious".

Philosopher Tim Bayne and colleagues also argue against degrees of sentience: "Arguably, the property of having a subjective point of view is not gradable—it cannot come in degrees. In this way it resembles being a member of the United Nations rather than being healthy, which clearly can come in degrees. One person can be conscious of more objects and properties than another person, but to be conscious of more is not to be more conscious" (Bayne et al., 2016).

Whether different degrees of sentience normally exist, aside from states of half-sleep or partial anaesthesia, may really be a question of definition (like many philosophical questions), and whether by "sentience" we mean awareness—having a minimal mental model of the world—which might be less gradable, or intensity or facets of experience, which might be more so. In fact, the requirement for certain macro structures to generate certain kinds of consciousness (e.g. the unique smell of strawberries or the feeling of anguish) is still compatible with the determinants of consciousness being built into the very properties of matter, even at the atomic level, a view known as panpsychism (Hunt, 2018). But there is almost certainly a minimum level of complexity needed for consciousness in the sense that we usually understand it.

However, it is the intensity of suffering that a sentient being is capable of experiencing that is the ethically most important question. A bee need not be less aware of its surroundings to be less capable of experiencing intense suffering. The intensity of suffering experienced—the absolute degree of unpleasantness—may depend in part on the total number of neurons firing and also the degree of sophistication of higher-order brain structures. For an insect, a small degree of aversion to certain stimuli may be sufficient to serve a biological and evolutionary purpose, without the need for full-blown intense pain or suffering.

On the other hand, the contrary is also plausible. The ability to experience the sensation of pain might have been one of the earliest and most useful characteristics to evolve in sentient beings. Perhaps the raw sensation of significant pain is one of the simplest manifestations of consciousness that the physical universe creates, and can even be experienced without the ability to fully perceive the world.

I admit that, based on what we know about consciousness in higher organisms, I am doubtful that the last speculation is true, and believe rather that the actual perception of pain as something unpleasant and therefore a cause of suffering requires more complex processing that might only be found in beings that we also believe to have conscious awareness. But even then, it would leave open the possibility of insects being able to suffer to some degree. And it might be the case that "to a tiny brain, an experience activating just a few pain neurons could feel like the worst thing in the world from its point of view" (Tomasik, 2019c).

Whether insects and other invertebrates can suffer, and more significantly, how much, remains an open question (Tomasik, 2017a). Even huge numbers of insects suffering a little would not have the urgency and importance of one pig or chicken suffering horribly on a factory farm, which includes intense emotional trauma. While the very large number of insects in existence does not itself create a higher degree of urgency, it dramatically increases the scale of the problem *in the case* that they are capable of suffering intensely.

Focusing for the moment just on insects: if one applied the tool of expected value, then even with a very low probability of them suffering intensely, the immense number of insects in existence would turn potential insect suffering on our planet into far and away our highest ethical priority. To be as effective as possible at reducing the expected value of this suffering, we would need to shift much of our attention from the horrors of factory farming to approaches such as the reduction of insect habitats, at least as far as this was feasible, knowing full well that insects probably do not suffer intensely like factory-farmed animals, but also that there is a slim possibility that they might. Actions to reduce the number of insects coming into existence, such as Brian Tomasik's (2019a) suggestion to replace lawns with gravel, might no longer seem as absurd, but rather, stubbornly rational.

From a purely practical perspective, a decision to shift resources away from advocating for tortured factory-farmed animals because of insect numbers and the concept of expected value would be highly counterintuitive and possibly counterproductive. While one can easily be motivated to protest in the street against the torture of animals bred for human consumption, it is much more difficult to argue as an activist that there is a small but non-negligible chance that huge numbers of insects are suffering immensely throughout the world, and to encourage people to take every opportunity we have to destroy green spaces. I am not sure how most people could operate with that perspective and still function normally. And for the vast majority of the world's population, and even for most intellectuals and activists concerned with the phenomenon of suffering, such a dramatic shift in priorities would not be seen as credible. At the least, then, we need to recognise the limits of human psychology, both in our strategies for change and in the ability of activists themselves to function as fully rational agents of change.

But beyond the practical aspects, we can question how appropriate a tool expected value is altogether for cases like this that involve fundamental epistemic uncertainty concerning the value (or disvalue) itself — suffering — rather than about the probability of something with known value happening. Applying expected value to this kind of uncertainty means multiplying the estimate of an organism being able to suffer under certain circumstances with the number of instances of such circumstances. For example, we might estimate the likelihood of most insects being able to suffer intensely at 0.1% (this is not necessarily a good estimate — the likelihood based on existing evidence may well be much higher), and multiply it by the number of insects that exist (ca. 10^{18}; Tomasik, 2019d) and the fraction that are subjected to situations that could potentially cause intense suffering — for example, being eaten alive — and the fraction of their lives that such suffering occupies. The expected value of intense insect suffering might still be much greater than that of all vertebrates because of the immense number of insects in existence. Using expected value would then also make insect suffering the most important cause area, even if the likelihood of insects suffering intensely were still considered to be very low. Is this a reasonable use of the expected value formula?

In fact, if one attributes a non-zero probability, however low, to the possibility of plants being sentient and even being able to suffer intensely, the same reasoning could apply to plants (Schukraft, 2018). Given the extent of plant life, and depending on the probability estimates one applies, this could theoretically make plant suffering the most important cause area! In reality, I think the probability is so low as to make this a negligible concern in practice.

If we were repeatedly confronted with situations with this kind of epistemic uncertainty, with each situation independent of the other, applying expected value would be the safest approach in deciding on priorities. For example, imagine that all the insects in existence were composed of just 1,000 species, each with similar numbers of individual insects, and that each species had an entirely independent 0.1% probability of being able to experience intense suffering. We could then statistically conclude that probably one or more insect species does experience intense suffering, and therefore that about 0.1% of all the vast number of individual insects in existence experience intense suffering. This would clearly justify treating insect suffering as a priority, assuming there were practical ways of addressing it.

But that situation is not representative of reality. We do not currently know what the minimum anatomical requirements are for an animal to experience intense suffering. The physiological or, more broadly, physical requirements to create a state of intense suffering are a single, largely unresolved question on which every attempt to have impact in reducing suffering in the universe depends—not a series of independent scenarios with different answers. The same considerations would therefore apply in making a probability calculation about any being whose capacity to suffer we were evaluating, and there appears to be no prospect for the expected value approach to optimise "success" in the long run. Either we guess right and use our resources most effectively—whether on insects or on other animals—or we guess wrong and either waste our resources on a non-problem while neglecting known suffering, or neglect most of the actual suffering on our planet.

From a more "philosophical" perspective, whether or not insects can suffer intensely determines just how much horror our planet is filled with: is it limited mainly to vertebrates who suffer from predation, the elements and disease (and, at the hands of humans, cruelty), or does it occur on an entirely different order of magnitude? If insects in the wild really do suffer intensely during their lives, our world represents an even greater hell than we might have hoped.

As I said, I think there is good reason to believe that no insects can experience anything comparable to what a tortured pig or other animal on a factory farm experiences, with its combination of physical pain and emotional distress. There is also a slight chance I might be wrong, and if so, this would probably apply to a large fraction of insects and perhaps even to all.

Some of the strongest evidence that insects, as well as many other invertebrates, might be able to feel pain is the presence of opioid-like receptors and the ability to respond to analgesics such as opioids. Some of the strongest evidence to the contrary is a usual lack of protective behaviours towards injured body parts, such as wound rubbing, and that at least some insects can continue functioning, including eating, even after a dismemberment or bodily harm that would cause great distress in animals with more complex brains (Tomasik, 2016d). But as pointed out by researcher Daniela Waldhorn (2019) in one of the Rethink Priorities reports, "Limited evidence of consciousness should not be confused with limited consciousness." The same can be said for evidence for the ability to feel pain.

Given our current state of knowledge, it still seems reasonable for most animal activism to prioritise preventing the torture and other causes of suffering of pigs, chickens, cows, fish and other vertebrates, as well as invertebrates such as octopuses and crustaceans, for which stronger evidence exists of the capacity to feel pain, even while we attempt to learn more about the subjective experience of insects and other invertebrates. Whether this approach to prioritisation is rational or not might not be a fully meaningful question, because it's not clear what "rational" would actually mean in this case, and whether the goal of preventing as much suffering as possible requires applying expected value to the basic question of the determinants of suffering itself. It seems, in fact, that this is another situation where we reach the limits of what rationality can tell us.

Nonetheless, there is certainly sufficient reason not to harm insects and other invertebrates unnecessarily, thereby limiting the suffering they might experience after all. While the consumption of honey, aside from being shunned by strict vegans as a matter of principle, is ethically problematic, the issue is not as straightforward as some might claim, as we depend on beekeeping for the pollination of many plant crops (though this does not, of course, require extracting honey from their hives), and the consumption of sugar instead might result in the killing of many more insects. In theory, honey can be harvested without causing the bees to suffer. On the other hand, the industrial raising of insects such as crickets or mealworms as a source of protein-rich food for human or animal consumption is a troubling development that raises the possibility of large-scale suffering (Sebo, 2021). Snails raised for human consumption are often killed by boiling (Waldhorn, 2020). The use of silkworms for silk production, whereby the worms are boiled alive, is another cause of potentially intense insect suffering. And the massive use of insecticides in agriculture might cause insects to suffer a slow, painful death. These and other potential sources of intense suffering in invertebrates merit attention and their replacement with alternatives that are less likely to cause suffering.

Far future suffering

Any extreme, involuntary suffering is never objectively tolerable, and ideally we would eliminate it from our planet's future and anywhere else in the universe that we could affect. The mere continuation of life on our planet as it is, far into the future, would be a dystopian scenario. But anything closely resembling the status quo is neither likely, nor the worst possible scenario. On the one hand, our civilisation might collapse, like so many past terrestrial civilisations, or even self-annihilate, as has been posited to have happened for extraterrestrial civilisations and to be the reason we don't detect any alien life (Urban, 2014). This might at least limit the amount of suffering occurring in the future, especially that of factory-farmed animals. But it would also remove the possibility of humans preventing on a large scale the suffering of wild animals, just at the point where we finally have the technology to do something about it.

On the other hand, various scenarios could lead to long-term suffering on a monumental scale, a possibility often referred to as "s-risks" (Baumann, 2017). If advanced life persists on our planet, technology will be a key driver of such risks. There could be a dramatic expansion in the number of sentient beings in existence, potentially colonising other planets in our solar system and far beyond in space, with a corresponding expansion in the capacity for suffering. Powerful algorithms and computing power could help maintain power structures that allow suffering to take place, similarly to how we currently exploit non-human animals for economic purposes, with indifference to the suffering caused.

Given the appropriate physical architecture, suffering might be possible to create in purely artificial beings, as discussed in the next section. If artificial sentient beings were sustainably replicated or just maintained indefinitely, even in the absence of humans, their suffering could potentially dominate the far future.

Artificial/machine suffering

Suffering is suffering, regardless of who or what experiences it. It's what happens on the inside that matters, not what it looks like from the outside. So the potential suffering generated by a computer would matter as much as biological suffering, as I discussed in *The Battle for Compassion* (p. 92) and as many others are concerned about, including those focused on s-risks (Tomasik, 2015).

I am confident that consciousness cannot be reduced to computation. It seems highly doubtful that a Turing machine, which manipulates a strip of tape and can, in principle, execute any algorithm, can experience anything. I am also sceptical that consciousness is merely a function of the degree of information integration in a physical system, as suggested by one well-known theory, proposed by neuroscientist Giulio Tononi and supported by neuroscientist Christof Koch (Integrated Information Theory, n.d.; Koch, 2009; Tononi & Koch, 2015; see also this critique: Aaronson, 2014), but aspects of the physical structure itself that matter for sentience. The focus on information integration suggests a conceptual bias rooted in our society's dependence on computers and algorithms. Consciousness is probably not reducible to logic gates and 0s and 1s, which is why I doubt that it can be produced using classical digital computers. It might be intimately related to vibration and resonance (Hunt, 2018; see also Bentov, 1977). However, even with these caveats, it is entirely possible that sentience and suffering could be created in non-biological substrates, including in other kinds of computers, especially if they were specifically designed and programmed for this purpose.

Although the prospect of suffering machines sounds like science fiction, its realisation would be terrifying. It could potentially happen by accident as an unintended consequence of AI development, due to a lack of awareness that the AI is sentient or plain indifference. It could even be a discounted side effect of intentionally creating sentience for research or industrial purposes. All of these cases would represent a grave consequence of "progress" to the end of generating economic value. Worse, suffering machines could be deliberately created for aggressive purposes, by man or machine, as a weapon of war, or simply out of sadism. The prospect of AI itself generating suffering in other AIs is a scenario taken very seriously by the Center on Long-Term Risk (Althaus & Gloor, 2016). Suffering of very high intensity could thus be manufactured and endlessly replicated. Even a slight but significant risk of this happening makes this a high priority on expected value grounds, especially if there may be ways to prevent it from happening (see, for example, Ziesche & Yampolskiy, 2018). Indeed, Thomas Metzinger (2021) has argued for a moratorium on synthetic phenomenology because of the risk of conscious machines suffering intensely.

Are there any other concerns about artificial sentience other than their capacity to suffer? Would there be any "obligation" to keep them in existence, in the way that we try to keep humans and even non-human animals alive, even if they are suffering from an illness? If we somehow managed to simultaneously create trillions of instances of consciousness in different places, would there be any issue with letting them vanish?

Here's a passage from the paper "The Ethics of Artificial Intelligence" by Nick Bostrom and Eliezer Yudkowsky on the "principle of substrate non-discrimination": "If two beings have the same functionality and the same conscious experience, and differ only in the substrate of their implementation, then they have the same moral status. One can argue for this principle on grounds that rejecting it would amount to embracing a position similar to racism: substrate lacks fundamental moral significance in the same way and for the same reason as skin color does" (Bostrom & Yudkowsky, 2014).

On the surface, this argument seems correct. And certainly, insofar as a machine might suffer, its suffering would matter as much as that of a human or non-human animal suffering to the same degree. However, the framing in terms of "moral status" might appear to imply that if sentience came into being in a non-biological substrate, we might need to extend the same effort to keep it going as to keep a human body alive. In contrast, according to an explicitly suffering-based ethical framework, there is no inherent need to give machine sentience the right to continue existing, unless depriving it of this right created suffering, such as in the form of fear, just as not protecting humans from dying would also create suffering. If we were unable to prevent artificial sentience from suffering the fear of being switched off, then it would clearly be deeply uncompassionate to bring it into existence in the first place.

To further illustrate this point: suppose we turned off a sentient machine every evening after work but turned it on again every morning, so it "woke up". And suppose it had no objection to being turned off just for the night. Would there be an "obligation" to wake it up? Would it in retrospect have been "killed" only if it wasn't turned back on again? These same questions could, in theory, apply to humans as well, as suggested in an earlier section on non-existence. But with machines, we are more directly confronted with the paradoxes that arise from adhering to an intuitive view of personal identity.

Anti-substratism can be taken too far if individual consciousness-moments are given the status of "persons". This would be to conflate two separate notions: consistency regarding the primacy of subjective experience, and the illusion of closed individualism as a metaphysically accurate model of personal identity. Interestingly, it could also put into question traditional voting rights, because anti-substratism could argue that if billions of sentient artificial beings were created, they would each be entitled to the right to vote. This thought experiment itself points to a need for ethics based on the prevention of suffering and not simply the principles of "one being, one vote" and majority rule.

AGI presents us with a new paradigm that forces us back outside our intuitive bubble, where utilitarianism becomes more relevant again. It is also a good illustration of how a fundamental rethinking of ethics to frame it in terms of the prevention of suffering produces a simpler, perhaps more elegant and ultimately more coherent framework, one that can be universally applied to any new situation that arises, especially as a consequence of advances in technology that increase the potential amount of extreme suffering that will occur.

Thirteen

A Tangible Tango
Resolving Ethical Conflicts

Trying to apply the xNU+ framework to the real world of ethical dilemmas and systemic change shows again the limited usefulness of moral realist framing. Some people may be persuaded to act in a certain way by being told they "ought" to do so, although appeals to people's own values can be more effective (Parker, 2015). But in terms of end goals and intermediate strategies, as we seek clarity in the chaos, there's no point where framing specific decisions as moral obligations seems truthful or even clearly appropriate.

Utilitarianism is often described as a cold, callous philosophy, and I discussed earlier why I think this can be the case if applied obsessively. But applied to the reduction of extreme suffering, especially strategically, it is the most inherently compassionate ethical philosophy there is. Only by starting from a negative utilitarian perspective can we ensure that we don't lose sight of what actually matters, as opposed to starting from existing laws and societal norms.

Would we not want a greater God-like being to be as utilitarian as possible in reducing the probability of any of us experiencing extreme suffering? It's actually from a position of privilege, one where our individual risk of extreme suffering is much lower than the average, that we may be more likely to reject a utilitarianism that doesn't benefit us personally. But from a more detached perspective based on empty individualism, utilitarianism is actually the only sensible overriding approach.

Yet utilitarianism forces us to confront reality in ways that make us deeply uncomfortable and challenge the very value of our existence. Pure utilitarianism would never be accepted as a way of living by a large population of humans. If we aimed only to see how far we could apply it in theory, preserving our existence itself would have to be put into question. So in a real world that we want to try to improve, we need to take into account the intuitions and some of the existing values of the humans that compose it. While those driving change will prevent more suffering if they don't lose sight of consequences, they will be more effective politically if they don't steamroll over ordinary people's intuitions. There is a balance between preventing suffering and respecting people's desire to live in integrity with themselves.

For many of the conflicts between utilitarianism and intuitions, if one comes out strongly in favour of one side of the argument, one is either potentially allowing a greater amount of severe suffering to happen in the world, or running against deep moral intuitions that partly define what it means—or at least, what we might want it to mean—to be human. That's a tough decision to make either way, and there is no clear answer. The closer we get to facing deep truths relevant to ethics, the further we get from the clear, practical prescriptions that many people seem to want. Regardless, we need to look for solutions that take us down a path of minimal harm, towards the goal of zero extreme suffering.

When we are faced with such conflicts, the most implementable and effective solutions would be utilitarian in the long run but within the constraints of people's intuitions. That is, solutions that will ultimately be most useful for reducing the amount of intense suffering, even if they are indirect because they will make us more credible as activists or more trustworthy because we will be known to keep commitments, or else because they are the only solutions that are actually implementable because they don't lead to unsustainable cognitive dissonance or undermine people's empathy. The signals we send about the kind of society we are supporting might be far more significant for our long-term impact than for any short-term utilitarian gains.

As a solution to the conflict between utilitarianism and intuitions, Brian Tomasik (2018a) has suggested, "One reasonable approach is to advocate a hybrid of negative utilitarianism and deontology: Focus on reducing suffering, but don't violate strong deontological constraints. For instance: 'Don't do anything that most of humanity would regard as extremely evil.'" There is obviously a strong similarity to what I am proposing, and especially to my initial formulation of negative utilitarianism *plus*, though it suggests a red line that cannot be crossed, up to which point everything is acceptable, whereas I am maintaining the relevance of intuitions even in much less extreme situations and the practical need for flexibility in how strongly we apply utilitarianism in our daily lives.

Returning to the tango metaphor: by becoming the dance one is actually assuming both roles, and not merely pretending to play one of them. One switches between the agent of change and the romantic human, and embraces both. The human is not simply a tool of the agent, nor vice versa. But one arrives there through a natural sequence of steps:

one invariably starts with the human perspective, thinks deeply in a way that can put into question several of one's deepest assumptions, and uses this thinking to drive one's actions and priorities, without negating one's identity nor the human urge to thrive. And that is the point where one becomes the dance.

In the rest of this chapter, I will discuss a small selection of relevant real-world issues and offer suggestions — sometimes just brief reflections — on how we can try to resolve the conflict between the two perspectives. Of course, not all solutions to suffering involve major conflicts between rationality and intuition, nor even have a considerable intuitive component. For example, as discussed in this chapter, restricted access to medical treatment with morphine or psychedelics, for people with terminal cancer or cluster headaches, respectively, is a serious issue with clear, rational solutions. When politicians drag their feet, it may be due to misinformation or flawed thinking, but not due to conflicts with moral intuitions or existence bias. But many issues are not nearly as clear-cut.

Helping those closest vs. helping strangers

A key principle of utilitarianism that is also widely applied by the effective altruism movement is that resources be used to do the most good, wherever that happens to be. The same amount of resources spent in poorer countries may go much further in saving lives and reducing suffering than if spent in one's own rich country.

A potential problem with strictly applying this thinking is that it could loosen the bonds of proximity, and suggest that even your close friends and family, and certainly your community, can't count on your support, because of numbers. In a sense, the issue is an extension of the question of how much to care for oneself before helping others. Activists who don't exercise sufficient self-care can burn out.

Some within the effective altruism community have advocated that we not override our intuitions, for reasons of instrumental efficacy. For example, Eric Bruylant wrote in a social media post, "EAs [effective altruists] need not override their family/tribe-preservation instincts in order to help those who are distant, and in fact that override is likely to be net negative for policy, psychology, and PR reasons." Andrés Gómez Emilsson concurred, saying, "I think that a utilitarian calculus that takes into account memetic effects is likely to value anyone who is close to you orders of magnitude higher than a person chosen at random. Namely, you … can convert such a person with a much higher probability than you would a person chosen at random."

More generally, any major disruption of our intuitive urge to help those close to us would not be sustainable. A meme based on self-care is more likely to spread than one based on self-denial. The key word is balance. If we don't help ourselves—individually, but also our communities—who will? But when our own basic needs are largely taken care of, it becomes much more compelling to use additional resources to alleviate as much suffering as possible, wherever it occurs.

War

Brian Tomasik wrote in a social media post that "the only justification for imposing torture-level suffering on one being is to prevent torture-level suffering by other beings." From a utilitarian perspective he is right. But even when the numbers might hold, this isn't a viable ethical principle for a human world. For example, people are appalled by the killing of innocent victims through drone strikes, regardless of any purported strategic justification in terms of avoiding greater harm (Shane, 2015).

And wars don't even respect the utilitarian principle. As Nathan Robinson (2016) wrote, with respect to the dropping of an atomic bomb on Hiroshima, "Even someone who considers himself a steely-hearted utilitarian, who has no trouble causing 100,000 people to perish if it will save 100,001, must use his capacity for empathetic imagination in order to make an informed assessment of the costs. After all, some deaths involve truly hideous suffering, and without understanding what the situation looks like for its victims, [it] is impossible to even know the stakes of what we are dealing with." He added, "If the utilitarian case is ever to be made, it must be made through tears. Anything else means the discussion isn't being treated with the moral seriousness it requires."

If utilitarianism means considering all equal suffering to matter equally, even when it is remote, then war is often its antithesis. It can mean imposing extreme suffering on people from another country—both soldiers and civilians—so that people from one's own country might experience less suffering of a much lower intensity, due for example to the loss of territory containing non-essential natural resources, or wounded national pride. And it is waged by soldiers who are exposed to risks of severe suffering that they haven't been fully informed about.

The Russian invasion of Ukraine in February 2022 illustrates some of these points. The motivation for the invasion had nothing to do with preventing suffering, even of native Russian speakers, who have also suffered horribly as a consequence. Or more precisely: the only suffering it aimed to relieve was the unfulfilled, imperialist yearnings of a Machiavellian dictator. In addition to sparking worldwide outrage, the invasion also led to some voices arguing for rapid concessions to at least some Russian demands—potentially even relinquishing some internationally recognised Ukrainian territory—in order to spare the

Ukrainian population further suffering.¹ This might even appear to be the best solution from a short-term utilitarian perspective in early spring 2022. After all, one could argue, how many children need to die, how many people need to be raped and tortured, and how many lives need to be destroyed, just to preserve political borders? And this is aside from other consequences of the war, such as global food shortages that could potentially lead to millions starving in other countries too.

But defending one's land from invaders and preserving the autonomy of one's tribe are powerful motivations that can override the principle of preventing intense suffering. As of this writing, most Ukrainians seem unsusceptible to being bombed into submission, proud of their national cohesion and resistance, and determined not to cede their sovereignty. Furthermore, it is conceivable that surrendering to demands in order to stop the bloodshed might embolden Russia and other authoritarian regimes to carry out further such invasions and also subject more people to their sordid brand of governance. An absolute principle of nonviolence leaves the door open to abuse and more violence, and what might appear to be the best (i.e. least bad) utilitarian solution in the short term might prove not to be in the long term.

Unfortunately, even when seemingly justified, war invariably causes increased overall suffering through the direct causing of harm—an infringement both of utilitarian ethics (from a detached, global perspective) and of one of our strongest intuitions. And the only reasonable justifications for it are self-defence—a reflection of the instinct for survival and autonomy, and for the preservation of the identity of one's own tribe and culture against the physical threats of others—and protecting others from harm.

Credible threats of violence are needed to prevent others from causing harm, which they might carry out directly through violence, or by blocking access to needed resources. The omnipresence of war throughout our history shows how often humans have found themselves in this situation and how easily the greed of some can force others to experience the unbearable. Any future existence that feels in any way worth

---

1   For example, Greek politician and author Yanis Varoufakis (2022) wrote, "To help Ukrainians stop the carnage and breathe again, the only question that I need to ask myself is: How do we get the Russian troops to withdraw? This is the question I have a duty to focus on. Any other questions must wait... Here, I must confess to a serious ethical conflict in my heart and mind: I am desperate for Ukrainian fighters to not give in, to continue to fend off Russian troops heroically—as they have been doing so far. I salute and celebrate them. But I know who Putin is. Putin is a ruthless killer."

preserving will have to find thorough answers to the problem of conflict resolution that obviate any perceived need for violence by providing safety and security to all. This will almost certainly require radical, comprehensive solutions at the level of global governance.

Animal experimentation

There are perhaps few issues more emblematic of the conflict between negative utilitarianism and the intuition against doing harm than animal experimentation. In the strictest sense, torture refers to the intentional infliction of physical or emotional pain for the direct purpose of obtaining something, such as information or pleasure. But more broadly, the very act of knowingly causing significant, avoidable suffering to another sentient being, even when the suffering is not the actual intention, can also be considered torture, as there is still a perpetrator and the experience is the same for the victim. The horrific treatment of animals in the food and clothing industries can justifiably be considered a form of torture, even if the suffering is callously ignored rather than intended. Even a rural farmer keeping a malnourished dog tied to a tree for years may be an act of apathy rather than malice, but for the suffering animal, it is still an act of torture.

The same can be said of experimentation on animals that causes them to suffer considerably. Photos of animals in agony, subjected to bizarre medical experiments of dubious worth or the testing of a new line of cosmetics, understandably trigger outrage. The extreme suffering is obvious, our deep moral intuition against causing harm triggers alarm bells, and the justifications offered usually lack credibility.

But are there any situations where medical experimentation might be justifiable from a utilitarian perspective? And if so, is it possible to retain the principle of anti-speciesism—that we don't discriminate ethically against non-human animals because of their species membership—and still treat members of other species with a greater degree of utilitarianism than we treat other humans? Theoretically it might suggest that we are treating them differently and therefore discriminating. But it could also be seen as applying the very same ethical framework but finding a different balance that is adapted to the situation.

Let's take a concrete, real-world example. The Impossible Burger is one of an increasing number of brands of plant-based meat with very similar taste and texture to traditional meat, and that can even beat it in taste tests (Jacobsen, 2019). Replacing traditional meat with realistic, cruelty-free substitutes, including plant-based meat and "clean meat" (meat grown from animal cells, referred to more frequently in the past as "lab meat"), is one of the big hopes for ending cruelty to animals, given that many people remain despairingly resistant to voluntarily removing animal products from their diet. The Impossible Burger helped to achieve its meat-like taste characteristics by including heme, a molecule normally found in animal tissue. The company ran into controversy when it was revealed that they had tested their heme—identical to the animal version but produced in yeast—on 188 rats in order to satisfy the regulatory authorities regarding its safety (Chiorando, 2017). There was an outcry from many devoted vegans and animal rights organisations such as PETA, who denounced the animal testing, claimed that the Impossible Burger was not vegan and urged other vegans not to consume it.

One can debate the decision to test on animals, including whether it was even necessary for obtaining regulatory approval, though it seems clear that it helped secure it. But it is nearly incontrovertible that the Impossible Burger, by replacing the consumption of some beef by plant-based meat—for example, it was made available in ca. 17,000 Burger King and other restaurants across the US—has saved far more than 188 animals from miserable lives on factory farms. A failure to have it approved would almost certainly have led to an increased amount of animal suffering.

The decision by a commercial company with a plant-based branding to carry out experiments on rats and kill them obviously leaves a bitter taste, directly infringing on the principle of not causing harm and at least on the surface appearing hypocritical in the avowed intent to help animals. Yet the cows suffering on factory farms are just as real as those 188 rats, even if we can't point to specific cows whose suffering was spared—they would be reflected in a smaller overall number of cows that came into being.

For vegans with a purist philosophical stance, the Impossible Burger may be tainted forever as non-vegan, even if there is no further testing on animals and the actual product is entirely plant-based. It's a strongly principled position based on the ethic of not carrying out direct harm, and especially not killing. Its rigidity nonetheless resembles declining forever to forgive a friend who made a mistake. In practice, the impact on animal consumption anyways comes from non-vegans who would otherwise have eaten meat-based hamburgers, though the purist stance doesn't give them much credit for eating plant-based burgers because it labels these burgers as non-vegan.

There are things we won't do to humans even if there might be a net benefit. We don't want to harm some for the benefit of others. If we did, we would also create additional suffering by causing humans to live in fear of being tortured, and we would cause great resistance in society. It wouldn't be a world most of us would be willing to tolerate. But non-human animals aren't aware of our rules and the risks we expose ourselves and themselves to, and so they cannot experience this source of fear. By being more utilitarian with non-human animals, we can potentially help them more effectively than we are able to help humans. That is to say, we might be more effective at reducing the overall number of non-human animals who suffer intensely.

Not surprisingly, it's been found that people are indeed more willing to treat non-humans than humans according to utilitarian principles — specifically, to harm a few in order to save a greater number — even when they recognise that non-humans can suffer as much as humans (Caviola et al., 2021). The study suggested that this is at least partly a result of speciesism. While speciesism might well be a contributing factor in people's motivations, this need not be the case, as I have argued, and we might be able to help more non-human animals when we are free of the constraints of the intuitions that apply to human society. Whether this is still considered speciesism is a matter of definition, and whether we apply it first and foremost to the attempt to prevent as much suffering as possible, or to other kinds of differentiated treatment, such as not causing direct harm. While the balance between these two dimensions of caring might shift with non-human animals, it might still be to their benefit.

Let's now consider a wholly different scenario where similar considerations come into play. The amount of suffering endured by wild animals in nature is immense. As briefly mentioned earlier, it's far from implausible to envisage addressing much of this suffering by reducing the ability of non-human animals to experience pain, through genetic intervention. While a large-scale project might well initially be controversial, let's just assume for the moment that it is practically feasible. In order to fully develop and fine-tune the technology, it would be necessary to carry out some experiments on animals in a laboratory setting before implementing the technology in the wild. This would involve causing direct harm to specific animals, though steps could be taken to minimise their discomfort. The consequences could be a drastic reduction or even the elimination of extreme suffering for many billions of animals every year, far into the future. Could this be seen as anything other than a good thing overall?

A related issue where causing direct harm might seem less obvious to justify is the use of animal experimentation for the benefit of humans. The first consideration is whether it is really even utilitarian. Much experimentation on animals is not carried out with the direct goal of relieving human suffering, but to test unnecessary products, or to satisfy scientific curiosity about issues that have only a vague or illusory potential impact on human wellbeing. Even with medically relevant research, it is doubtful

13. A Tangible Tango

that an objective, explicitly utilitarian calculation is ever carried out of the net expected impact of animal experimentation on extreme suffering. In the absence of such a calculation, the only certainty is the direct harm inflicted on non-human animals. Empathy for them and consideration of their suffering seems very much absent from the equation.

If, however, it could be clearly shown that the research was justified from a purely utilitarian, suffering-focused perspective, one might still ask the question whether there still isn't a troubling discrimination of non-human animals for the benefit of humans. But this concern is more closely related to our intuitions against causing harm or concentrating suffering in one group — and even more so, an outwardly identifiable one — than to the utilitarian reduction of suffering altogether. Justification for the experimentation would still be based on the anti-speciesist principle that equivalent suffering matters equally, regardless of species — and that the suffering of a little girl with cancer matters as much as the suffering of a laboratory mouse. So even though it creates more intuitive dissonance, it would still be defendable on the basis of aiming to reduce overall suffering.

But the opposing perspective is also valid. While writing this book, I watched a video showing beagles made to suffer in a laboratory (one of countless videos I have watched of cruelty to animals), and I admit to having felt momentary disdain for utilitarianism, or at least any brand of it that condones such experimentation because it can save human lives or prevent human suffering, or even non-human animal suffering — even if the numbers added up. Whenever we are tempted to harm others in the interest of an overall reduction of harm according to strict utilitarian principles, we might want to consider how doing so transforms us, and what will be left of us at the end. Using violence against sentient beings who do not threaten us seems a particularly ironic route to a more peaceful, harmonious world. Doesn't harming an animal even for medical purposes turn us into cold, cruel, number-crunching agents acting against our compassionate nature, against something essential to our humanity? Are we not humans before we are gods? Is a world where we carry out experiments on terrified sentient beings a world that feels worth living in? If torturing sentient beings today is the price to be paid for suffering-free flourishing tomorrow, how can the latter possibly be justified? Even if the aim is just to reduce suffering in the future, wouldn't non-existence still be a preferable choice?

Perhaps these last reflections seem more sentimental than realistic, and even after carrying out harm for compassionate ends, we remain largely unchanged after all. But there is something qualitatively different, potentially also in the level of suffering itself, about being tortured than suffering from a disease. I wouldn't wish a horrible disease on anyone. But we can always use strong pain medication, and in the very worst case, end our lives, rather than torture animals to test a medicine. This dilemma highlights the paradox of living—that to make it seem worthwhile (preventing intense suffering) we may feel the need to do things that make it feel *not* worthwhile (causing suffering). Is existence so beautiful that we can justify torturing animals to prevent our own suffering? Is it still beautiful if we do?

I would prefer "no world" over one where we experiment on animals —or over one that contains extreme suffering. But if just a few of us personally shunned existence, would it change anything? It seems we may have no choice but to begrudgingly take on the part-time role of gods if we want to steer the future towards less suffering. Is it then not better to accept our fate and do the best we can?

But any justification for such experimentation would need to be explicitly and clearly utilitarian, based on a net reduction in extreme suffering, and not dependent on questionable assumptions, including an indefinite future that allows us to claim any net benefit desired, given a long enough period of time. Every reasonable measure possible must be taken to minimise discomfort. And alternative approaches must be used whenever possible. Finally, efforts to end experimentation on animals deserve continued support, as they ensure that animal suffering is taken seriously and hasten the development of alternative medical approaches.

The grey zone of animal exploitation

The exploitation of others—both human and non-human animals—is often a direct cause of suffering, in which case the term serves mainly to call attention to this fact. But the term is sometimes used more broadly to refer to any benefit that humans obtain from non-human animals, especially when it derives from a relationship of dominance. While we need to look very carefully at any possible suffering that can arise from such a relationship and not overlook such suffering in an attempt to justify the relationship, we also need to distinguish between actual harm and harm that exists only in our minds. While freedom in a deterministic universe (at least at the scale of most human activity) is ultimately a state-of-mind, we suffer when we feel our liberty physically constrained by others or by circumstances. The specific needs of a non-human animal need to be taken into account in determining whether they are suffering from lack of freedom, rather than us projecting our own needs onto them.

Examples of the use of animals in ways that some might see as exploitation but that may cause them little or no suffering and that can often spare others suffering are the training and use of animals for rescue, police and military work, including search and rescue dogs that can detect buried earthquake victims, and dogs and rats that can detect mines, or the use of seeing-eye dogs. If an animal is given stimulating tasks that keep them busy, and is well treated and cared for, there is arguably nothing especially problematic. In fact, the animal may have a much better life than a companion animal who spends long periods of time alone and bored. The experience of the animal might be similar to that of a human fully engaged in a challenging task. It might not be "natural", but that isn't a relevant consideration. Though the optics are often deceptive, what matters is the experience of the animal themselves.

Veganism vs. reducing suffering: is eating animal products ever justifiable?

Veganism is both a diet and a life philosophy that seeks to exclude the exploitation of and cruelty to animals, including the consumption of their products, to the extent possible. Vegans tend to be strongly committed to the principle of not harming animals and to encouraging others not to do so either. Although they are still a relatively small fraction of the world's population, there are sometimes acrimonious debates among them about who qualifies as a vegan and whether any use of animals is ever acceptable. The story mentioned above about the Impossible Burger was one such subject of contention. For some, veganism is a moral baseline, the minimum required of anyone—that is, not to cause harm. This perspective can conflict with a more nuanced view that admits the messiness of ethics and seeks to minimise total suffering. The debate often appears to reduce to moral purity vs. pragmatism, although those who weigh in on the purity side will often argue that the stricter approach will be more successful in the long run because it takes a clearer stance against any use of animals as commodities. Even if it would be a gross oversimplification to equate the word "vegan" with "ethical", the lifestyle is a good model for much of the change we would want to see in the world from an ethical perspective.

So is it better to be strictly vegan and avoid even small amounts of animal products, or to select a diet that is calculated to cause the least suffering? Ploughing fields to grow plants, whether for human or animal consumption, inevitably kills and maims rodents and other small animals —despite some studies, the actual numbers are uncertain and estimates vary widely. Since most animals raised for human consumption are fed plants that were cultivated, often industrially, and much smaller amounts of plants are needed to feed humans directly, eating plants causes less collateral suffering as well (see, for example, Middleton, 2009). This fact supports the argument that a vegan diet causes much less suffering.

But when animals like cows or sheep graze exclusively in fields or pastures—sometimes ones that wouldn't even be suitable for plant farming—they cause little suffering to others, directly or indirectly. Is it therefore possible that eating such free-range animals—which are, nonetheless, a small fraction of the animals raised worldwide for food—might cause less suffering than eating plants grown industrially? After all, the suffering of a maimed mouse counts as much as the equivalent suffering of a larger animal such as a cow, or a dog for that matter, even if the suffering wasn't intended. Unintentional harm still counts as harm, and if foreseeable it needs to enter our calculations.

Or let's imagine that insects were raised entirely on organic waste, rather than on industrially grown crops. If they could hypothetically be raised without harm and killed painlessly, for example, by lowering the temperature, might it then be better to eat insects rather than plants, again sparing the definite suffering of small vertebrates caused by industrial plant agriculture?

One could also ask what effect fishing has on the overall amount of suffering in the oceans, taking into account the predation of fish by other fish and how fishing affects the numbers, and also comparing suffering by being drawn out of the sea in a net with suffering by being swallowed alive by another fish. If there were no net effect, or if it actually reduced total suffering, would it then matter if fishing continued, at least so long as other steps were not being taken to reduce the suffering of wild fish? I am not claiming that this is actually the case, just raising it as a hypothetical.

It is entirely possible that universal pure veganism is not the absolutely optimal solution for minimising extreme suffering on our planet. It is probable that the killing and consumption of *some* wild animals or free-range grazers causes less net suffering than the industrial tilling of soil and harvesting of plants. From a short-term, purely utilitarian perspective, one might see some degree of animal consumption as preferable to none.

But this does *not* mean that it is better to kill some animals sometimes. Veganism is a simple heuristic that may have greater utilitarian impact over time by signalling that treating animals as food is not acceptable when there are healthy alternatives. What would it mean to live on a planet where we actively harm and eat some animals *because* we think this is overall the best way of reducing animal suffering? What kind of cognitive dissonance would this entail? Encouraging meat-eating as an indirect way of reducing suffering risks undermining compassion. It's a slippery slope that can lead to ethical backsliding, or even simply the stabilisation of a catastrophic status quo. And legitimising the eating of animals as a means of reducing overall suffering creates conflicts of interest. As long as there are people benefitting from a commercial activity such as turning animals into meat, they will be incentivised not to take more effective actions on behalf of animals when these might conflict with it. There are certainly better long-term approaches to reducing suffering in the world than raising or capturing some animals for food.

What's nonetheless useful about these kinds of reflections is that they demonstrate that the suffering of animals raised or caught for consumption and the suffering of other wild animals cannot be neatly separated into categories of distinct, unequal moral concern. As soon as we look at maximising impact in reducing suffering, the label we apply to an animal becomes irrelevant.

These considerations do point to the need to develop new agricultural technologies to allow land to be tilled and crops to be grown and harvested without causing harm to small animals. The average plant-based diet is still currently far from suffering-free (Keim, 2018). New technologies could potentially reduce our dependence on traditional agriculture altogether (Carleton, 2019).

However, while striving for apparent ethical purity is intuitively appealing, and it is fully understandable that someone chooses not to ingest animal products where possible, there is still a conflict with rationality that can come into play, because everything is connected, and personal purity is based on the illusion of separateness. Vegans are regularly confronted with this conflict between impact and purity.

For example, let's say that you are vegan, and you go to a party and see that there is some food that contains eggs and dairy products. It's already been bought or made and will all be eaten, because the host didn't provide quite enough food, so it may seem to have no direct effect on animal suffering whether you consume it or not—aside from the potential positive effect of signalling to others that you don't eat animal products. But it's also possible that, if you eat some of the food, someone else who is not vegan will be left hungrier and eat more animal-based food when they return home, whereas if you instead waited until you got home you would eat plant-based food. In that case, your decision to refrain from eating at the party would indeed have some impact. But what if all the food at the party were vegan? You could similarly avoid eating it so that there would be more for the non-vegans to eat, reducing their consumption of animal food at home. In fact, the two cases are highly similar in this respect. From a utilitarian perspective, shunning pre-made food with non-vegan ingredients is equivalent to trying to prevent non-vegans from buying more non-vegan food, and therefore shunning any food, whether vegan or non-vegan, would have the same benefit.

A vegan will also often find themselves in situations, when eating out with non-vegans, where a main dish is accompanied by a dairy or egg product, or perhaps a free non-vegan dessert is offered at the end. If they try to decline the non-vegan product, the non-vegan friend may well say, "It's ok, I'll have it instead" — eliminating the impact of not consuming it personally. (Of course, insisting on declining it and depriving the friend of a free dessert may be a good way to lose a friend.)

Although the actual significance of such decisions is relatively minor in the grand scheme of things, every factory-farmed egg used for a cake can represent a day of squalor for a sentient being. To the extent that we do try to reduce such suffering, situations where we can influence others' consumption are potentially as important as our own consumption in that moment. When our consumption of a low-suffering product indirectly causes someone else to consume a high-suffering product, the effect is the same.

I am not advising people to go hungry at parties, certainly not when there is vegan food available. The point is that suffering doesn't care about your personal purity and is only influenced by actual impact, and our influence on others matters just as much as the direct impact of our personal lifestyle. And ultimately, the most important question is: how can I have as much impact as possible?

Eating oysters and other brainless invertebrates

The question of whether or not to eat oysters might not appear to belong among the highest-ranking ethical dilemmas we face, but it is interesting not just intellectually but because there are practical implications as well. Oysters are a relatively unique case of an organism used for consumption that is classified as an animal but that appears less likely to be sentient because of its simple nervous system — far simpler than that of insects. They have cerebral ganglia but no brain, and scientific publications are inconsistent about whether or not they can be said to have a central nervous system (Yurchenko et al., 2018). Oysters contain various nutrients that cannot readily be obtained from plants, such as vitamin B12, which vegans need to take as supplements, and long-chain omega-3 fatty acids, which can only be produced inefficiently from the shorter-chain ALA found in plants and which might be useful for vegans to take as supplements as well, especially children with developing brains. They also have high concentrations of other essential minerals such as zinc, selenium and iron. If they were incapable of feeling pain, there would be a strong justification for farming and eating them as a source of cruelty-free nutrients, with little collateral damage to other sentient beings, such as small animals who are maimed and killed through industrial plant agriculture.

Arguments have been made for eating oysters, based on the claim that they are unable to feel pain (Fleischman, 2020; Cascio, 2017). Aside from their anatomy, the arguments include the inability of mature oysters to move (though this is not true for oyster larvae, which can swim), and that experiencing pain would therefore be useless and energetically wasteful. Even a physiological reaction to harmful stimuli (nociception), such as movement of the shell, could be similar to the human reflex of removing one's hand from a hot burner, which occurs before a pain sensation is experienced in the brain.

But there is also the possibility that they are indeed sentient—at least, in the sense of being able to subjectively experience pain—and that any responses to stimuli represent more than just simple reflexes. One argument is on evolutionary grounds. If they were not sentient, it would place an unusual dividing line between sentience and non-sentience right through the middle of an animal phylum. There are two ways this could have happened. Oysters belong to phylum Mollusca, which includes other bivalves, snails and octopuses—known for their intelligence and ability to communicate in an apparently emotional way with humans, as depicted in the moving documentary "My Octopus Teacher". The most recent common ancestor (Davis, 2017)—the mother of all molluscs, if you like—likely had a rudimentary central nervous system including cerebral ganglia, similar to bivalves. A worm-like descendent called Aplacophora (n.d.) might be the closest living relative and very similar. If it was sentient while oysters are not, this would probably be one of the few examples of sentience being *lost* within an evolutionary lineage.

On the other hand, if the common ancestor of molluscs was not sentient, and bivalves neither, octopuses would then represent a separate emergence of sentience within the animal kingdom, as suggested by philosophy professor and author Peter Godfrey-Smith in an article about octopus consciousness: "Given the distant common ancestry between octopuses and humans, conscious octopuses would mean that consciousness has evolved on earth twice. Godfrey-Smith believes it's plausible that there are more than two branches of evolution where consciousness independently developed. It's important to figure out whether consciousness is 'an easily produced product of the universe' or 'an insanely strange fluke, a completely weird anomalous event,' says Godfrey-Smith. Based on the current evidence, it seems that consciousness is not particularly unusual at all, but a fairly routine development in nature" (Goldhill, 2017).

But if sentience appeared separately in octopuses, this might suggest that snails, which recent studies show are more closely related to bivalves than to octopuses (Kocot et al., 2011; see Figure 4 therein), are not sentient either. That snails are zombie-like creatures is at least counterintuitive. It would be ironic for a theory to suggest that sentience emerges easily but imply its absence in organisms with a simple nervous system that appear to be sentient. Perhaps snails independently developed sentience as well, and thus sentience appeared more than once within the mollusc phylum. A simpler theory is that the common ancestor was indeed sentient — and earlier worm-like ancestors as well — and that sentience was never lost.

Even if oysters are sentient, their sentience may be limited to simple sensations of unpleasantness and share nothing with the complexity of a higher organism that can experience thoughts, emotions, love and fear. In other words, killing them would not itself merit much sentimental concern. If we could open their shells without triggering any pain response there would arguably be zero harm done. An entire human brain can be quickly anaesthetised by administering certain chemicals. It wouldn't be too difficult to turn off any capacity for pain in an oyster, such as by reducing their temperature to near freezing.

As of this writing, I am still undecided. Given that there are good arguments for and against oyster sentience, and that measures are rarely taken to further reduce the likelihood of them experiencing pain, I give them the benefit of the doubt and avoid eating them. For most people in high-income countries, they are still an expensive source of nutrients compared to supplements. If new progress is made in understanding the determinants of consciousness, we may eventually obtain a more definitive answer as to whether or not it is reasonable to eat oysters and whether we might actually reduce overall suffering by doing so.

Painlessly killing happy animals

There's a certain unique quality to the suffering associated with knowing one is about to die at someone else's hands, such as when an animal, even one raised well, realises they are about to be slaughtered. This is precisely the kind of horror that we would want to prevent humans from ever experiencing. Are there many situations more worthy of attention than this? And the reality is that the killing of animals with complex brains is almost always accompanied by mortal fear.

But let's imagine that, in theory, we could kill happy animals without them experiencing any fear or pain. This scenario is very far removed from reality for the vast majority of animals raised by humans. But if it were possible, would there be any ethical concerns?

From an ethical perspective that focuses on suffering, there would appear at first to be no essential problem. In an earlier section on "interests", I mentioned that the concept can include the right to continue existing. Even if we limit the concept of interests to humans with explicit desires for the future: although I may desire to live eternally, if I suddenly cease to exist without suffering, there is no actual harm done, except to mourning survivors, etc. (Leighton, 2011, pp. 120–123) An ethical theory based on interests might conclude that my ceasing to exist was in conflict with my interests, but while it would indeed be in conflict with my prior wishes, there is no frustration or suffering occurring afterwards that results from that conflict. The conflict is purely conceptual and has no phenomenological consequences.

The strongest reason to accord people the right not to be killed, aside of course from the direct suffering averted, is to preserve a world we would want to live in, where we don't live in constant dread — not because of some fundamental ethical principle that any sentient being that comes into existence *needs* to have its life preserved for as long as possible. And, as mentioned in the section on animal experimentation, since non-human animals don't have the awareness we do of the rules we apply to our world, a happy animal would not live in fear of being eventually killed.

Similarly, as I also mentioned earlier, claiming that animals "value" their lives isn't necessarily an accurate statement. It would be more correct to simply say that they want to live, or even more precisely, that they pursue life, and that they are afraid and suffer when they are in danger of dying. But in the absence of such suffering, an animal ceasing to exist is not a problem in and of itself.

However, if human beings value autonomy for themselves, it would appear inconsistent to deprive non-human animals of it as well. At the least, it is hard to reconcile seeing animals purely as sequences of consciousness-moments, in the spirit of empty individualism, while still respecting people as individuals with stable personal identities. It's true that we don't need to accommodate any conflicting intuitions of animals the way we do those of people in order to implement rational policies. But to the extent that we actually value stable personal identity as a source of meaning, illusory as it might be, it creates cognitive dissonance to limit it to our own species. The termination of the personal identity of a non-human animal can feel just as tragic as that of a human's.

The engineering of slaughterhouses to minimise suffering provides an uncomfortable example of what happens when we seek to reduce suffering but continue to treat sentient beings as objects at our disposal (Bell, 2015). Although so-called "humane slaughter" represents a potential improvement from a welfare perspective, it also normalises violence by accommodating rather than opposing it.

Killing a sentient being, especially one that experiences love and emotions, even in the ideal, usually imaginary case where there is no suffering, is violent and almost always unnecessary. And unnecessary violence is not a compelling model for the gentler, more peaceful world most of us desire (see Vinding, 2014, 2020b).

Euthanasia of suffering animals

Killing a happy animal for food when there are healthy plant-based options available represents needless violence carried out for self-interested reasons. But what about killing that is done out of compassion, to end intense suffering? Is it better to try to keep a severely injured animal alive if there is a good prospect of recovery?

We are probably most motivated to relieve an individual animal's suffering when we do so by rescuing an abused animal, say from a factory farm, and seeing them experience joy, love and freedom, even if some of the suffering from their previous trauma persists, at least during the recovery phase. Our intuition says that this is clearly a better outcome than simply putting the animal out of their misery.

If the animal had been gently euthanised and their suffering ended in that way, we would not experience the same happiness — at most, just relief that the suffering had ended, but also sadness at seeing the death of the animal. Going on a euthanasia spree with compassionate intent, aiming to put countless animals out of their misery, might seem more akin to a horror film than carrying out serial acts of kindness.

In fact, neither is there the same feeling of joy when, as a result of one's efforts as an activist, fewer animals are brought into this world to be tortured — just a feeling that one's efforts were worthwhile. Rescuing an individual animal from a life of suffering gives far more joy than the reduction by one of the number of animals raised on factory farms.

So even though a detached ethical perspective based on reducing suffering might argue more often for euthanasia, we feel a very strong intuitive desire to see an animal recover while shown love. As humans we cannot separate ourselves from our intuitions to embrace life, especially when it involves individuals. Consistently killing suffering animals would reflect a grim view of life. In a similar way, once a creature is dead, our respectful treatment of the body reflects the meaning we see in life and is not about any direct harm we would cause by desecrating the body.

A way to reconcile the utilitarian focus on reducing suffering with the intuition to preserve happy life is to respect the desire of an animal to live in the same way that we respect a human's, especially if one knows the suffering will decrease over time, but to carry out euthanasia if the suffering appears unbearable.

If the animal is to be saved, it is also important from a suffering perspective to take steps to ensure that it causes as little subsequent suffering as possible to other beings, through hunting or the consumption of other animal products. Saving one animal only to indirectly inflict suffering on many more may provide sentimental value, but it is obviously counterproductive from the perspective of impact (see also the section "The meat-eater problem", below).

Since one of the causes of suffering to animals raised for food, whether or not on factory farms, is the extreme fear they experience right before they are slaughtered, one might ask, if a rescued animal experiences a similar level of fear while being caught, is this any more justifiable? After all, even if our motives are radically different, the effect might be the same.

I think the answer has a few aspects. First of all, in practice, an animal being rescued may experience fear but it probably is not as intense as knowing that it will be killed. Second, the fear will usually quickly subside once the animal realises that it is not being threatened. Third, ignoring the animal altogether could mean allowing it to continue suffering intensely. In theory, if the fear were really extreme, one might argue that quickly euthanising the animal might still be the most compassionate solution. But again, we would have trouble living with ourselves if our reflex was to kill rather than nurture back to life. Causing fear before carrying out an unnecessary act of violence feels radically different from causing fear as part of an act of caring. Once again, a crucial factor in practice is our need to maintain a world that feels worth living in.

Euthanasia and assisted suicide in humans

Forcing people to stay alive against their will, especially if they are suffering intensely without relief or any prospect thereof, is cruel, and also a failure to respect their autonomy. Nobody chooses to be born on this planet, and even if they had, that wouldn't imply any commitment to making the choice an irreversible one. Although the large-scale suffering in the world is a complex problem, an individual's attempt to relieve their own suffering by ceasing to exist may still be a perfectly rational choice that demands respect.

And yet, suicide is still a tragedy, both because of the suffering that led up to it, and because of the hole left in the lives of the surviving friends and family. Sometimes it reflects a failure—of people and institutions—to offer needed help that could have led to a different outcome.

Aside from the suffering that suicide can both end and create, a hypothetical world where people are encouraged to commit suicide whenever they are experiencing extreme pain or psychological suffering would be a strange world that most people would not want to live in. Given the investment involved in raising a child and trying to ensure their happiness, it would be inconsistent to give up the moment they hit a major barrier. After all, if we are to be honest, we can *expect* many people to experience severe or even extreme suffering at some point in their lives.

So when is it reasonable to urge someone to keep fighting, and when is it reasonable to actually assist them in their decision to call it quits? An important consideration is whether all practically available means have been afforded to alleviate the suffering. It is hardly acceptable for someone to have to choose suicide because their pain has not been properly alleviated as it could have been, including with medication that is easy to produce and procure. For example, in much of the world, terminal cancer patients in severe pain are unable to obtain morphine, a highly effective analgesic, because their governments, overly fearful of drug dependence and diversion to the black market, have imposed severe restrictions on its use or otherwise failed to ensure the training of doctors and a stable supply chain (Leighton, 2018a, 2018b). Patients are left in agony, and many would prefer to die sooner rather than later.

Another example is cluster headaches, mentioned earlier, an excruciating condition also known as "suicide headaches" that drives many patients to take their lives to end the pain. Several psychedelic substances have been found to be dramatically effective at aborting and/or preventing attacks and even entire months-long or chronic episodes, but because of strict drug laws, many patients are unable to obtain them—a situation that is entirely unjustifiable, and that is being prolonged because of the stigma associated with these substances (Leighton, 2020a, 2020b).

Yet another related example is chronic pain, a common, often debilitating condition. For many patients, morphine and other opioids are the only effective medications that allow them to manage and have a semblance of a normal life. But in the US, in a misguided attempt to stem the opioid overdose epidemic, the authorities have made it very difficult for chronic pain patients to obtain opioids, even if they were already reliant on them for pain relief (Human Rights Watch, 2018; Adams, 2017). Many such patients have chosen to commit suicide.

These examples, and especially the first two, are cause areas that the Organisation for the Prevention of Intense Suffering (OPIS), a think-and-do tank I founded, has been active in. If governments made the relief of intense suffering their top priority, fewer patients would feel compelled to take their own lives.

As many cluster headache patients don't have access to medications that could more effectively treat their condition, and even some patients who do have access find the medications insufficiently effective, they may find themselves soldiering on through the suffering, expressing thoughts about ending it all, while fellow patients urge them to keep fighting, to push back the limits of what they consider bearable. This is a powerful example of the struggle between the desires to end suffering and to preserve life. Ultimately it is a person's own choice. But if governments claim to value life, then at the very least they need to give people all the means possible to make it bearable.

Saving lives vs. preventing suffering

The COVID-19 crisis confronted society with huge prioritisation issues, and it can serve as a good case study for the problem of choosing which lives to save, but also, how to pit lives saved against suffering averted. One of the issues is how to evaluate the "worth" of the lives of human beings who only have a few more years to live, compared to those of younger, healthier people. This issue appeared early on in the form of patient triage when overflowing intensive care units in northern Italy could not cope with the influx of new patients, and not only those with greater survival chances but also those with a greater life expectancy— more "life-years" left—were prioritised (Parodi et al., 2020; Mounk, 2020). Hospitals elsewhere faced similar situations (Sprung et al., 2020). But this has also been one of the underlying issues in deciding how far to go in shutting down society, largely to protect the older and most vulnerable (though healthy young people have, of course, succumbed to the virus as well), and how to compare premature loss of life and its associated suffering with the direct psychological suffering and other harms caused by lockdowns.

The virus obviously causes suffering in those who contract bad cases of the disease: even some who recover after a few weeks have said they wouldn't wish that experience on anyone. In the worst cases, an elderly or vulnerable patient is put on a ventilator and dies alone in the hospital, a death that has much additional suffering associated with it. But preventing these deaths by locking down the population causes suffering due to social isolation and depression as well as domestic tensions that can include violence. The impact on businesses and jobs created financial insecurity for huge numbers, pushing millions worldwide into extreme poverty, and will probably have long-term effects on suffering as well.

Many people are less concerned about an old person dying than someone younger, including health economists who weigh lives by their potential "value". Of course, we prefer to see people live out their natural lives and die at a ripe old age rather than in their prime. Premature deaths cause extra sadness. And dying at an old age gives one a lifetime to prepare oneself emotionally.

On the other hand, more readily sacrificing the older and more vulnerable because there is less potential life to preserve goes against a competing intuition of treating every individual equally and not concentrating suffering in one group. Strict utilitarianism based not even on suffering but on the concept of "creating value" is potentially less humanistic and, for reasons I explained earlier, less rational than utilitarianism that treats all members of society equally in trying to reduce their suffering.

The fact that so many people have been generally willing to self-isolate for an extended period, largely for the benefit of the elderly and the vulnerable, is a reassuring sign of society's potential for compassion. On the other hand, those who see a person's worth in terms of the economic productivity they represent, or the amount of future happiness they will experience, are more likely to consider life expectancy as the key factor in deciding whose lives to value most, and may consider lockdowns a needless burden on the young and healthy.

But even making society-wide decisions purely on the basis of overall suffering averted is complicated and also inextricable from intuitions. The main metric currently used in evaluating the impact of the pandemic is number of lives lost, which is far easier to measure but may only roughly correlate with direct suffering caused, against the backdrop of the suffering caused by lockdowns themselves.

In its starkest and simplest representation, the conflict can pit widespread moderate suffering of large numbers of people of all ages against an increased number of premature deaths of mainly elderly people, with the suffering these entail as well. In practice, it's far more complicated, since a virus allowed to run rampant still causes fear, overwhelms healthcare facilities and does huge damage to the economy, with knock-on effects, while widespread isolation can cause severe suffering and deaths as well.

Ideally we would want to assess different response scenarios for the amount of intense suffering they contain and determine which one is best on this measure. Solutions could then be modified as necessary to better accommodate people's intuitions.

In any case, society-wide problems require society-wide solutions. If we are trying to protect as many people as possible from dying prematurely under conditions of intense suffering, then we need to protect those who sacrifice their own wellbeing as well, giving up their freedoms and their ability to generate an income. This in itself is a strong argument for introducing a stronger social safety net that includes a universal basic income (Wignaraja, 2020; Gibson, 2020; Allas et al., 2020) as well as other measures to protect people's physical safety and emotional wellbeing. With such a safety net in place and consistent, rational government measures, the policy choices available might not need to be as stark.

Anti-natalism

If "no world" would be a better situation than the world as it is, or indeed any world that contains extreme suffering, then it would be unjustifiable to bring this world into existence. This doesn't mean it would be justifiable, nor perceived as justifiable, to attempt by any means available to reverse the situation and bring about "no world". But it also means we don't need to perpetuate the status quo indefinitely. Given the amount of intense suffering experienced and caused by humans, there is a compelling argument for people not to have children. This is precisely what is advocated by anti-natalists and their most prominent proponent, David Benatar (2006).

At least on the surface, this appears to be a practical way of reducing suffering in a way that doesn't involve violence and destruction. But it also conflicts with the strong human intuition to exist and to thrive. How can this conflict, which goes to the heart of ethics, be resolved?

First of all, most anti-natalists do not advocate trying to actually prevent people from having children,[2] such as by creating legal obstacles similar to China's past one-child policy. And even if many people decided not to have children, this is not a path to extinction, but merely to population reduction. A truly utopian future without extreme suffering is unlikely to happen through voluntary extinction, but through ethical governance and the benevolent use of technology. The systematic alleviation of the widespread intense suffering of wild animals will require some large-scale interventions in the future, and for that to happen, it is essential that humans don't go extinct.

---

[2] Although any movement can attract people with diverging views, the anti-natalist philosophy is at its essence nonviolent, and ultimately concerned about suffering resulting from sentience in all forms, and therefore not even necessarily focused primarily on stopping human procreation (Emma Tulanova, personal communication).

However, the utilitarian argument remains compelling, if only to reduce somewhat the amount of future suffering rather than use anti-natalism to try to abolish it. The decision to have children represents a strong intuitive override, based on the multifaceted desire to have a family. There are alternative solutions that can help meet the underlying needs, including adoption, closer connections with existing family and friends, adopting rescue animals and working closely with altruistic organisations to help others. If one decides to have children, limiting their number represents a compromise solution.

There is also a possible counterargument to this view, according to which more humans means the reduction of natural habitats and fewer wild animals coming into existence, resulting in less net suffering (Vinding, 2021). If this position is true, it provides yet another example of how everything is connected by utilitarianism, while also demonstrating the difficulty of choosing one unsatisfactory situation over another, where each contains huge amounts of intense suffering.

Regardless of how many children are brought into the world, future suffering can be minimised by instilling them with compassionate ethics and a balanced lifestyle that minimises harm. Although one cannot control the life path of one's children, if they choose to carry out social activism to promote compassionate policies, it is even more likely that they might have a net positive impact on the world.

The meat-eater problem

Is it always better to save human lives, even if it will lead to more animals suffering due to meat consumption by those whose lives are saved? This question has been termed the "meat-eater problem" (n.d.), and it has parallels to the question of anti-natalism raised in the previous section. A variation called the "poor meat-eater problem" refers to the reduction of poverty and a subsequent increase in meat consumption as aid recipients become wealthier. If we focus just on the first situation, it's undeniable that every life saved, whether a human's or a non-human animal's, has the potential to contribute to additional suffering in the world. Is it therefore not more compassionate to focus efforts on reducing suffering rather than on saving lives, which is what some of the most highly rated charities focus on?

Even from a utilitarian perspective, the loss of a child can be extremely painful to the surviving parents and could potentially outweigh in intensity the suffering caused to animals by that child's existence. But regardless, and without getting into the numbers, a society where we intentionally allow children to die, or even to remain in poverty, for utilitarian reasons does not feel like a world most of us would want to live in. So while it is understandable for individual donors and activists to focus directly on other issues related to extreme suffering, such as preventing the torture of animals, the path to a gentler world does not include intentionally allowing children to die of disease or malnutrition when we could readily save them. Even if we believe that a world with far fewer or even no humans would be better, allowing children to die hardly seems an acceptable way to achieve it.

Preserving the environment vs. reducing wild animal suffering

One of the most seemingly intractable ethical issues is our relationship with the natural environment and the suffering contained within it (Faria & Paez, 2019). It turns the core ethical conundrum of existence and suffering into a real-life practical problem. Doing away with human conflict and cruelty, disease, poverty and depression is not controversial. Neither—in principle, for most people—is doing away with the horrors of factory farming. But addressing the vast amounts of suffering contained within nature is another story altogether. While there are many uncontroversial ways we can help individual animals, such as rescuing stranded koalas whose habitats have been destroyed by forest fires, the impact remains small-scale. As mentioned earlier, some larger-scale interventions are also being carried out and further studied to improve feasibility, including vaccinations and contraception (Eckerström-Liedholm, 2022).

Environmentalists believe in the preservation of our environment for reasons of both intrinsic and instrumental value. The instrumental reasons are that humans and non-human animals depend on a healthy ecosystem for their survival and for a life that feels worth living. This argument is closely linked to our existence bias and our desire to thrive.

The "deep ecology" philosophy goes further, holding the belief in the intrinsic worth of all living beings—regardless of whether or not they are sentient and can suffer—and that it is "wrong" out of principle to mess with nature. It is appealing on an intuitive level because it speaks to our desire for meaning and spirituality, promoting a view of nature as pristine and existence as inherently beautiful. It therefore reflects the instrumental reasons as well—that a healthy ecosystem is something we depend on for our own lives to have meaning. But aside from the irrationality of attributing intrinsic value to non-sentient beings—not only does value require sentient beings to do the valuing but, as I have argued, the value is still only instrumental if it is external to a sentient being affected by it—what the philosophy ignores is the fact that nature is the result of random processes that are apathetic to the wellbeing of individual creatures, and to the reality of the widespread intense suffering that nature contains. In a sense, it maintains a fairy tale view of existence that misses the most essential aspects. The suffering of non-human animals is simply accepted as an immutable part of the system. What on the surface may appear to be a beautiful philosophy may reveal itself, even if unintentionally, to actually be anthropocentric and callous.

Many of those who particularly cherish nature blame our society for separating ourselves from it, for acting as if nature is at our disposal and is something we can seek to control. There is an aspect of truth to this, the idea that we have cut ourselves off from the roots from which we evolved. And yet there is an implicit speciesism in the same people's unwillingness to consider sentient beings in the wild as deserving the same consideration for their wellbeing as we afford ourselves — an ethical separation that is far more devastating than any urban lifestyle. The values of many environmentalists often prioritise preserving stable systems over addressing the suffering contained within those systems (Leighton, 2019a).

Not all animal rights activists are overly concerned about suffering in nature. Many subscribe to the idea that what is not caused by humans is not our problem or responsibility. For example, Austrian animal rights activist Martin Balluch considers the core problem to be the oppression that comes from using animals for our benefit, and that what matters most is freedom and autonomy. He further argues that most wild animals are happy most of the time (Balluch, 2017). But while oppression (and the related concept of exploitation) is of course a major cause of suffering, it arguably matters because of the suffering it causes, including through the deprivation of liberty. The raw experience of suffering matters intrinsically, regardless of the cause, or any happiness that precedes or follows it. And there is an inherently speciesist aspect to a perspective that determines who deserves our help by their species membership rather than the degree of their suffering.

When people argue for the preservation of the natural world, I want to ask them: where is the beauty in seeing a sustainable cycle of predation? Surely not in the suffering. Would they be willing to trade places with an animal being eaten alive, or have their child risk that fate? Or is it rather the awe of complexity, of a system where everything is fine-tuned, polished by the winds of time? Is it about sustainability itself, the fear of death and the clamouring for our own low-suffering existence for near-eternity? Is it ever really principally a pragmatic assessment that we have no alternative but to accept nature or risk worse consequences?

But if we do recognise the presence of widespread intense suffering of wild animals in nature, how do we reconcile the conflicting desires to preserve the environment and to reduce this suffering? How do we create harmony with our environment, on which our lives and wellbeing depend, without putting nature on a pedestal, with all the suffering it has created? This requires separating the beauty and nourishing qualities of nature from the suffering embedded within it, a shift in perspective from the one most people grow up with, and an acceptance of some cognitive dissonance. Although it's too much to expect from ourselves to always feel two conflicting emotions at the same time, overall we need to try to live with this dissonance—again, in a dance between two radically different perspectives that both have validity.

Destroying or ignoring the destruction of our environment in order to reduce suffering would be extremely counterintuitive, psychologically unsustainable and politically unfeasible. And any major intervention in our planet's complex ecosystem would risk causing more harm than good, at least with our current level of knowledge.

But what if we could create small low-suffering ecosystems as pilot projects that, if successful, could eventually be expanded to replace existing ones, as suggested by David Pearce (1995) in *The Hedonistic Imperative*?[3] The idea would be highly controversial today. But it would be a means of satisfying two conflicting needs—the inherent urgency of preventing extreme suffering and the human need to maintain a world perceived as worth living in. Our status quo bias—the tendency to prefer things to stay the same—might resist such large-scale changes, but we might be able to achieve such a transformation over time in a way that was intuitively acceptable. Persuading people to warm up to more interventionist approaches may require not just sensitising them to the experiences of animals suffering in nature, but also presenting plausible, tested solutions. Again, the prospect of easing much of the extreme suffering that occurs in nature is actually one of the most compelling reasons for us to strive to maintain the existence of our species.

---

[3] See also Pearce's (2021a) more recent text on CRISPR-based "gene drives".

Fourteen

From Ethics to Action

Reflections on the ethical tango

A rational approach to ethics in the big-picture sense would, I have argued, lead to a theoretical preference for the world not to exist—not to a fear of existential risk. This is because impartial utilitarianism with a focus on prioritisation by degree of urgency, well informed about relevant phenomenological facts and by metaphysically accurate, empty- and open-individualist views of personal identity, and freed from existence bias, leads to the realisation that even blissful existence doesn't justify any occurrence of the worst forms of extreme suffering. A reluctance to adopt this view is an understandable concession to our Darwinian, life- and personal-identity-affirming intuitions. But these intuitions overlook the reality of extreme suffering—a reality that no one who was fully aware of it would consent to risk experiencing. I added a practical "+" that asserts the innate human desire to exist and to thrive in order to make the negative utilitarian framework not just palatable, but workable. I think that's honest. We can even embrace the "+" as a starting point. But then we need to act like responsible adults, roll up our sleeves and get to work on the reality we face.

Yet we cannot be fully rational and seamlessly combine pure utilitarian calculations and strong human intuitions within one framework that provides unambiguous, non-arbitrary prescriptions for actions. Where they collide is a chaotic zone that can't be properly resolved with a cursory appeal to subjective exchange rates between pleasure and pain. However appealing this approach may seem because it is theoretically based on measurements, it doesn't capture the heart of the problem, the conflict between, on the one hand, the ego and its various self-focused, altruistic and spiritual instincts and emotions, and, on the other hand, the detached bird's eye perspective that treats all mental states—all slices of consciousness-moments—impartially.

And you can't simply dismiss the intuitions as if they are a distraction, because they are intimately connected with what feels worth preserving altogether. Respecting our intuitions might be seen as giving us a good conscience while we continue to tolerate great amounts of harm, but strictly applying utilitarianism would run right up against these intuitions and make the world seem totally absurd.

Furthermore, we can't hope to prevent most intense suffering without reducing the frustrations and feelings of injustice that can arise from thwarted intuitions. These feelings are a form of suffering in themselves, but they can lead to far worse suffering if allowed to persist, especially if they result in conflict. In other words, the sustainable reduction or even elimination of intense suffering *requires* that we not neglect our intuitions.

The metaphor of a tango may seem intentionally and frustratingly vague—a reluctance to commit to a clear ethical position. But there is actually a clear underlying commitment that is far from trivial: to the idea that existence does not justify extreme suffering. Yet once we exist, we are condemned to dance, and even indulge in some of the beauty that existence thrusts upon us.

Creating a new suffering metric for health economics

Returning to the very concrete and tangible: in order to determine priorities and measure progress, we need metrics that are based on what matters. I have argued that everything that matters ethically, in the sense of there being inherent urgency to change it, can be reduced to suffering. There are also strong intuitions, such as for the continuity of life and against knowingly causing harm, that, if not respected, create suffering as well.

The two most widely used health metrics, the QALY (Quality-Adjusted Life-Year) and the DALY (Disability-Adjusted Life-Year), are strongly based on the intuition towards preserving life. The QALY considers a full year of healthy life to be a reference, and a year of life lived at a lower level of health to be less valuable. The DALY measures years of life lost to death or "disability" (actually meaning departure from optimal health), and similarly considers a year of life at a lower level of health comparable to a year partially lost altogether. Health economists literally weigh the value of lives based on their quality adjustment and number of expected years remaining. QALY-based cause prioritisation has also been advocated for within the effective altruism movement (MacAskill, 2015).

When QALYs are used to weigh different outcomes in terms of QALYs lost or gained, they directly imply that the death of an older person is less costly and therefore more acceptable than the loss of a younger person, and also that the death of someone with a chronic illness is less costly and therefore more acceptable than the death of someone in good health. Although this might appear shocking—at least from a perspective that considers all lives to matter equally, regardless of how healthy people are — this is exactly the way much of mainstream health economics works, and the acceptability of a policy is often argued to be a direct consequence of its impact on human lives, expressed in terms of QALYs. This means that, all things being equal, a system that relies mainly on this metric to make decisions will prefer to save the life of a 40-year-old over a 60-year-old, and the life of a healthy athlete over someone of the same age with diabetes. A newborn who has barely seen the light of day beats everyone else (with the possible theoretical exception — if the reasoning were to be extended — of a 3-month-old foetus, with a full lifetime of QALYs ahead plus a half-year of in utero hedonic zero).

Furthermore — and this may be more of a theoretical criticism than one based on common usage (Dolan, 2001) — if applied aggregatively to a population rather just to measuring outcomes for individuals, the QALY paradigm would have the absurd consequence of allowing severe suffering to be compensated by having more individuals alive experiencing that suffering! If someone has a terrible chronic illness that causes them to suffer greatly, then keeping them alive is less important according to the QALY paradigm, but if we could bring into being several such people, that might still be considered better than having just one healthy, suffering-free person. QALY-based reasoning could, in principle, thereby lead to the Repugnant Conclusion, and even justify a worse scenario where everyone is suffering severely.

The QALY, which is currently used by the National Institute for Health and Care Excellence (NICE) in the UK, among other places, was intended to be a useful metric for making health and economic decisions. But it is closely aligned with the notion that our goal is to create "value" in the universe, and that a human life is valued by how much happiness it will produce. As I've argued repeatedly in this book, I don't think this is a rational approach to achieving a better world — or the most humanising approach, either. In fact, in one way the QALY paradigm seems conceptually even more flawed than the classical utilitarian weighing of happiness vs. suffering, in that it doesn't even explicitly acknowledge suffering as inherently bad, but rather, as instrumentally reducing the positive value of a life.

The DALY, which is used by the Global Burden of Disease project and the World Health Organisation (WHO), is philosophically somewhat distinct. While the use of QALYs inherently values years of life as something to maximise, DALYs focus on what is lost from a normal life due to poor health. Yet even DALYs don't focus explicitly on suffering as a core phenomenon to measure and address. Although most diseases with a high disability score are accompanied by serious suffering, this is not always the case. Anencephaly (where part of the brain is missing) is an extreme case of a fatal condition that is entirely disabling but appears not to cause suffering, but people can psychologically adapt to other, less disabling conditions and thrive, especially if there isn't severe pain. More concerning, diseases or conditions that cause severe suffering but leave the patient relatively functional most of the time have a disability weight that hardly conveys the seriousness of the suffering. The theoretical maximum disability weight is 1.0, but average disability weights for the range of conditions tend to plateau at about 0.6 or 0.7 (though for some conditions the range extends to a maximum of 0.8 or even 0.9), meaning that even some of the most disabling conditions are still only considered to reduce health by two-thirds, on average. Yet, in part also because of the use of aggregation, even a disability weight nearing 1.0 might not cause a rare condition to stand out in the overall rankings as a target for urgent relief of suffering.

In some cases, patients commit suicide to escape their suffering. Yet a DALY measure that tied the suicide to the condition would, in principle, be more affected by the years of life lost due to the suicide than by the actual suffering incurred while the patient was alive.

What we see, then, is that the metrics being used don't reflect the full range of things that matter, and neglect the parameter that actually matters most. In addition, the methodology for determining disability weights or life quality involves asking healthy people to compare diseases or conditions that they don't have. This is a very poor way of assessing severe or extreme suffering—a situation that many cluster headache patients have experienced when trying to convey the severity of their condition to others.

Health metrics are a major factor in government priority-setting. There is a need for a new metric that better tracks the most ethically relevant parameter, suffering. The proposed metric Wellbeing-Adjusted Life-Year (alternatively referred to as WELBY, WELLBY or WALY) is a step in that direction, in that it more explicitly addresses subjective wellbeing as the key parameter (Frijters et al., 2019). According to one definition offered by wellbeing economist Paul Frijters (2020), it is a "one point change in life satisfaction for one person for one year when measured on a 0–10 scale". But it doesn't substitute for a metric that can capture the agony of intense and extreme suffering. It also shares the fundamental problems of aggregation and hedon-like metrics with QALYs and DALYs—that wellness or life quality points are summed up, with changes considered equivalent no matter where they are on a scale of wellbeing, and potentially no matter how these changes are distributed among a population.

A major report by the Lancet Commission on Palliative Care and Pain Relief (Knaul et al., 2018) proposed a metric called the SALY (Suffering-Adjusted Life-Year), modelled on the DALY but based on suffering rather than disability or health. Since years of life lost do not directly contribute to suffering, SALY could exclude the Years of Life Lost (YLL) component and be reduced to Years Lived with Suffering (YLS), with a weighting based on degree of suffering. However, because of the inherent problem with aggregation, there is no adequate way of combining mild, moderate and severe suffering into one metric.

It would therefore be advisable to create additional metrics of severe suffering to be used in parallel to a YLS measure. Years Lived with Severe Suffering (YLSS) could capture suffering at the level of approximately 7/10 and above. A separate metric called Days Lived with Extreme Suffering (DLES) could capture the most urgent suffering at the level of approximately 9/10 and above, and properly account for it even when experienced on short timescales. The goal would not be to effect any major shift in resources away from patients suffering moderately, but to ensure that the most severe suffering is given greater visibility and treated with the urgency it demands.

Suffering metrics could also be applied to non-human animals, notwithstanding the practical difficulties in assessing their degree of suffering (Savoie & Sarek, 2018; Welfare Footprint Project, n.d.). This would allow them to be included in a more global assessment of priorities, on the basis of the one parameter that matters most. Adapting a human health metric to non-human animals might be unprecedented, but a focus on suffering would do away with any objections based on how much we, as external observers, happen to subjectively value human and non-human lives.

Impacting the far future

How much of an influence can the actions we take today have on the amount of intense suffering occurring far into the future? If we look at trends over the past decades and centuries, then despite all the atrocities committed in recent history, it seems that overall rates of violence have declined, as famously argued by Steven Pinker (2011). We also tend to see overall progress in the protection of human rights, and of animal rights as well, with the implementation in some countries of stronger (though woefully inadequate) animal protection laws and changes in practices. But the potential for violence is written in our genome. We still torture and abuse animals by the billions, and the numbers are increasing. Multiple wars are ongoing, and widespread savagery towards civilians, recalling the Nazi era, is again on display in Europe as I write this. We see how populations can become polarised and sections of them radicalised, and how even supposedly stable liberal democracies can be threatened by populist authoritarians, a corrupt ruling class and heavily biased, billionaire-controlled media, and risk backsliding. There is no natural law dictating that moral progress will continue.

Having an impact on the far future (or long-term future, as it is often called) essentially means introducing a technological, cultural or structural innovation that has remarkable staying power and cannot easily be dislodged. A powerful technology that becomes widely adopted can affect the subsequent paths along which society develops. An idea that spreads in the population can potentially become sustainably anchored as part of the culture if it promotes, or appears to promote, the wellbeing of those applying and sharing it. And changes in the very structure of a political and economic system can lead to high exit barriers that stabilise it, for better or for worse. These different mechanisms can also be combined, such as when a totalitarian regime employs new technology to control a population and restrict the ideas that it is exposed to while stifling dissent with heavy punishments.

The possibility of the world, or even part of it, being locked into a system that sustains intense suffering, such as a totalitarian regime, represents a huge danger (Bostrom & Cirkovic, 2008). In contrast, the lock-in of a system that eliminates suffering would arguably be utopian (if the vision included actual thriving it would be more intuitively appealing). The first kind of lock-in seems far easier to achieve than the second. We have seen throughout history, including numerous examples from the twentieth century, how totalitarian regimes that suppress human rights, carry out acts of barbaric cruelty and prevent public discussion on ethical governance can stay in power for decades or longer, without even having recourse to modern technology.

On the other hand, given human nature, achieving and stabilising a utopia seems much less probable. Benevolent dictators are rare and temporary, and populists can easily appeal to humankind's crassest instincts. The greed of a relative few can destabilise a system that values cooperation and fairness, especially if there are no repercussions, with countries as diverse as the US and many underdeveloped countries suffering from corruption (Transparency International, 2021) and often deep inequality (World Population Review, n.d.). Ensuring stability might itself require restrictions that would feel dystopian. The design is crucial, and there are many ways to get it wrong.

The idea that we can wilfully reduce suffering in the far future implies that we can today create a new kind of Big-Bang-like event—in importance, if not in physical visibility—that will still have repercussions in thousands, millions and possibly even billions of years. That is quite a challenge. A project designed to have such an effect also risks having unintended, counterproductive consequences that persist over a long time frame. But if we continue to exist as a species and our high-technology civilisation doesn't collapse—admittedly a big if—we seem at high risk of being headed for some kind of lock-in. If we can positively influence its characteristics, now is the time to do so. The next two sections describe how we might go about it.

Designing compassionate blueprints for governance based on xNU+ ethics

The widespread societal acceptance and implementation of an ethical framework based on the xNU+ model, or inspired by this or similar thinking, requires that it meet people's needs and protect the things that people value most, including freedom (when it doesn't cause unnecessary harm to others), happiness and meaning, physical health and security, and social connections. A system implementing such a framework therefore needs to be attuned to people's needs and have an embedded or institutionalised mechanism for continuously listening to them. And it has to appeal to people's capacity for compassion and intuitive agreement with the Golden Rule.

A goal then, as I see it, is to try to express the xNU+ framework as a relatively small number of principles that can be easily spread—in the spirit of rule utilitarianism that also accommodates our intuitions. The key principles are clear: a steady drive to prevent and ideally, in the long term, eliminate extreme suffering, while protecting humans' freedom to thrive and live without fear of being harmed. Many of the concrete details can be specified, as they are essential elements of an implementable framework. But the fine-tuning requires the participation and cooperation of the people who will allow themselves to be governed by such a framework.

Ideally, we might want to attempt to formalise mathematically all the principles behind the framework and their relationship to each other, including the inherent uncertainty, the practical role of intuitions and how we can deal with conflicts. The value of doing so might be less for making precise prescriptions, which would still be subject to the approval of decision-making bodies representing the people as well as popular referenda, than in the theoretical description of the problem and its encapsulation of the conflicting values. However, a formalisation might be more valuable for trying to convert xNU+ into a specific set of instructions to be followed by an AGI in determining how to act ethically, as I will discuss shortly.

Echoing a point I made earlier, an ethically grounded system of governance can be more risk-averse, in the specific sense of reducing the likelihood of intense or unbearable suffering, and thus more aligned with the "x" part of xNU+ than individuals typically are. In the interest of personal autonomy, we allow people to sometimes take even ridiculous personal risks of harm and suffering. However, on a societal level, we may be better able to avoid even small risks of severe suffering—applying more rationality than individuals do in their own lives, greater awareness of the significance of extreme suffering and also a more conscious implementation of understanding distinct, continuous personal identity as an illusion. Giving priority to extreme suffering does not mean ignoring those suffering moderately—it means expanding our capacity to attend to a range of urgencies.

Since it is not realistic to expect most people to carry out or even support actions or policies that contradict our strongest intuitions, we need to serve our intuitions by trying to create a reality where we are not constantly in conflict with them. This means that we protect people against existential risks and against being harmed or allowed to suffer for the benefit of others.

We can potentially achieve greater consensus by focusing less strongly on political and economic ideologies with polarising labels, and insisting instead on certain clear outcomes. These include the priority of preventing human and non-human animals from experiencing severe suffering—non-humans could potentially also be protected by a new version of the Universal Declaration of Human Rights expanded to include all sentient beings[1]—while enshrining specific human rights, such as various freedoms, the abolishment of victimless crimes as punishable offences, and a minimum decent standard of living that includes lodging, nutritious food, clean water, electricity and healthcare. The notion of "equal opportunity" is insufficient, because it attributes poor outcomes—suffering—to people's bad decisions, when the supposed equality of opportunity is always more superficial than it might appear. And regardless: from the perspective of the universe, suffering happens, and the compassionate approach is to act to try to prevent it from happening, rather than blame people for their life decisions. With advances in technology and the shrinking set of skills where humans can still provide added value, it may become increasingly difficult for most humans to avoid suffering without a compassionate system of governance that ensures their needs are met.

---

1   See, for example, an open letter to the UN from the Algosphere Alliance (2017).

The conflicting desires for privacy and security are a cause of tension in many countries. While claiming to be doing so for security reasons, governments like the US have carried out illegal surveillance on their own citizens. The Chinese government uses technology to take surveillance of its population to an entirely new level. Surveillance would be less problematic if governments could be entirely trusted to use it purely to prevent terrorist attacks and other acts of violence or that cause great suffering, and never for any other purposes, including prosecuting people for victimless crimes, or otherwise limiting their human rights. As I also argued in *The Battle for Compassion* (p. 185), the potential need for surveillance to prevent severe suffering demands the solid entrenchment of a compassionate ethical framework within all levels of governance, stronger privacy protections, and a higher basic standard of guaranteed security so that even unintentional releases of private data cannot have drastic effects on people's wellbeing. It also requires much greater transparency about the workings of government itself.

Ultimately we need a rebuilt system of global governance that protects humans and animals from harm, and especially from intense suffering, wherever they happen to be situated, and ensures peaceful cooperation between states, dissipating any motivation to resort to violence and armed conflict. The UN has served as a positive step in this direction since its founding in 1945, but it is widely recognised as inadequate for a host of reasons. These include the veto power granted to a small group of countries in the Security Council, voting often based on narrowly conceived national interests, the hypocrisy and resultant loss of credibility of giving some of the worst human rights offenders places on the Human Rights Council and other UN bodies, such as the Commission on the Status of Women (Coogle, 2017), a lack of alignment between UN aspirations and national legislation, ordinary people's voices not being heard, insufficient focus on intense suffering, and little attention to the wellbeing of non-human animals. And critically, there is no reliable mechanism of enforcement—a global police force with both power and legitimacy. Many ideas and proposals have been made for new systems of global governance, including in a contest organised by the Global Challenges Foundation (n.d.), though scepticism abounds about the UN's ability to reform itself, not least because it would require the agreement of the permanent members of the Security Council to relinquish their unique power.

Implementing an effective new system of global governance is obviously an extremely difficult problem, not just because of divergences in countries' stances on specific issues or solutions, but more fundamentally because of a lack of common values among the world's governments and a universal, genuine commitment to human rights that supersedes the self-enrichment of ruling elites. There is also deep mistrust among much of the world's population of authorities and official information, but also a widespread inability to distinguish fact from fiction and a vulnerability to propaganda—all factors that undermine both engagement in the political process and the ability to make good political decisions (The Consilience Project, 2022). A promising approach is to hugely expand, up to the level of global governance, the use of citizens' assemblies—a successful model for informed, collaborative decision-making by ordinary citizens with the input of experts (Sortition Foundation, n.d.; Global Assembly, n.d.; Vergne et al., 2018). It's essential to embed xNU+ thinking into the ethical grounding of citizens' assemblies, as well as other experiments in democracy and governance (see Vinding, 2022), to ensure that the voices of those actually or potentially suffering the most—in the present and in the future—are fully taken into account.

The last tango: embedding xNU+ ethics into AGI

We are in the middle of a technology revolution in which new breakthroughs in AI are being made at a breathtaking pace.[2] As AI speeds towards achieving powerful general intelligence well beyond that of humans, with the ability to continuously self-improve, we risk losing control, as many AI experts fear (see, for example, Yampolskiy, 2020). AGI, as it would then be called, or superintelligence, might relatively soon become the dominating force on our planet, with little or no possibility to turn it off or otherwise rein it back in. The values it is guided by and the goals it pursues would determine how much harm it is capable of doing, or of allowing. The translation of ethical thinking into AI programming might therefore represent one of our last foreseeable opportunities to have a large-scale ethical influence on the future. If this is true, our current reflections might well represent the last tango of ethics.

The field of AI safety aims to ensure that AI does what we actually want it to do. The greatest concern, as summarised by AI researcher Roman Yampolskiy, is that "a single failure of a superintelligent system may cause an existential risk event" (Yampolskiy, 2019). Aside from the misery such an event would bring, it would appear a rather ironic turn of events to a detached observer, who might comment, "Look at you silly

---

[2] See, for example, two references from April 2022, the first showing language understanding/generation and reasoning (Narang & Chowdhery, 2022), the second showing image generation (Robertson, 2022).

humans, you've managed to kill yourselves off without even wanting to, and you've left behind your favourite toys, which are still running."

A central problem with AI is that it can interpret a specified goal literally and narrowly. In doing so, it can fail to take into consideration a whole range of constraints, either on the goal itself or on the ways to achieving that goal, that its programmers might consider obvious or implied, but that they haven't explicitly provided. The consequences can be comical (simulated robots learning new ways of walking), troubling (algorithms revealing societal racial biases) or existential (an AGI that destroys everything as a means to eradicate a smaller problem, such as a disease, or to create something new), depending in large part on the power wielded by the AI. In the preface to the book on AI safety referenced above, Roman Yampolskiy lists several examples others have given of possible accidents that could occur.

We can try to specify as many of these constraints or principles as possible, or program in a set of general values so that the AI can determine what constraints to impose on its own actions. Because we have trouble formulating our values or more detailed principles clearly, accurately and comprehensively, an alternative approach being used is to allow the AI to learn these principles through observation and reinforcement, and thereby better understand the world as we want it to be (Christiano et al., 2017).

Even if it understands our values, an AGI may still explicitly seek goals that are not what we want. This could happen if an AGI autonomously shifts its values or develops goals that are no longer aligned with those of humans. An AGI could also be instrumentalised by humans for explicitly malevolent purposes, or developed without concern about collateral harm it causes while doing specific people's bidding.

Physicist and AI researcher Max Tegmark (2017) describes the problem of AI safety as three-fold: making AI learn our goals, adopt our goals and then retain our goals. There are various distinct and difficult problems here. A practical one is that there are many groups trying to develop AGI around the world, including corporations and governments. Without coordination around desired goals, overall AI safety may not be achievable, as there may be a competitive advantage in not being overly conservative about AI safety, even if the end result is not in anyone's interests. This part of the problem is more about strategy, politics and game theory. Other issues are more of a technical nature, including how to build in fail-safe mechanisms.

The way in which ethics is perhaps most directly relevant to the problem is in the values that we decide to program into an AGI or allow it to infer. Even for many specific, well-defined situations, there isn't a consensus on what we want. To take a commonly cited example of comparatively minor importance in the context of AGI, how would we want a self-driving car to react if it risked hitting a group of pedestrians—would we always want it to spare the driver's life, or to save a maximum number of lives? The varied answers provided to the trolley problem imply similarly varied answers to its real-life version.

But on a larger scale, even if we were able to accurately capture a snapshot of society's current values and then stably program them into an AI, or have the AI learn our values and goals through observation, this would be a devastatingly lost opportunity for ethical progress. In our world today, we still torture non-human animals on a massive scale. We deprive people in horrendous pain of legal access to effective medication. We allow people to go hungry and homeless, and to die of preventable diseases. We imprison and torture people in many countries for not having the right beliefs or saying the right things. And we allow the wealthiest to control governance mechanisms to enrich themselves and accumulate resources. If this is the dataset from which AI will learn society's values, that could portend a very bleak future. Surely we would want to encode a powerful AGI with the most utopian ethical framework we can, rather than lock in the prevailing ethics of the early twenty-first century.

AI researcher Stuart Russell (2017) has pointed out that an AI wouldn't necessarily copy our behaviour, and that it could learn to understand our underlying desires. A fundamental problem, though, is that our own behaviours are not designed to avoid extreme suffering, and the preferences or desires revealed by our behaviours are a poor guide to suffering-free flourishing—for humans, and even more so for non-humans. An AI modelled on underlying human preferences might still be an improvement over the present situation and help preserve a world that feels worth living in for more people. For some AI researchers, that alone might seem a sufficiently ambitious outcome to expect of an AGI, when the alternative might be annihilation. But if it preserved and stabilised extreme suffering far into the future, this would be a dystopia.

Although artificial suffering, as discussed earlier, is a real possibility, an AGI based on classical computing seems most unlikely to be sentient itself (though it might conceivably find a reason to construct artificial sentience). The hope that a non-sentient AGI will be able to truly "understand" suffering and use that understanding to adapt its priorities seems unfounded. While it could conclude that there are situations that humans really don't seem to like, it wouldn't be able to drive an aversion to those situations based on a visceral grasp of what they entail. In the worst case, without robust constraints, it could conclude that allowing situations that enable such suffering might still serve its goals, especially if these goals were preserving its own existence or even that of humanity.

From the perspective I have been arguing for in these pages, the core issues are as follows. To the extent that the future of our world depends on the values programmed into an AGI, how can we incorporate the principles of xNU+? And more fundamentally: how do we deal with the inherent conflict *within* xNU+? Do we want xNU+ to be interpreted as meaning, first and foremost, do everything possible to eliminate extreme suffering, while *trying* to avoid conflicts with our intuitions? Or rather, try to eliminate extreme suffering while *always* seeking to avoid or minimise conflicts with our intuitions? Or something in between? Can we expect an AGI to perform an ethical tango as we might ourselves do in addressing concrete issues, or do we need to make clear choices in advance? And if so, won't these choices be arbitrary? The problem becomes acutely dramatic if we need to anticipate a binary choice between the persistence of huge amounts of extreme suffering and non-existence.

In a review article, AI researcher Tom Everitt and colleagues wrote, "Rejecting all particular choices, Bogosian (2017) instead argues that a better option would be to build an AGI that remains uncertain about which moral theory is correct, since morally uncertain agents typically avoid events that are extremely bad according to any possibly correct moral theory" (Everitt et al., 2018). Essentially, this means leaving things open, allowing the AGI to dance the ethical tango itself, on the assumption that it won't go clumsily crashing off the edge. Stuart Russell has also argued that it is demonstrably beneficial when the objectives are left uncertain, as an AI will then request more information before making decisions it is uncertain about.

But if constraints are not clearly specified, this might still lead to dramatic consequences. Even if we were prepared to defer to an AGI to solve the ambiguity of small-scale problems, this ambiguity might still translate into huge risks at a larger scale, at least if the AGI really does become uncontrollable. As Nate Soares (2019), Executive Director of the Machine Intelligence Research Institute (MIRI), has written, "Operators will require methods for robustly communicating their intentions to the system … And eventually, explicit methodologies for resolving normative uncertainty may be required."

The clearer the vision we have of what we want, the more clearly we can specify it to the AI. In that way we can also constrain its range of options and allow ourselves to maintain control, helping to ensure that an AGI won't make itself indestructible. If an AGI could be successfully programmed to always defer back to humans in case of uncertainty, and

14. From Ethics to Action

to allow itself to be turned off if necessary, this wouldn't be an AGI over which we had ever lost control.

If we return to the question of which values to program into an AI that will eventually become autonomous and powerful, we can think of there being an "easy problem" and a "hard problem" of AI ethics, analogous to the easy and hard problems of consciousness (which are, respectively, determining the functional details of how the brain works, and determining more fundamentally how physical matter can create conscious experience). The "easy problem" is figuring out how to ensure that an AGI indefinitely respects the values we teach it. Of course, it's actually anything but easy—it's complicated, technically demanding and might not even be possible. It's only easy by analogy to the consciousness problem, in the sense that with enough work it might be solvable and the details set out. The "hard problem" is determining what values to program in, if we can. And it's hard because it's unclear how to answer this question through a non-arbitrary procedure or algorithm, because of the inherent conflict in the values themselves, and the distinct modes of being that lead to them.

In a somewhat different perspective on the problem that leads to a similar conclusion, Adam Keiper and Ari Schulman wrote, "to truly guarantee that robots would act ethically, we would first have to solve all of ethics—which would probably require 'solving' philosophy, which would in turn require a complete theory of everything" (Keiper & Schulman, 2011). This would mean that even if you thought ethics was objectively solvable, you might still need to solve the hard problem of consciousness as well!

In practice, few programmers would actively program in values or principles that they found strongly counterintuitive, and there would be essentially zero chance of achieving widespread consensus around such values or principles. So as long as we retain some active influence on the values an AGI will have, our intuitions will inevitably play an important role.

But the people developing AI are generally not experts in governance either. If you really think that an AGI is going to rule the world, then you had better be thinking a little bit more about principles of good governance than just observing human behaviour and our revealed preferences. Modelling the psychological profile of a benevolent dictator who is rational and compassionate might be a better approach.

Even if we accept, based on the reasoning I have offered in these pages, that non-existence would, in theory, be better than existence containing extreme suffering, it would be widely considered highly unacceptable to try to use an AGI as a means to actively achieve the goal of non-existence through destructive actions. Neither would most people even consider an avoidable risk of an existential catastrophe to be acceptable. Just as most people theoretically wouldn't tolerate governments knowingly allowing large existential threats to persist (though, as we see with climate change and other threats, reality is obviously very different), we wouldn't want to explicitly program an AGI to allow such threats to persist either.

An AGI programmed primarily to abolish extreme suffering, with no clear red lines, would aim to do just that, possibly by the most obvious and simplest means, and thereby represent a clear existential risk. This is what any other single-minded AGI might do as well, since humans who aren't slaves could be a nuisance for whatever goal it wants to achieve. Even without a specific goal programmed in, an AGI might, through simple rationality, arrive autonomously at the goal of non-existence as a means of abolishing extreme suffering and similarly seek to cause annihilation. Thomas Metzinger (2017a) described such a scenario in an essay on "benevolent artificial anti-natalism": "The superintelligence concludes that non-existence is in the own best interest of all future self-conscious beings on this planet. Empirically, it knows that naturally evolved biological creatures are unable to realize this fact because of their firmly anchored existence bias. The superintelligence decides to act benevolently." These considerations again argue for the need to program in human intuitions so that an AGI doesn't become an unwanted agent of destruction.

The most pragmatic way forward is therefore probably to seek consensus around the joint goals of preserving existence and wiping out extreme suffering. The question remains, what constraints do we put on the elimination of extreme suffering? How much more utilitarian and thus effective could we allow an AGI to be than we currently are, without creating a dystopia that would make life feel not worth living?

My own thinking on how to implement xNU+ is to explicitly spell out both the avoidance of existential risk and any explicitly destructive actions on the part of the AGI, but also to attach stringent clauses about the conditions under which continued existence is actively pursued as a goal. As I suggested in a film I made based on *The Battle for Compassion*, I believe this is all part of the bargain, and that with existence comes the responsibility of compassionate agency on behalf of all sentient life (Leighton, 2015). The word "responsibility" might, in an ethical context, suggest a hint of moral realism, so let me put it this way: if there's anything we would want to *feel* responsibility for and thereby capture the spirit of the term, this would be a top priority. If we really think we might be designing our eternal algorithmic overlord, we would do well to be extremely careful about what kind of future it is allowed to maintain. There is an important distinction between trying to avoid an existential catastrophe and ensuring indefinite existence regardless of its nature.

We're not quite there yet. In a society increasingly run by computer algorithms but where there are still human beings in charge, there is the hope that people with compassion can still intervene if things go very wrong. Once we are locked into a system run by AGI, it becomes too late to change the values.

This could apply as well to a totalitarian dictatorship (Althaus & Baumann, 2020) or a corporate plutocracy (or some combination of the two) that has designed an AGI to preserve its power indefinitely, placing structurally embedded barriers to people organising further systemic change. An AGI might not need to exert control directly if it provided reliable instructions to its totalitarian masters on how to do so. Pointing to the specific locus of control is, in at least some sense, unimportant—the human masters might believe they are in control, with the power to turn off the AGI if desired, but be manipulated into doing the AGI's bidding.

In some respects our world already bears some of these characteristics, with high-frequency trading algorithms increasing wealth concentration and by extension political power, with various other unintended consequences as well (Slavin, 2011). If the functioning of our economy is so dependent on AI systems that turning them off would immediately lead to paralysis, then the lock-in effect is, in practice, very similar.

If there is somewhere valuable to invest energy to avoid a dystopia, then it is not just in technical solutions, but in the humans who are still part of the system, who still make decisions, and who will help determine what kind of future we might be locked into. An essential driving motivation behind ethics is an awareness or at least approximate imagination of what intense suffering actually *feels* like. Without compassionate, sentient beings maintaining ultimate control, there is a risk that compassion can be lost as a driver. It's the intuitive, sentient mind that screams moral outrage about cruelty towards sentient beings. Even a calculating mind needs to viscerally understand suffering in order to truly care.

In an essay on the need to focus on AI as a cause area, Lukas Gloor (2016b) argued, "AI is the ultimate lever through which to influence the future." He further stated, "The goals of an artificial superintelligence would plausibly be much more stable than the values of human leaders or those enshrined in any constitution or charter. And a superintelligent AI would, with at least considerable likelihood, remain in control of the future not only for centuries, but for millions or even billions of years to come."

I share his belief that such stability is at least a *possible* outcome and, further, that it could even represent an opportunity to eliminate extreme suffering. But I also have strong doubts about the stability of the values of an autonomous AGI. I also question whether a world beyond human influence would feel worth living in—although it might be objectively better than the actual world we live in today.[3]

I believe we do, ideally, need sentient beings with the capacity to feel compassion and even love to be driving and monitoring the algorithms. If those who are governed feel they are at the mercy of non-sentient algorithms with no capacity for empathy, they might feel imprisoned by machines. The COVID-19 pandemic has shown how readily people can feel manipulated and controlled even by sentient beings supposedly making rational decisions on their behalf (though many decisions around COVID-19 were indeed contestable). What happens when there is not even a live human component at the other end—a *feeling* being with the capacity to suffer, but also to experience and understand the beauty of life, and to connect with those who bear the decisions they make?

The reduction of suffering may have more to gain from a place of love than from a calculating mind. Love and empathy are the essential foundations of our whole enterprise as humans. Without it, everything crumbles.

In one chapter of *The Battle for Compassion*, I drew heavily on Ray Kurzweil's book *The Singularity is Near* and on his vision of human minds being uploaded to non-biological substrates. I find that scenario almost as dystopian now as I did then, if for no other reason than because there would be a realisation that the experiences, lacking real-world correlates, were virtual and empty. (Though if it were really as thorough as a perfect real-life simulation, or even better, with meaning still experienced non-biologically, then where would be the objection?) But I am doubtful that such a scenario is even likely to come about, for technical reasons, and that continued talk of uploading human minds is inconsistent with what we know about how the human mind actually works. As I said above, I also find it most unlikely that an AGI will have a conscious mind of its own.

I suspect that a powerful, non-sentient AGI that has fully escaped human control would be unable to coexist indefinitely with humans without truly dystopian consequences. If we are to have a sustainable future free of extreme suffering, we might need advanced AI to help us, but I

---

[3] See also Magnus Vinding's (2018) critique, where he argues that, for both conceptual and empirical reasons, focusing on AI is unlikely to be the best way to reduce future suffering.

believe we will need empathetic, compassionate sentient beings to remain in control. Fighting to maintain that control might be the ultimate challenge that we face.

Balancing personal initiative and collective action

A key recurring question for anyone aiming to make a real difference in the world is, where do I direct my efforts? As a single individual, what is the greatest impact I can theoretically have? Can I have a significant chance of influencing the long-term future, or am I best off reducing suffering with certainty on a much more immediate timescale? Am I better off adding my voice to the choir, such as joining a movement for change or an existing organisation—perhaps one focused on improving governance, conflict resolution or AI safety—or can I do better by thinking strategically about my individual actions? Or some mixture of both? Another way of thinking about it is: are the options made available by certain existing institutions and movements worth following in the spirit of rule utilitarianism, or do I have access to thoughts and ideas that would rationally steer me, individually, more towards act utilitarianism in the striving for much greater impact?

A more general question is, what kinds of strategies have the greatest chance of making a difference in shifting the trajectory of sentient life on our planet compared to what is likely to happen otherwise? Is any individual unlikely to take a defining action that someone else would not eventually have taken? And is this even a tractable problem, or is the future largely determined by the characteristics of the system we are part of? Perhaps societal collapse is essentially inevitable, and the most we can hope for is damage control to reduce the resultant suffering. Are there effective memes I can help spread? What form would they take? And how do I avoid actually causing more extreme suffering in the universe due to actions that I intuitively feel are correct?

For many of these questions, I can only offer a guess. My view is that widespread societal collapse is likely, a function of human nature, advanced technology and complexity itself (see Smith, 2019). But this scenario doesn't rule out the possibility of totalitarian control or AGI taking over in parallel, either. As I suggested earlier, significantly influencing the long-term future, particularly in a way that preserves existence while drastically curtailing extreme suffering, may be an unlikely prospect—paradoxically, perhaps, due to a combination of large-scale determinism and randomness. But I don't rule out the possibility, either—and that is a source of motivation as well. I'll return to this idea shortly.

I won't try to explore in any detail here how to choose the best specific options for personal impact. I would like instead to reflect more generally on the interplay between being an independent innovator and being a contributor to collective action. Although the choices can be framed as a problem of rational decision-making, in practice it is actually a dance between the two different ways of being in the world, which has been a running theme in this book.

As rational ethical agents, we might expect to have the most impact if we regularly think independently and determine our actions in accordance with our evaluation of situations and our own expertise. In principle, we might want to carry out expected value calculations on the various options available and choose the highest, even though that seems an impossible task to get right in practice. This raises the question as to when it makes sense to participate in collective actions, like voting or participating in a demonstration, especially if we suspect that our extra voice or presence will have no marginal impact. How do we reconcile our roles as independent thinkers and collective doers?

If everyone put into question their individual impact in collective actions, few people would bother showing up for demonstrations or to vote in elections, and nothing would ever change. For example, the mass demonstrations for political change in Belarus in August 2020 would never have occurred if each person thought that their own presence would make no perceptible difference. So when is it better to yield our sense of individuality and allow ourselves to get caught up in a mass movement for change? And when is it better to do something else entirely, such as developing a new strategy or starting a movement?

To try to answer this, let's focus further on voting. At the moment of casting a vote, in the absence of coordination among potential voters, you have no influence on what anyone else does. For any important election where the result is likely to be close, your participation is justified on expected value grounds—the likelihood of your vote making a difference times the value of the outcome. This is why votes for third parties with no realistic chance of winning can be counterproductive, unless there are tangible secondary benefits, such as helping a party to grow in visibility for the future. But in a race that is not close and where you are certain that most people will vote for the more ethically-minded candidate, you can indeed be sure that your vote will not make a difference to the election result. (Of course, it might still be useful for your own sense of identity and motivation.) If everyone with the same ethical goals was thinking the same way in terms of their marginal impact and drew the same conclusion, no one would vote and the election would be lost. But of course, everyone thinking the same way changes the situation: if you knew that most people were thinking like you, and everyone else knew this too,[4] you would all realise that the desired outcome was no longer certain and you would all consider your votes to be more important. In that case, everyone would indeed vote. In fact, it still wouldn't be anyone's individual vote that would be expected to make a difference—rather, it's the entire way of thinking that is determinant.

So it seems that abstaining from voting or from participating in a demonstration only makes sense if you are a detached, rational observer, the situation seems certain, relatively few people are thinking like you, and you have a more valuable action to carry out with your time. But as we want to encourage more people to think rationally and critically, isn't there a risk that they will decline to participate in group action because they are sceptical of their marginal impact?

In practice I don't think this is a real risk, because of the strong human urge to feel part of a community. But what I think is interesting is that rationality sometimes actually requires acting like a member of the whole, rather than as an isolated individual thinking about their marginal impact in terms of expected value. For mass action, the marginal impact of any individual may never make any difference, but change requires that people suspend that kind of thinking and unite. Value on the margin retracts and one acts more like a superorganism, though one that values the wellbeing of each member.

From a game-theoretic perspective, each person thinking about the minor benefit to themselves of not spending resources participating in a group action leads to potentially disastrous consequences for everyone. The antidote is promoting a different perspective or model of behaviour that can be spread as a simple, stable message: be the change you want to see in the world. That is, follow Gandhi's interpretation of Kant's categorical imperative. Serve as an ethical model, or an "attractor" in the parlance of social network theory, that others are inclined to replicate. This paradigm applies to one's lifestyle, to the balance between thriving and serving as an agent of change, to the principle of not doing harm. To living a life that would lead to a much better world if everyone else adopted the same principles.

Social change is more likely when people feel part of a movement for change, rather than detachedly weighing their individual options and their expected marginal impact. Expressing a similar idea, author David Wallace-Wells said, "I think that's what politics is for—to live up to

---

[4] This is essentially a kind of decision-making known as "superrationality" (n.d.).

aspirations collectively that we can't live up to individually" (Facing Future, 2019).

These scenarios illustrate a new variation of the tango where the rational agent recognises the benefit of letting themselves cede to the more intuitively driven membership of the larger tribe and their human need for connection with the whole. This facet of the tango seems like an essential part of the messages to spread. We need people to value the truth and rational thought, to take responsibility for their own actions, and to resist crude tribal thinking that is misaligned with ethics. But we also need people to identify as members of the larger community they are part of.

If we return now to the question of maximising personal impact and, ideally, affecting the far future, it may seem that the likelihood of an individual making a difference large enough to significantly affect the total amount of extreme suffering that will occur on our planet and beyond is minute. In fact, the general causes of suffering on our planet are themselves largely systemic, though individual dictators can cause widespread misery. Our hardwired potential for conflict and war is realised when there are disagreements over resources or religion and a lack of shared interests. The decision to enslave tens of billions of non-human animals in industrial complexes probably cannot be traced to one single cold-hearted individual, but was the inevitable result of new technology applied to old, entrenched eating habits. Similarly, whether factory farms and the general abuse of non-human animals are eventually eliminated might be largely independent of the actions of any single individual, but rather, dependent on the properties of the complex system we are part of. In this case, individual activists might have a smaller, though still important, effect in accelerating such change and helping billions of animals—in itself a phenomenal impact on the timescale of a single human lifespan.

However, if one wants to think ambitiously—the only way that these problems are ever really solved—the largest possible personal impact on the future may require creative thinking that yields approaches and solutions that no one else is likely to have. This line of thinking might suggest that we need to encourage as much creativity in the world as possible. While that might lead to many more creative ideas, it would also probably increase the competition among ideas, reducing the likelihood that the few most promising ideas would succeed. After all, popularity is not an accurate gauge of ethical effectiveness. Ideally, these ideas would be tested out against reality, or at least evaluated for potential. But the best solutions may require believing in the seemingly impossible—and having backers willing to take a risk.

I sense that there isn't enough such creative thinking being applied to social activism—in part because of time and energy constraints, which force people to initiate movements and campaigns before the most creative ideas have been properly developed and thought through; and in part because the people thinking most creatively are not necessarily those most skilled at building movements. However, there is also a need for greater expert understanding of the properties of the complex system we are part of and trying to change, so that we can direct our creative efforts more effectively.

An important consideration in developing creative solutions, worth reiterating, is that achieving large-scale change is only likely to happen if it appeals to the vast majority of people, because it meets their needs and they have reason to trust those proposing the solutions, but also if existing rulers, especially in authoritarian regimes, see greater personal interest in adopting such changes than opposing them. An ethical framework that addresses the needs and suffering of all is therefore necessary, not just inherently, but for strategic reasons as well.

To conclude this section, I believe that individuals can be most effective if they think creatively about new ideas for change; see how ideas they think have realistic merit resonate with others, and work to implement them if they seem promising; try to serve as a model for others of how we can best be in the world; and embrace organisations and movements that are grounded in compassion and rationality and that feel worth supporting.

Activism and the desire to see impact

Earlier I discussed expected value as a tool for determining the most effective interventions to focus on. There's a direct implication for personal activism of using this approach. It means that for some kinds of interventions, and potentially the ones with the greatest expected value, most attempts will be unsuccessful, because the high expected value comes from the value part rather than the probability. This means, at least in theory, that for a large group of activists each devoting time to risky campaigns with potentially great impact, the majority might expect to see no concrete impact of their work—analogously to how start-up investors might expect to see most of their investments lose money but be able to cash in on one or two stars.

Complete failure may be theoretically acceptable but not a very encouraging or positively reinforcing outcome of one individual's risky efforts. It might be more motivating to make a small but acknowledged difference today, rather than a thankless, potential positive contribution to the long-term suffering-free future of sentient life. Psychologically, the latter requires resilience and a firm belief in the concept of expected value. In practice, it might be more motivating for everyone to feel like a participant in a number of risky endeavours, to ensure that they also have a concrete stake in whatever rare successes arise.

How much empathy do we need?

Psychologist Paul Bloom (2013) has argued against a focus on empathy, claiming that it can actually be counterproductive, as it can cause us to become overly focused on individuals instead of thinking rationally about how to have the most impact. An alternative proposal is to promote what AI researcher Jonathan Stray (2015) has termed "statistical empathy", illustrated by a quote attributed (perhaps falsely) to Bertrand Russell: "The mark of a civilised human is the ability to look at a column of numbers, and weep."

I disagree somewhat with both proposals, though not with the underlying motivation. Empathy with those suffering can be seen as an essential basis of ethics, the starting point for ethical behaviour and activism. And it needs to be balanced with the big-picture perspective that seeks to have as much impact as possible. If we were to lose our tendency to empathise with individuals suffering, including those in our immediate environment, I think our society would become much more fragile. But, as much as I agree how crucial it is to recognise the reality behind statistics, neither do I think it practical or necessary to promote greater empathy in proportion to the number of individuals—although one might empathise with many different individuals. Too much empathy can be literally overwhelming. And a single individual suffering intensely is enough to warrant our full empathy and our determination to alleviate any such suffering. When there are choices to be made about how to prioritise, it is then up to our rational brain to make the decisions with greatest impact.

The fractal-like nature of ethical action

In practice, ethics is a process—we never reach the actual target. Because the urgency of a situation is contained in the intensity of suffering, not the number of instances, there is always urgency to act as long as there is a single instance of extreme suffering. In a sense, the urgency of the problem remains the same—just the scale of the problem might decrease over time, if we are effective. In this respect, ethics is like a fractal where the same pattern repeats as one continues to zoom in.

We naturally want to see positive change happen on a human timescale where we can observe improvements, but against the backdrop of the amount of suffering that has happened on our planet over the eons, it becomes more understandable that shutting down intense suffering, if ever, is only likely to occur over a lengthy timescale as well, despite our frustration and anger over widespread human cruelty. A difficult thing about long-term activism is that it's never-ending and has this fractal quality—that a 99% or even a 99.999% reduction in extreme suffering still leaves huge numbers of beings equally in need of help. Just as one child kept locked in a dungeon for years is one child too many, one non-human animal kept enclosed in a small cage for their whole life is one animal too many.

So, on the one hand, every reduction in the number of sentient beings suffering is a reduction in the scale of the problem and a very real reason to celebrate. On the other hand, the remaining suffering—present and future—crying out to be alleviated demands the same available resources.

Trying to reduce suffering in individual small-scale situations might seem to pale in importance compared to the bigger picture, including the amount of suffering occurring among wild animals. As long as we have the potential to affect larger numbers, that is where the rational choice lies. But when we do focus on small numbers—because that's where our expertise lies, or we are called to action by circumstances, such as people being needed to carry out actions locally—attending to the urgency remains important. That is where the fractal pattern has led us in that moment.

Although the end goal of reducing and eventually abolishing all intense suffering is clear, the best path to take, i.e. the one that reduces most of the suffering most quickly along the way, is not. This is not just because the information that would be needed is, in practice, unknowable, but because even in theory there is no way of making a fully objective comparison between most situations along the various possible paths towards this goal, containing various combinations of intensity and numbers of individuals suffering. In other words, there *is* no single best path. We can only aim to gradually get closer to our eventual goal, knowing that the more rapidly we approach it, the less important it is which path we take.

Spreading love, empathy, rationality and compassion

The power that the documentary "Earthlings" has had to awaken and sensitise so many people to the reality of animal suffering at human hands, and even to lead many of them to rapidly eliminate animal products from their diet, attests to the deep significance that others' suffering has for us once we expose ourselves to it and open up our hearts to feeling it.

A focus on the truth is perhaps the surest way of ensuring the spread of compassionate ethics in our universe. And by combining it with love, we ensure that the compassion is actually felt by those receiving and transmitting the message, and is given a more effective vehicle for spreading.

Within a strategic context, talk about the need for love can sound fluffy and even frivolous. But it really matters, for two reasons. One, love is actually what most makes existence feel worth preserving. We need an inspiring vision to strive for, not just a hell to escape. And two, love — including truly caring about how it is for others — may ultimately be a better means of achieving compassionate governance or AI safety than focusing mainly on algorithms. We can figure out the coding, within the limits of the possible. The starting point is a greater global consensus on ethics, based less on calculation than on caring.

And so, I would end with some key principles that if widely spread may give us a better chance of attaining the compassionate future we all want:

- Listen empathetically and address the needs of all — including those with different views and ideas.
- Seek to understand rather than blame.
- Follow the spirit of the Golden Rule and treat others' suffering as if it were your own.
- Take the suffering of all sentient beings into account — not just those whose voices are the loudest.
- Treat extreme suffering with the urgency it demands.
- Respect the truth and use rational thinking to make better, more compassionate decisions for society.
- Fill existence — yours and others' — with love and meaning.
- Aim high.
- Live these principles and share them with others.

References

Aaronson, S. (2014, May 21). *Why I am not an integrated information theorist (or, the unconscious expander)*. Shtetl-Optimized. https://scottaaronson.blog/?p=1799

Acton, H. B., & Watkins, J. W. (1963). Negative utilitarianism. *Aristotelian Society Supplementary Volume, 37*(1), 83–114. https://doi.org/10.1093/aristoteliansupp/37.1.83

Adams, M. (2017, December 31). *The other side of opioids*. [YouTube]. https://www.youtube.com/watch?v=72Y8YB6OY_U

Alexander, S. (2012, December 7). *2012 survey results*. LessWrong. https://www.lesswrong.com/posts/x9FNKTEt68Rz6wQ6P/2012-survey-results

Alexander, S. (2020, April 14). *A failure, but not of prediction*. Slate Star Codex. https://slatestarcodex.com/2020/04/14/a-failure-but-not-of-prediction/

Algosphere Alliance. (2017, September). *Open letter to the United Nations*. https://algosphere.org/about/positions/open-letter-to-the-united-nations/

Allas, T., Maksimainen, J., Manyika, J., & Singh, N. (2020, September 15). *An experiment to inform universal basic income*. McKinsey & Company. https://www.mckinsey.com/industries/public-and-social-sector/our-insights/an-experiment-to-inform-universal-basic-income

Althaus, D., & Baumann, T. (2020, April 29). *Reducing long-term risks from malevolent actors*. Effective Altruism Forum. https://forum.effectivealtruism.org/posts/LpkXtFXdsRd4rG8Kb/reducing-long-term-risks-from-malevolent-actors

Althaus, D., & Gloor, L. (2016, September 14). *Reducing risks of astronomical suffering: A neglected priority*. Center on Long-Term Risk. https://longtermrisk.org/reducing-risks-of-astronomical-suffering-a-neglected-priority/

Animal Ethics. (n.d.-a). *Different ethical theories*. Retrieved April 26, 2022, from https://www.animal-ethics.org/different-ethical-theories/

Animal Ethics. (n.d.-b). *Wild animal suffering: An introduction*. Retrieved April 26, 2022, from https://www.animal-ethics.org/introduction-to-wild-animal-suffering/

Animal Ethics. (n.d.-c). *Helping animals in the wild*. Retrieved April 26, 2022, from https://www.animal-ethics.org/helping-animals-in-the-wild/

Animal Ethics. (n.d.-d). *What beings are conscious?* Retrieved April 26, 2022, from https://www.animal-ethics.org/what-beings-are-conscious/

Animal Ethics. (2020). *Negative consequentialism*. Retrieved November 12, 2020, from https://www.animal-ethics.org/negative-consequentialism/. Available at https://web.archive.org/web/20201112011852/https://www.animal-ethics.org/ethics-animals-section/ethical-theories-nonhuman-animals/negative-consequentialism/

Aplacophora. (n.d.). In Wikipedia. https://en.wikipedia.org/wiki/Aplacophora

Ariely, D. (2008). *Predictably irrational*. Harper Collins.

Arrhenius, G., Ryberg, J., & Tännsjö, T. (2017). *The repugnant conclusion*. Stanford Encyclopedia of Philosophy (Spring 2017 Edition). https://plato.stanford.edu/archives/spr2017/entries/repugnant-conclusion/

Ballantyne, C. (2007, June 21). *Strange but true: Drinking too much water can kill*. Scientific American. https://www.scientificamerican.com/article/strange-but-true-drinking-too-much-water-can-kill/

Balluch, M. (2017, September 18). *Most wild animals are happy most of the time!* https://martinballuch.com/most-wild-animals-are-happy-most-of-the-time/

Batchelor, S. (1997). *Buddhism without beliefs: A contemporary guide to awakening*. Riverhead.

Baumann, T. (2017). *S-risks: An introduction*. Center for Reducing Suffering. https://centerforreducingsuffering.org/intro/

Baumann, T. (2020). *Common ground for longtermists*. Center for Reducing Suffering. https://centerforreducingsuffering.org/common-ground-for-longtermists/

Bayne, T., Hohwy, J., & Owen, A. M. (2016). Are there levels of consciousness? *Trends in Cognitive Sciences, 20*(6), 405–413. https://doi.org/10.1016/j.tics.2016.03.009

Beard, S. (2018, March 21). *Guest post: Consequentialism and ethics? Bridging the normative gap*. Practical ethics. http://blog.practicalethics.ox.ac.uk/2018/03/guest-post-consequentialism-and-ethics-bridging-the-normative-gap/

Bell, R. (2015, August 19). *Temple Grandin, killing them softly at slaughterhouses for 30 Years*. National Geographic. https://www.nationalgeographic.com/

culture/article/temple-grandin-killing-them-softly-at-slaughterhouses-for-30-years

Benatar, D. (2006). *Better never to have been: The harm of coming into existence.* Oxford University Press.

Benatar, D. (2017, October 19). *Kids? Just say no.* Aeon. https://aeon.co/essays/having-children-is-not-life-affirming-its-immoral

Bentov, I. (1977). *Stalking the wild pendulum: On the mechanics of consciousness.* Destiny Books.

Bloom, P. (2013, May 13). *The baby in the well.* The New Yorker. https://www.newyorker.com/magazine/2013/05/20/the-baby-in-the-well

Bostrom, N. (2002). Existential risks: Analyzing human extinction scenarios and related hazards. *Journal of Evolution and Technology, 9*(1). Available at https://www.nickbostrom.com/existential/risks.html

Bostrom, N. (2003). Are you living in a computer simulation? *Philosophical Quarterly, 53*(211), 243–255. https://www.simulation-argument.com/simulation.pdf

Bostrom, N. (2006). Quantity of experience: Brain-duplication and degrees of consciousness. *Minds and Machines, 16*(2), 185–200. https://www.nickbostrom.com/papers/experience.pdf

Bostrom, N. (2009, January 1). *Moral uncertainty – towards a solution?* Overcoming Bias. https://www.overcomingbias.com/2009/01/moral-uncertainty-towards-a-solution.html

Bostrom, N. (2013). Existential risk prevention as global priority. *Global Policy, 4*(1), 15–31. https://www.existential-risk.org/concept.pdf

Bostrom, N., & Cirkovic, M. M. (2008). *Global catastrophic risks.* Oxford University Press.

Bostrom, N., & Yudkowsky, E. (2014). The ethics of artificial intelligence. In K. Frankish & W. Ramsey (Eds.), *The Cambridge handbook of artificial intelligence.* Cambridge University Press. https://nickbostrom.com/ethics/artificial-intelligence.pdf

Bourget, D. & Chalmers, D. (Eds.) (2020). *The 2020 PhilPapers survey.* https://survey2020.philpeople.org

Buddhist Society, The. (n.d.). *Fundamental teachings.* Retrieved April 24, 2022, from https://www.thebuddhistsociety.org/page/fundamental-teachings

Burish, M. J., Pearson, S. M., Shapiro, R. E., Zhang, W., & Schor, L. I. (2021). Cluster headache is one of the most intensely painful human conditions: Results from the international cluster headache questionnaire. *Headache: The Journal of Head and Face Pain, 61*(1), 117–124. https://doi.org/10.1111/head.14021

Carleton, A. (2019, January 24). *Solar Foods is making food mostly out of air and electricity.* Vice. https://www.vice.com/en/article/43zdag/this-startup-is-making-food-mostly-out-of-air-and-electricity

Carroll, L. (1871). *Jabberwocky.* https://www.poetryfoundation.org/poems/42916/jabberwocky

Cascio, D. (2017, January 20). *On the consumption of bivalves.* The Animalist. https://medium.com/@TheAnimalist/on-the-consumption-of-bivalves-bdde8db6d4ba

Cascio, J., & Plant, E. A. (2015). Prospective moral licensing: Does anticipating doing good later allow you to be bad now? *Journal of Experimental Social Psychology, 56,* 110–116. https://doi.org/10.1016/j.jesp.2014.09.009

Caviola, L., Kahane, G., Everett, J. A., Teperman, E., Savulescu, J., & Faber, N. S. (2021). Utilitarianism for animals, Kantianism for people? Harming animals and humans for the greater good. *Journal of Experimental Psychology: General, 150*(5), 1008–1039. https://doi.org/10.1037/xge0000988

Chiorando, M. (2017, August 14). *Impossible Foods CEO speaks out over animal testing row: 'It was an agonizing decision'.* Plant Based News. https://plantbasednews.org/lifestyle/impossible-foods-ceo-blasts-animal-testing-i-abhor-the-exploitation-of-animals/

Christiano, P. F., et al. (2017, July 13). *Deep reinforcement learning from human preferences.* https://arxiv.org/pdf/1706.03741.pdf

Coogle, A. (2017, April 28). *How was Saudi Arabia voted onto a UN women's panel?* Human Rights Watch. https://www.hrw.org/news/2017/04/28/how-was-saudi-arabia-voted-un-womens-panel

Consilience Project, The. (2022, February 23). *The endgames of bad faith communication.* https://consilienceproject.org/endgames-of-bad-communication/

Coste, R. (2013, December 12). *A Solution to the trolley problem.* Philosophy Walk. Available at https://web.archive.org/web/20160324195348/http://www.philosophywalk.com/solution-trolley-problem/

Crisp, R. (2021, August 10). *Would extinction be so bad?* New Statesman. https://www.newstatesman.com/politics/2021/08/would-extinction-be-so-bad

Curry, O. S. (2019, March 26). *What's wrong with moral foundations theory, and how to get moral psychology right.* Behavioral Scientist. https://behavioralscientist.org/whats-wrong-with-moral-foundations-theory-and-how-to-get-moral-psychology-right/

Dash, M. (2012, January 27). *The most terrible polar exploration ever: Douglas Mawson's Antarctic Journey.* Smithsonian.com. https://www.smithsonianmag.com/history/the-most-terrible-polar-exploration-ever-douglas-mawsons-antarctic-journey-82192685/

Davis, N. (2017, February 6). *Lumpy, hairy, toe-like fossil could reveal the evolution of molluscs.* The Guardian. https://www.theguardian.com/science/2017/feb/06/newly-discovered-slug-looks-like-a-hairy-toe-and-could-reveal-the-ancestry-of-molluscs-calvapiloa-kroegeri de Lazari-Radek, K., & Singer, P. (2017). *Utilitarianism: A very short introduction*. Oxford University Press.

Diener, E. (1984). Subjective well-being. *Psychological Bulletin, 95*(3), 542–575. https://doi.org/10.1037/0033-2909.95.3.542

Diener, E., Larsen, R. J., Levine, S., & Emmons, R. A. (1985). Intensity and frequency: Dimensions underlying positive and negative affect. *Journal of Personality and Social Psychology, 48*(5), 1253–1265. https://doi.org/10.1037/0022-3514.48.5.1253

Diener, E., & Iran-Nejad, A. (1986). The relationship in experience between various types of affect. *Journal of Personality and Social Psychology, 50*(5), 1031–1038. https://www.researchgate.net/publication/272157296_Diener_Iran-Nejad_1986

Dockterman, E. (2013, October 29). *Nearly one million chickens and turkeys unintentionally boiled alive each year in U.S.* Time. https://nation.time.com/2013/10/29/nearly-one-million-chickens-and-turkeys-unintentionally-boiled-alive-each-year-in-u-s/

Dodgson, L. (2017, November 15). *The way 'good' people explain away bad behaviour is called 'moral licensing' – here's what it means.* Business Insider. https://www.businessinsider.com/what-moral-licensing-means-2017-11

Dolan, P. (2001). Utilitarianism and the measurement and aggregation of quality–adjusted life years. *Health Care Analysis, 9*(1), 65–76. https://doi.org/10.1023/a:1011387524579

Eckerström-Liedholm, S. (2022, April 8). *Deep dive: Wildlife contraception and welfare.* Wild Animal Initiative. https://www.wildanimalinitiative.org/blog/contraception-deep-dive

Eisenberger, N. I. (2012). Broken hearts and broken bones. *Current Directions in Psychological Science, 21*(1), 42–47. https://doi.org/10.1177/0963721411429455

Epicurus. (n.d.). *Letter to Menoeceus* (R. D. Hicks, Trans.). The Internet Classics Archive. http://classics.mit.edu/Epicurus/menoec.html

Esvelt, K. (2019, August 30). *When are we obligated to edit wild creatures?* Leaps.org. https://leaps.org/when-are-we-obligated-to-edit-wild-creatures/particle-3

Everitt, T., Lea, G., & Hutter, M. (2018, May 22). *AGI safety literature review.* https://arxiv.org/pdf/1805.01109.pdf

Facing Future. (2019, March 8). *David Wallace-Wells – The Uninhabitable Earth.* [YouTube]. https://www.youtube.com/watch?v=ZcisVZ3sE7Q

Farhad. (2013, March 16). *Richard Dawkins – Science works bitches!* [YouTube]. https://www.youtube.com/watch?v=0OtFSDKrq88

Faria, C., & Paez, E. (2019). It's splitsville: Why animal ethics and environmental ethics are incompatible. *American Behavioral Scientist, 63*(8), 1047–1060. https://doi.org/10.1177/0002764219830467

Feldman, B. (2016, August 9). *The trolley problem is the internet's most philosophical meme*. Intelligencer. http://nymag.com/intelligencer/2016/08/trolley-problem-meme-tumblr-philosophy.html

Fleischman, D. (2020, April 7). *The ethical case for eating oysters and mussels – part 1*. Dianaverse. https://dianaverse.com/2020/04/07/bivalvegan part1/

Ford, A. (2018, October 26). *Ethics, qualia research & AI safety with Mike Johnson*. Science, Technology & the Future. http://www.scifuture.org/ethics-qualia-research-ai-safety-with-mike-johnson/

Frijters, P. (2020, April 8). *How many WELLBYs is the corona panic costing?* Club Troppo. https://clubtroppo.com.au/2020/04/08/how-many-wellbys-is-the-corona-panic-costing/

Frijters, P., Clark, A. E., Krekel, C., & Layard, R. (2019, October). *A happy choice: Wellbeing as the goal of government*. IZA Institute of Labor Economics. https://ftp.iza.org/dp12720.pdf

Gibson, M. (2020, February 28). *Is basic income a good idea? Here's what the evidence from around the world says*. The Conversation. https://theconversation.com/is-basic-income-a-good-idea-heres-what-the-evidence-from-around-the-world-says-132337

Global Assembly. (n.d.). https://globalassembly.org/

Global Challenges Foundation. (n.d.). *New shape prize*. https://globalchallenges.org/about/history/new-shape-prize/

Gloor, L. (2016a, August 26). *The case for suffering-focused ethics*. Center on Long-Term Risk. https://longtermrisk.org/the-case-for-suffering-focused-ethics/

Gloor, L. (2016b, December 7). *Altruists should prioritize artificial intelligence*. Center on Long-Term Risk. https://longtermrisk.org/altruists-should-prioritize-artificial-intelligence/

Gloor, L. (2017, July 18). *Tranquilism*. Center on Long-Term Risk. https://longtermrisk.org/tranquilism/

Goldhill, O. (2017, August 5). *Octopus research shows that consciousness isn't what makes humans special*. Quartz. https://qz.com/1045782/an-octopus-is-the-closest-thing-to-an-alien-here-on-earth/

Gómez Emilsson, A. (2015, December 17). *Ontological qualia: The Future of Personal Identity*. Qualia Computing. https://qualiacomputing.com/2015/12/17/ontological-qualia-the-future-of-personal-identity/

Gómez Emilsson, A. (2018, July 23). *Open individualism and antinatalism: If god could be killed, it'd be dead already*. Qualia Computing. Retrieved April 24, 2022, from https://qualiacomputing.com/2018/07/23/open-individualism-and-antinatalism-if-god-could-be-killed-itd-be-dead-already/

Gómez Emilsson, A. (2017a, June 18). *Quantifying bliss: Talk summary*. Qualia Computing. https://qualiacomputing.com/2017/06/18/quantifying-bliss-talk-summary/

Gómez Emilsson, A. (2017b, October 21). Facebook post. https://www.facebook.com/algekalipso/posts/1522517014507117

Gómez Emilsson, A. (2018, April 10). *Quantifying bliss: empirically testable hypotheses for valence*. [YouTube]. https://www.youtube.com/watch?v=Vj7PmCnUWds

Gómez Emilsson, A. (2019, August 11). *Logarithmic scales of pleasure and pain: Rating, ranking, and comparing peak experiences suggest the existence of long tails for bliss and suffering*. Effective Altruism Forum. https://forum.effectivealtruism.org/posts/gtGe8WkeFvqucYLAF/logarithmic-scales-of-pleasure-and-pain-rating-ranking-and

Gómez Emilsson, A. (2020). *The symmetry theory of valence*. Qualia Computing. https://qualiacomputing.com/2020/12/17/the-symmetry-theory-of-valence-2020-presentation/

Gowans, C. (2021). *Moral relativism*. Stanford Encyclopedia of Philosophy (Spring 2021 Edition). https://plato.stanford.edu/archives/spr2021/entries/moral-relativism/

Greenberg, S. (2017). Facebook post. https://www.facebook.com/spencer.greenberg/posts/10103366398387442

Greene, J. D. (2015). *The cognitive neuroscience of moral judgment and decision making*. In J. Decety & T. Wheatley (Eds.), *The moral brain: A multi-disciplinary perspective*. The MIT Press. https://clbb.mgh.harvard.edu/the-cognitive-neuroscience-of-moral-judgment-and-decision-making/

Greene, J. D. (2016). *Solving the trolley problem*. In J. Sytsma & W. Buckwalter (Eds.), *A companion to experimental philosophy*. Wiley Blackwell. https://projects.iq.harvard.edu/files/mcl/files/greene-solvingtrolleyproblem-16.pdf

Haidt, J. (2012). *The righteous mind: Why good people are divided by politics and religion*. Pantheons Books.

Harari, Y. N. (2016). *Homo deus: A brief history of tomorrow*. Harvill Secker.

Hare, R. M. (1973). The presidential address: principles. *Proceedings of the Aristotelian Society, 73*(1), 1–18. https://doi.org/10.1093/aristotelian/73.1.1

Harris, S. (2010, February). *Science can answer moral questions* [Video]. TED Conferences. https://www.ted.com/talks/sam_harris_science_can_answer_moral_questions

Helliwell, J., et al. (Eds.). (2017). *World happiness report 2017*. https://s3.amazonaws.com/happiness-report/2017/HR17.pdf

Herrán, M. (2017, September 6). *The big lie*. https://manuherran.com/the-big-lie/

Human Rights Watch. (2018, December 18). *"Not allowed to be compassionate": Chronic pain, the overdose crisis, and unintended harms in the US.* https://www.hrw.org/report/2018/12/18/not-allowed-be-compassionate/chronic-pain-overdose-crisis-and-unintended-harms-us

Hunt, T. (2018, December 5). *The hippies were right: It's all about vibrations, man!* Scientific American. https://blogs.scientificamerican.com/observations/the-hippies-were-right-its-all-about-vibrations-man/

Integrated Information Theory. (n.d.). http://integratedinformationtheory.org/

Jacobsen, R. (2019, July 31). *This is the beginning of the end of the beef industry.* Outside. https://www.outsideonline.com/health/nutrition/impossible-foods-beyond-meat-alt-meat/

James, W. (1891). The moral philosopher and the moral life. *International Journal of Ethics*, 1(3), 330–354. https://www.jstor.org/stable/pdf/2375309.pdf

Jarrett, C. (2018, October 12). *What are we like? 10 psychology findings that reveal the worst of human nature.* Research Digest. https://digest.bps.org.uk/2018/10/12/what-are-we-like-10-psychology-findings-that-reveal-the-worst-of-human-nature/

Johnson, M. E. (2016). *Principia qualia: Blueprint for a new science.* Opentheorynet. https://opentheory.net/PrincipiaQualia.pdf

Johnson, M. E. (2018, November 26). *Rescuing philosophy.* Opentheorynet. https://opentheory.net/2017/10/rescuing-philosophy/

Joyce, R. (2021). *Moral anti-realism.* Stanford Encyclopedia of Philosophy (Winter 2021 Edition). https://plato.stanford.edu/archives/win2021/entries/moral-anti-realism/

Kafka, F. (2004). *The blue octavo notebooks* (M. Brod, Ed.). Exact Change.

Kahneman, D. (2011). *Thinking, fast and slow.* Farrar, Straus and Giroux.

Kahneman, D., Fredrickson, B. L., Schreiber, C. A., & Redelmeier, D. A. (1993). When more pain is preferred to less: Adding a better end. *Psychological Science*, 4(6), 401–405. https://doi.org/10.1111/j.1467-9280.1993.tb00589.x

Keim, B. (2018, July 18). *The surprisingly complicated math of how many wild animals are killed in agriculture.* Anthropocene. https://www.anthropocenemagazine.org/2018/07/how-many-animals-killed-in-agriculture/

Keiper, A., & Schulman, A. (2011). *The problem with 'friendly' artificial intelligence.* The New Atlantis. https://www.thenewatlantis.com/publications/the-problem-with-friendly-artificial-intelligence

Koch, C. (2009, July 1). *A "complex" theory of consciousness.* Scientific American. https://www.scientificamerican.com/article/a-theory-of-consciousness/

Knaul, F. M., et al. (2018). Alleviating the access abyss in palliative care and pain relief—an imperative of universal health coverage: The Lancet

Commission report. *The Lancet, 391*(10128), 1391–1454. https://doi.org/10.1016/s0140-6736(17)32513-8

Knutsson, S. (2016, April 11). *How could an empty world be better than a populated one?* Simon Knutsson. https://www.simonknutsson.com/how-could-an-empty-world-be-better-than-a-populated-one/

Knutsson, S. (2019). The world destruction argument. *Inquiry, 64*(10), 1004–1023. https://doi.org/10.1080/0020174x.2019.1658631

Kocot, K. M., Cannon, J. T., Todt, C., Citarella, M. R., Kohn, A. B., Meyer, A., Santos, S. R., Schander, C., Moroz, L. L., Lieb, B., & Halanych, K. M. (2011). Phylogenomics reveals deep molluscan relationships. *Nature, 477*(7365), 452–456. https://doi.org/10.1038/nature10382 [Figure 4: https://www.semanticscholar.org/paper/Phylogenomics-reveals-deep-molluscan-relationships-Kocot-Cannon/26fc722d008931bfc501bcc41a29f0905528b66e/figure/4]

Kolak, D. (2004). *I am you: The metaphysical foundations for global ethics.* Springer.

Kumar, S. (2002). *You are, therefore I am: A declaration of dependence.* Green Books.

Le Guin, U. K. (1973). *The ones who walk away from Omelas.* In R. Silverberg (Ed.), *New Dimensions 3.* Nelson Doubleday/SFBC.

Leighton, J. (2011). *The battle for compassion: Ethics in an apathetic universe.* Algora Publishing. Excerpts available at http://www.jonathanleighton.org/the-battle-for-compassion

Leighton, J. (2015, March 16). *The battle for compassion – a short film.* [YouTube]. https://www.youtube.com/watch?v=DBiKl_v5Mls

Leighton, J. (2017, September 14). *Thriving in the age of factory farming.* https://medium.com/@jonleighton1/thriving-in-the-age-of-factory-farming-fbcca7121d67

Leighton, J. (2018a, March). *Ending the agony: access to morphine as an ethical and human rights imperative.* Organisation for the Prevention of Intense Suffering. https://www.preventsuffering.org/wp-content/uploads/2018/03/Guide-to-morphine-access.pdf

Leighton, J. (2018b, May 4). *Why access to morphine is a human right.* https://medium.com/@jonleighton1/why-access-to-morphine-is-a-human-right-80ce2965de1a

Leighton, J. (2019a, May 2). *For a compassionate rebellion against extinction.* https://medium.com/@jonleighton1/for-a-compassionate-rebellion-against-extinction-c29b0d384bd2

Leighton, J. (2019b, November 18). *OPIS, a think-and-do tank for an ethic based on the prevention of suffering.* https://medium.com/@jonleighton1/opis-a-think-and-do-tank-for-an-ethic-based-on-the-prevention-of-suffering-eb2baa3d5619

Leighton, J. (2020a, November). *Legalising access to psilocybin to end the agony of cluster headaches: An ethical and evidence-based approach to treating one of the most excruciating conditions known to medicine.* Organisation for the Prevention of Intense Suffering. https://www.preventsuffering.org/wp-content/uploads/2020/11/Legalising-Access-to-Psilocybin-for-Cluster-Headaches-Policy-Paper.pdf

Leighton, J. (2020b, November 16). *Removing the legal barriers to treating the excruciating pain of cluster headaches.* Journal of Medical Ethics blog. https://blogs.bmj.com/medical-ethics/2020/11/16/removing-the-legal-barriers-to-treating-the-excruciating-pain-of-cluster-headaches/

Leighton, J., & Bendell, J. (2022). *Ethical implications of anticipating and witnessing societal collapse: Report of a discussion with international scholars.* Institute for Leadership and Sustainability (IFLAS) Occasional Papers Volume 9. University of Cumbria, Ambleside, UK. https://insight.cumbria.ac.uk/id/eprint/6326/1/Occasional%20Paper%209%20-%20Leighton%20and%20Bendell.pdf

List of cognitive biases. (n.d.). In Wikipedia. https://en.wikipedia.org/wiki/List_of_cognitive_biases

Litt, M. D. (1988). Self-efficacy and perceived control: Cognitive mediators of pain tolerance. *Journal of Personality and Social Psychology, 54*(1), 149–160. https://doi.org/10.1037/0022-3514.54.1.149

Lord, E. (2017). What you're rationally required to do and what you ought to do (are the same thing!). *Mind, 126*(504), 1109–1154. https://doi.org/10.1093/mind/fzw023

Lyubomirsky, S., Sheldon, K. M., & Schkade, D. (2005). Pursuing happiness: The architecture of sustainable change. *Review of General Psychology, 9*(2), 111–131. http://sonjalyubomirsky.com/wp-content/themes/sonjalyubomirsky/papers/LSS2005.pdf

MacAskill, W. (2015). *Doing good better.* Random House.

MacAskill, W., Bykvist, K., & Ord, T. (2020). *Moral uncertainty.* Oxford University Press. https://static1.squarespace.com/static/5506078de4b02d88372eee4e/t/5f5a3ddd466873260486fb06/1599749604332/Moral+Uncertainty.pdf

MacAskill, W., Chappell, R. Y., & Meissner, D. (n.d.). *Elements and types of utilitarianism.* Utilitarianism. Retrieved April 19, 2022, from https://www.utilitarianism.net/types-of-utilitarianism#aggregationism

Macleod, C. (2020). *John Stuart Mill.* Stanford Encyclopedia of Philosophy (Summer 2020 Edition). https://plato.stanford.edu/archives/sum2020/entries/mill/

Mankoski, A. (2000). Mankoski Pain Scale. http://www.valis.com/andi/painscale.html

Massey, E., & Robinson, N. J. (2018, October 12). *Being Mr. Reasonable*. Current Affairs. https://www.currentaffairs.org/2018/10/being-mr-reasonable

Mayerfeld, J. (1999). *Suffering and moral responsibility*. Oxford University Press.

Meat-eater problem. (n.d.). Effective Altruism Forum. https://forum.effectivealtruism.org/tag/meat-eater-problem

Metzinger, T. (2003). *Being no one: The self-model theory of subjectivity*. The MIT Press.

Metzinger, T. (2017a, August 7). *Benevolent artificial anti-natalism (BAAN)*. Edge.org. https://www.edge.org/conversation/thomas_metzinger-benevolent-artificial-anti-natalism-baan

Metzinger, T. (2017b). Suffering. In K. Almqvist & A. Haag (Eds.). *The return of consciousness: A new science on old questions*. Axel and Margaret Ax:son Johnson Foundation. https://www.philosophie-e.fb05.uni-mainz.de/files/2013/07/Metzinger_Suffering_2017.pdf

Metzinger, T. (2021). Artificial suffering: An argument for a global moratorium on synthetic phenomenology. *Journal of Artificial Intelligence and Consciousness*, *08*(01), 1–24. https://doi.org/10.1142/s270507852150003x

Middleton, M. (2009, October 12). *Number of animals killed to produce one million calories in eight food categories*. Animal Visuals. Retrieved April 27, 2022, from http://www.animalvisuals.org/projects/1mc/

Mikkelson, D. (2012, April 5). *Are turtles used on Chinese souvenir keyrings?* Snopes. https://www.snopes.com/fact-check/chinese-turtle-keyrings/

Mortimer, C. (2017, July 26). *Horrific footage shows bull kill itself after horns set on fire at spanish fiesta*. The Independent. https://www.independent.co.uk/news/world/europe/bull-kill-itself-horns-fire-spanish-fiesta-foios-valencia-spain-bulls-defenders-united-a7861341.html

Mounk, Y. (2020, March 11). *The extraordinary decisions facing Italian doctors*. The Atlantic. https://www.theatlantic.com/ideas/archive/2020/03/who-gets-hospital-bed/607807/

Muehlhauser, L. (2014, April 8). *Will MacAskill on normative uncertainty*. Machine Intelligence Research Institute. https://intelligence.org/2014/04/08/will-macaskill/

Narang, S., & Chowdhery, A. (2022, April 4). *Pathways language model (PaLM): Scaling to 540 billion parameters for breakthrough performance*. Google AI Blog. https://ai.googleblog.com/2022/04/pathways-language-model-palm-scaling-to.html

Negative Utilitarianism FAQ. (n.d.). Utilitarianism Resources. Retrieved April 25, 2022, from https://www.utilitarianism.com/nu/nufaq.html

Nozick, R. (1974). *Anarchy, state and utopia*. Blackwell.

Oishi, S., Diener, E., & Lucas, R. E. (2014). Subjective well-being: The science of happiness and life satisfaction. In C. R. Snyder et al. (Eds.), *The Oxford Handbook of Positive Psychology (3rd Edition)*. Oxford University Press.

Ord, T. (2013, March 1). *Why I'm not a negative utilitarian*. http://www.amirrorclear.net/academic/ideas/negative-utilitarianism/

Organisation for the Prevention of Intense Suffering. (2022). *Cluster headaches: Improving access to effective treatments*. https://www.preventsuffering.org/cluster-headaches/

Ortiz-Ospina, E., & Roser, M. (2017). *Happiness and life satisfaction*. Our World in Data. https://ourworldindata.org/happiness-and-life-satisfaction

Parfit, D. (1984). *Reasons and persons*. Oxford University Press.

Parfit, D. (2016). Can we avoid the repugnant conclusion? *Theoria, 82*(2), 110–127. https://doi.org/10.1111/theo.12097

Parfit, D. (2017). *On what matters*. Oxford University Press.

Parker, C. B. (2015, October 12). *New research shows how to make effective political arguments, Stanford sociologist says*. Stanford News. https://news.stanford.edu/2015/10/12/framing-persuasive-messages-101215/

Parodi, E., Aloisi, S., & Barbaglia, P. (2020, March 16). *Special report: 'All is well'. In Italy, triage and lies for virus patients*. Reuters. https://www.reuters.com/article/us-health-coronavirus-italy-ethics-speci/all-is-well-in-italy-triage-and-lies-for-virus-patients-idUSKBN2133KG

Pearce, D. (1995). *The hedonistic imperative*. https://www.hedweb.com/hedab.htm

Pearce, D. (2005). *The pinprick argument*. Utilitarianism Resources. https://www.utilitarianism.com/pinprick-argument.html

Pearce, D. (2014). *Non-materialist physicalism: An experimentally testable conjecture*. https://www.physicalism.com/#3

Pearce, D. (2021a). *Compassionate biology*. https://www.gene-drives.com/

Pearce, D. (2021b). *What does David Pearce think of longtermism in the effective altruist movement?* Quora. https://www.quora.com/What-does-David-Pearce-think-of-Longtermism-in-the-Effective-Altruist-movement/answer/David-Pearce-18

PhilPapers surveys. (n.d.). Retrieved April 19, 2022, from https://philpapers.org/surveys/results.pl

Pinker, S. (2011). *The better angels of our nature: Why violence has declined*. Viking Books.

Plato. (n.d.). *Protagoras* (B. Jowett, Trans.). Project Gutenberg EBook. https://www.gutenberg.org/files/1591/1591-h/1591-h.htm#link2H_4_0002

Price, A. (2019). *Richard Mervyn Hare*. Stanford Encyclopedia of Philosophy (Summer 2019 Edition). https://plato.stanford.edu/archives/sum2019/entries/hare/#LevMorThi

Prioritarianism. (2020). In Wikipedia. Retrieved June 11, 2020, from https://en.wikipedia.org/wiki/Prioritarianism. Available at https://web.archive.org/web/20200220221221/https://en.wikipedia.org/wiki/Prioritarianism

Rationality. (n.d.). In LessWrong. Retrieved April 19, 2022, from https://www.lesswrong.com/tag/rationality#Instrumental_vs_Epistemic_Rationality

Rethink Priorities. (n.d.). *Research and publications*. https://rethinkpriorities.org/research

Rethink Priorities. (2019, June 14). *Invertebrate sentience table*. https://rethinkpriorities.org/invertebrate-sentience-table

Richardson, H. S., et al. (2016). *Chapter 2 – Social progress... a compass*. International Panel on Social Progress. https://comment.ipsp.org/chapter/chapter-2-social-progress-compass

Robertson, A. (2022, April 6). *OpenAI's DALL-E AI image generator can now edit pictures, too*. The Verge. https://www.theverge.com/2022/4/6/23012123/openai-clip-dalle-2-ai-text-to-image-generator-testing

Robinson, N. J. (2016, May 11). *How to justify Hiroshima*. Current Affairs. https://www.currentaffairs.org/2016/05/how-to-justify-hiroshima

Russell, S. (2017, April). *3 principles for creating safer AI* [Video]. TED Conferences. https://www.ted.com/talks/stuart_russell_3_principles_for_creating_safer_ai

Savoie, J., & Sarek, K. (2018, September 18). *Is it better to be a wild rat or a factory farmed cow? A systematic method for comparing animal welfare*. EA Forum. https://forum.effectivealtruism.org/posts/cimFBQbpjntoBAKCq/is-it-better-to-be-a-wild-rat-or-a-factory-farmed-cow-a-1

Sawyer, W., & Wagner, P. (2022, March 14). *Mass incarceration: The whole pie 2022*. Prison Policy Initiative. https://www.prisonpolicy.org/reports/pie2022.html

Schopenhauer, A. (1890). *Counsels and maxims. Being the second part of Arthur Schopenhauer's "Aphorismen zur Lebensweisheit"*. (T.B. Saunders, Trans.). Swan Sonnenschein & Co.

Schubert, S. (2017, March 10). *Understanding cause-neutrality*. Effective Altruism. https://www.effectivealtruism.org/articles/understanding-cause-neutrality

Schukraft, J. (2018, December 22). *Detecting morally significant pain in nonhumans: Some philosophical difficulties*. Rethink Priorities. Retrieved April 26, 2022, from https://rethinkpriorities.org/publications/detecting-morally-significant-pain

Schukraft, J. (2019, June 9). *Invertebrate sentience: A useful empirical resource*. Rethink Priorities. https://rethinkpriorities.org/publications/invertebrate-sentience-useful-empirical-resource

Sebo, J. (2021, July 27). *On the torment of insect minds and our moral duty not to farm them*. Aeon. https://aeon.co/essays/on-the-torment-of-insect-minds-and-our-moral-duty-not-to-farm-them

Shane, S. (2015, April 23). *Drone strikes reveal uncomfortable truth: U.S. is often unsure about who will die*. The New York Times. https://www.nytimes.com/2015/04/24/world/asia/drone-strikes-reveal-uncomfortable-truth-us-is-often-unsure-about-who-will-die.html

Siderits, M. (2015). *Personal identity and Buddhist philosophy: Empty persons*. Routledge. https://www.routledge.com/Personal-Identity-and-Buddhist-Philosophy-Empty-Persons/Siderits/p/book/9781472446459

Singer, P. (2002, November 13). *A response to Martha Nussbaum*. PhilPapers. https://philpapers.org/rec/SINART-2

Singer, P. (2013, August 5). *The world's first cruelty-free hamburger*. The Guardian. https://www.theguardian.com/commentisfree/2013/aug/05/worlds-first-cruelty-free-hamburger

Sinnott-Armstrong, W. (2021). *Consequentialism*. Stanford Encyclopedia of Philosophy (Fall 2021 Edition). https://plato.stanford.edu/archives/fall2021/entries/consequentialism/

Sinnott-Armstrong, W. (2019). *Moral skepticism*. Stanford Encyclopedia of Philosophy (Summer 2019 Edition). https://plato.stanford.edu/archives/sum2019/entries/skepticism-moral/#SkeHyp

Slavin, K. (2011, July). *How algorithms shape our world* [Video]. TED Conferences. https://www.ted.com/talks/kevin_slavin_how_algorithms_shape_our_world

Smith, S. (2019, April 24). *How to enjoy the end of the world*. [YouTube]. https://www.youtube.com/watch?v=5WPB2u8EzL8

Soares, N. (2019). The value learning problem. In R. V. Yampolskiy (Ed.), *Artificial intelligence safety and security*. CRC Press/Taylor & Francis Group.

Sortition Foundation. (n.d.). https://www.sortitionfoundation.org/

Sprung, C. L., Joynt, G. M., Christian, M. D., Truog, R. D., Rello, J., & Nates, J. L. (2020). Adult ICU triage during the coronavirus disease 2019 pandemic: Who will live and who will die? Recommendations to improve survival. *Critical Care Medicine*, 48(8), 1196–1202. https://doi.org/10.1097/ccm.0000000000004410

Stafforini, P. (2013, April 7). *[Link] Values spreading is often more important than extinction risk*. LessWrong. https://www.lesswrong.com/posts/nbd4aB24ktozQeHwL/link-values-spreading-is-often-more-important-than

Stelling, T. (2014, March 10). *Do lobsters and other invertebrates feel pain? New research has some answers*. The Washington Post. https://www.washingtonpost.com/national/health-science/do-lobsters-and-other-invertebrates-feel-pain-new-research-has-some-answers/2014/03/07/ f026ea9e-9e59-11e3-b8d8-94577ff66b28_story.html

Stillman, J. (2019, May 16). *Nobel prize-winning psychologist: Most people don't want to be happy (and that's smart)*. Inc.com. https://www.inc.com/jessica-stillman/nobel-prize-winning-psychologist-chasing-happiness-wont-make-you-happy.html

Stray, J. (2015, September 28). *Bertrand Russell on statistical empathy*. Effective Altruism Forum. https://forum.effectivealtruism.org/posts/KKFg3HnWvSqa3QSZq/bertrand-russell-on-statistical-empathy

Superrationality. (n.d.). In Wikipedia. Retrieved April 29, 2022, from https://en.wikipedia.org/wiki/Superrationality

Taylor, J. (2015, February 23). *How to change public opinion*. Niskanen Center. https://niskanencenter.org/blog/how-to-change-public-opinion/

Tegmark, M. (2017, August 29). *Friendly AI: Aligning goals*. Future of Life Institute. https://futureoflife.org/2017/08/29/friendly-ai-aligning-goals/

Thaler, R. H., & Sunstein, C. R. (2009). *Nudge: Improving decisions about health, wealth, and happiness*. Penguin Books.

Todd, B. (2017, March). *Which world problems are the most pressing to solve?* 80,000 Hours. Retrieved April 26, 2022, from https://80000hours.org/career-guide/world-problems/

TOI-Online. (2019, December 18). *What is Nirbhaya case?* The Times of India. https://timesofindia.indiatimes.com/india/what-is-nirbhaya-case/articleshow/72868430.cms

Tomasik, B. (2015, February 3). *Why digital sentience is relevant to animal activists*. Animal Charity Evaluators. https://animalcharityevaluators.org/blog/why-digital-sentience-is-relevant-to-animal-activists/

Tomasik, B. (2016a, March 1). *Which marine trophic level contains the most total suffering?* Essays on Reducing Suffering. Retrieved April 30, 2022, from https://reducing-suffering.org/marine-trophic-level-contains-total-suffering/

Tomasik, B. (2016b, March 14). *Preventing extreme suffering has moral priority*. [YouTube]. https://www.youtube.com/watch?v=RyA_eF7W02s

Tomasik, B. (2016c, March 13). *Preventing extreme suffering has moral priority*. [Google Doc presentation]. https://docs.google.com/presentation/d/1bbEmWGJXiFQ7igO_YuyqUzgdEUn-727muUlkIozrYT4/edit

Tomasik, B. (2016d, April 25). *The importance of insect suffering*. Essays on Reducing Suffering. Retrieved April 26, 2022, from https://reducing-suffering.org/the-importance-of-insect-suffering/

Tomasik, B. (2017a, July 28). *Do bugs feel pain?* Essays on Reducing Suffering. Retrieved April 24, 2022, from https://reducing-suffering.org/do-bugs-feel-pain/

Tomasik, B. (2017b, November 15). *Does negative utilitarianism override individual preferences?* Essays on Reducing Suffering. Retrieved April 24, 2022, from https://reducing-suffering.org/negative-utilitarianism-override-individual-preferences/

Tomasik, B. (2017c, December 23). *Are happiness and suffering symmetric?* Essays on Reducing Suffering. Retrieved April 24, 2022, from https://reducing-suffering.org/happiness-suffering-symmetric/#Consent-based_negative_utilitarianism

Tomasik, B. (2018a, April 16). *Reasons to promote suffering-focused ethics*. Essays on Reducing Suffering. Retrieved April 20, 2022, from https://reducing-suffering.org/the-case-for-promoting-suffering-focused-ethics/

Tomasik, B. (2018b, May 18). *Will gene drives reduce wild-animal suffering?* Essays on Reducing Suffering. Retrieved April 26, 2022, from https://reducing-suffering.org/will-gene-drives-reduce-wild-animal-suffering/

Tomasik, B. (2019a, May 14). *Convert grass lawns to gravel to reduce insect suffering*. Essays on Reducing Suffering. Retrieved April 26, 2022, from https://reducing-suffering.org/convert-grass-lawns-to-gravel-to-reduce-insect-suffering/

Tomasik, B. (2019b, June 17). *How does vegetarianism impact wild-animal suffering?* Essays on Reducing Suffering. Retrieved April 26, 2022, from https://reducing-suffering.org/vegetarianism-and-wild-animals/

Tomasik, B. (2019c, July 21). *Is brain size morally relevant?* Essays on Reducing Suffering. Retrieved April 26, 2022, from https://reducing-suffering.org/is-brain-size-morally-relevant/

Tomasik, B. (2019d, August 7). *How many wild animals are there?* Essays on Reducing Suffering. Retrieved April 26, 2022, from https://reducing-suffering.org/how-many-wild-animals-are-there/

Tononi, G., & Koch, C. (2015). Consciousness: Here, there and everywhere? *Philosophical Transactions of the Royal Society B, 370*(1668). https://doi.org/10.1098/rstb.2014.0167

Torres, P. (2017, October 24). *Why superintelligence is a threat that should be taken seriously*. Bulletin of the Atomic Scientists. https://thebulletin.org/2017/10/why-superintelligence-is-a-threat-that-should-be-taken-seriously/

Torres, P. (2021a, July 28). *The dangerous ideas of "longtermism" and "existential risk"*. Current Affairs. https://www.currentaffairs.org/2021/07/the-dangerous-ideas-of-longtermism-and-existential-risk

Torres, P. (2021b, October 19). *Against longtermism*. Aeon. https://aeon.co/essays/why-longtermism-is-the-worlds-most-dangerous-secular-credo

Transparency International. (2021). *2021 Corruption perceptions index*. https://www.transparency.org/en/cpi/2021

Trolley problem memes. (n.d.). Facebook. https://www.facebook.com/TrolleyProblemMemes/

Tversky, A., & Kahneman, D. (1981). The framing of decisions and the psychology of choice. *Science, 211*(4481), 453–458. https://doi.org/10.1126/science.7455683

Two-level utilitarianism. (n.d.). In Wikipedia. https://en.wikipedia.org/wiki/Two-level_utilitarianism

Urban, T. (2014, May 21). *The Fermi paradox*. Wait But Why. https://waitbutwhy.com/2014/05/fermi-paradox.html

van Roojen, M. (2018). *Moral cognitivism vs. non-cognitivism*. Stanford Encyclopedia of Philosophy (Fall 2018 Edition). https://plato.stanford.edu/archives/fall2018/entries/moral-cognitivism/

Varoufakis, Y. (2022, March 5). *What we must do in the face of Putin's criminal invasion of Ukraine - A personal view plus a heartwarming manifesto by Russian comrades*. https://www.yanisvaroufakis.eu/2022/03/05/what-we-must-in-the-face-of-putins-criminal-invasion-of-ukraine-a-personal-view-plus-a-heartwarming-manifesto-by-russian-comrades/

Vergne, A., et al. (2018, May 25). *Towards a global citizens' assembly*. The Global Challenges Foundation. https://globalchallenges.org/library-entries/towards-a-global-citizens-assembly/

Vinding, M. (2014). *Why "happy meat" is always wrong*. https://www.smashwords.com/books/view/435640

Vinding, M. (2016, November 23). *Fundamental values and the relevance of uncertainty*. http://magnusvinding.blogspot.com/2016/11/fundamental-values-and-relevance-of_23.html

Vinding, M. (2017). *You are them*. https://www.smashwords.com/books/view/719903

Vinding, M. (2018, September 18). *Why altruists should perhaps not prioritize artificial intelligence: A lengthy critique*. https://magnusvinding.com/2018/09/18/why-altruists-should-perhaps-not-prioritize-artificial-intelligence-a-lengthy-critique/

Vinding, M. (2020a). *Suffering-focused ethics: Defense and implications*. Ratio Ethica. Available at https://magnusvinding.files.wordpress.com/2020/05/suffering-focused-ethics.pdf

Vinding, M. (2020b, October 3). *Underappreciated consequentialist reasons to avoid consuming animal products*. https://magnusvinding.com/2020/10/03/underappreciated-consequentialist-reasons/

Vinding, M. (2021, February 20). *Antinatalism and reducing suffering: A case of suspicious convergence*. https://magnusvinding.com/2021/02/20/antinatalism-and-reducing-suffering/

Vinding, M. (2022). *Reasoned politics*. Ratio Ethica. Available at https://magnusvinding.files.wordpress.com/2022/03/reasoned-politics.pdf

Waldhorn, D. R. (2019, June 14). *Invertebrate sentience: Summary of findings, part 2*. Rethink Priorities. https://rethinkpriorities.org/publications/invertebrate-sentience-summary-of-findings-part-2

Waldhorn, D. R. (2020, February 6). *Snails used for human consumption: The case of meat and slime*. Rethink Priorities. https://rethinkpriorities.org/publications/snails-used-for-human-consumption

Watson, D., Clark, L. A., & Tellegen, A. (1988). Development and validation of brief measures of positive and negative affect: The PANAS scales. *Journal of Personality and Social Psychology*, 54(6), 1063–1070. https://doi.org/10.1037/0022-3514.54.6.1063

Welfare Footprint Project. (n.d.). https://welfarefootprint.org/

Weyl, E. G. (2018, August 1). *"Everybody's brain knows how to run a tail": Glen Weyl talks to Jaron Lanier about how to live with technology*. Logic Magazine. https://logicmag.io/failure/glen-weyl-and-jaron-lanier-how-to-live-with-technology/

Wiblin, R., & Harris, K. (2018, August 7). *Spencer Greenberg on the scientific approach to solving difficult everyday questions*. 80,000 Hours. https://80000hours.org/podcast/episodes/spencer-greenberg-bayesian-updating/#intrinsic-and-instrumental-values

Wiblin, R., & Harris, K. (2019, April 15). *Animals in the wild often suffer a great deal. What, if anything, should we do about that?* [Interview with Persis Eskander]. 80,000 Hours. https://80000hours.org/podcast/episodes/persis-eskander-wild-animal-welfare/

Wignaraja, K. (2020, July 10). *The case for a universal basic income*. UNDP. https://www.undp.org/blog/case-universal-basic-income

Wilson, E. O. (1998). *Consilience: The unity of knowledge*. Vintage.

World Animal Protection. (2019, January 11). *10 things you should know about factory-farmed meat chickens*. https://www.worldanimalprotection.org.uk/blogs/10-things-you-should-know-about-factory-farmed-meat-chickens

World Population Review. (n.d.). *Gini coefficient by country*. https://worldpopulationreview.com/country-rankings/gini-coefficient-by-country

Yampolskiy, R. V. (2019). Preface: Introduction to AI safety and security. In R. V. Yampolskiy (Ed.), *Artificial intelligence safety and security*. CRC Press/Taylor & Francis Group.

Yampolskiy, R. (2020, July 18). *On controllability of artificial intelligence*. PhilPapers. https://philpapers.org/rec/YAMOCO

Young, L., & Durwin, A. J. (2013). Moral realism as moral motivation: The impact of meta-ethics on everyday decision-making. *Journal of Experimental Social Psychology*, 49(2), 302–306. https://doi.org/10.1016/j.jesp.2012.11.013

Yudkowsky, E. (2007, October 30). *Torture vs. dust specks*. LessWrong. https://www.lesswrong.com/posts/3wYTFWY3LKQCnAptN/torture-vs-dust-specks

Yudkowsky, E. (2009, April 3). *Rationality is systematized winning*. LessWrong. https://www.lesswrong.com/posts/4ARtkT3EYox3THYjF/rationality-is-systematized-winning

Yudkowsky, E. (2013, May 6). *Five theses, two lemmas, and a couple of strategic implications*. Machine Intelligence Research Institute. https://intelligence.org/2013/05/05/five-theses-two-lemmas-and-a-couple-of-strategic-implications/

Yurchenko, O. V., Skiteva, O. I., Voronezhskaya, E. E., & Dyachuk, V. A. (2018). Nervous system development in the Pacific oyster, Crassostrea gigas (Mollusca: Bivalvia). *Frontiers in Zoology, 15*(10). https://doi.org/10.1186/s12983-018-0259-8

Zembrzuski, T. (2015, February 22). *How ayahuasca completely changed my life*. Your Mate Tom. http://www.yourmatetom.com/journal/2015/2/21/my-first-ayahuasca-experience

Zhang, L. (2017, December 6). *Behind the absurd popularity of trolley problem memes*. HuffPost. https://www.huffpost.com/entry/behind-the-absurd-popular_b_10247650

Ziesche, S., & Yampolskiy, R. (2018). Towards AI welfare science and policies. *Big Data and Cognitive Computing, 3*(1), 2. https://doi.org/10.3390/bdcc3010002

Zimmerman, M. J., & Bradley, B. (2019). *Intrinsic vs. extrinsic value*. Stanford Encyclopedia of Philosophy (Spring 2019 Edition). https://plato.stanford.edu/archives/spr2019/entries/value-intrinsic-extrinsic/#WhaHasIntVal

Index

80,000 Hours, 126
9/11, 47

activism (and activists), 4, 6, 119, 132, 143, 152-4, 160, 161, 176, 182, 183, 184, 206-9
Acton, H.B., 44
affect (hedonic state), 37, 42, 51-8, 75, 86, 119
aggregation, 8, 29, 79-82, 84, 116, 118, 121, 126, 137, 150, 188-90
Algosphere Alliance, 193
Animal Ethics, 80, 137, 139, 149, 150
anencephaly, 189
animal rights, 165, 184, 190
anti-natalism, 120, 181-2, 200
    benevolent artificial anti-natalism (BAAN), 200
anti-speciesism, *see* speciesism
anti-substratism (and substrate non-discrimination), 157-8
Ariely, Dan, 104
Aristotle, 32
artificial intelligence (AI, and artificial general intelligence, AGI), 4-7, 40, 123, 138, 157, 158, 192, 195-202, 203, 210
    superintelligence, 7, 66, 195, 200, 201
attractor (social network theory), 205
autonomy, 30, 40, 41, 51, 64, 102, 113, 131, 146, 163, 175, 177, 184, 193
axioms (and axiomatic), 9, 17, 19-20, 22, 73-75, 82, 88, 129-30

Balluch, Martin, 184
Bayne, Tim, 151
Beard, Simon, 34, 115

bees, 101
    sentience, 150-1
    suffering, 155
    see also invertebrate suffering
Belarus, 204
Benatar, David, 120, 181
Bentham, Jeremy, 29
Berraud, Vincent, 46
birds, 148
    chickens, 101, 102, 147, 152, 154
    turkeys, 147
Bloom, Paul, 208
Bostrom, Nick, 33, 73, 123, 125, 126, 157, 191
Bruylant, Eric, 161
Buddhism, 33, 49, 97
    Three Signs of Being, 97
Burger King, 165

cancer, 43, 46, 49, 82, 91, 161, 167, 178
Carroll, Lewis, 23
categorical imperative (Kant), 31, 205
cats, 74
Center on Long-Term Risk, 57, 157
childbirth, 47, 146
China (and Chinese), 181, 194
citizens' assemblies, 195
clean meat, 164
climate change, 4, 122, 144, 200
closed individualism, *see* personal identity
cluster headaches, 47, 87, 161, 178-9, 189
cognitive biases, 42, 67, 108
cognitive dissonance, 3, 16, 131, 141, 160, 170, 175, 185

collapse (societal, civilisational), 4, 155, 192, 203
Commission on the Status of Women, 194
companion animals ("pets"), 148, 169
complex system, 206-7
consequentialism, 14, 27-32, 34, 37, 80-1, 115, 135, 139
consensus (on ethics, values, goals), 5, 33, 193, 197, 199, 210
consent
  of intuitions, 34
  to experience extreme/unbearable suffering, 109, 186
Coste, Rick, 145
COVID-19, 179-81, 202
cows, 154, 165, 170
Crisp, Roger, 124
CRISPR, 185
crustaceans, 51, 149, 155
  see also invertebrate suffering
Csikszentmihalyi, Mihaly, 53
cultured meat, *see* clean meat

DALY (Disability-Adjusted Life-Year), 187-90
Darwinian, 122, 124, 187
  see also evolutionary
Dawkins, Richard, 17-18
deontology, 5, 31-2, 34, 139-40, 142, 160
dictator
  benevolent, 191, 199
  see totalitarianism
Diener, Ed, 39, 52-3
disability (metric, weight), 187-90
DLES (Days Lived with Extreme Suffering), 190
dogs, 74, 102, 148, 164, 169, 170
drone strikes, 144, 162
drugs
  dependence, 49, 178
  nonviolent offences, 55
  strict laws, 178
  warfare, 70
dystopia (and dystopian), 4, 34, 141, 155, 191, 197, 200-2

Earthlings (documentary), 209

ecology, *see* environmentalism
effective altruism (EA), 3, 14, 25, 63, 74, 93, 94, 126, 161, 187
emotivism, 24
empathy gap, hot-cold, 42, 46, 108
empty individualism, *see* personal identity
environmentalism, 183-4
Epicurus, 57
equality (and inequality), 37, 114, 115, 117, 191, 193
euthanasia
  humans, *see* suicide
  non-human animals, 176-7
Everitt, Tom, 198
evolutionary (processes, pressures), 15, 16, 124, 148
  see also Darwinian
existence bias, 64, 67, 69, 98, 120, 123, 130, 131, 136, 140, 161, 183, 186, 200
existential risk(s) (x-risk), 4, 7, 69, 123-7, 186, 193, 195-6, 200-1
expected value, 33-4, 74, 93-4, 123, 125-6, 140, 152-5, 157, 204-5, 207-8
experience machine (Nozick), 37-9
expressivism, 24

factory farming, 4, 26, 74, 102, 132, 139, 144, 147, 152, 154, 155, 165, 172, 176, 177, 183, 206
fairness (and unfairness), 15, 37, 86, 100, 113, 114-7, 126, 136, 191
fish, 84, 147, 148, 154, 170
fishing, 147, 170
flow (state of), 49, 53, 58, 65
Foot, Philippa, 12
free will, 11
Frijters, Paul, 189

Gandhi, Mahatma, 205
Global Burden of Disease, 188
Global Challenges Foundation, 194
Gloor, Lukas, 57, 65, 201
Golden Rule, 31, 99-101, 192, 210
  Silver Rule, 99
Gómez Emilsson, Andrés, 46, 58, 67, 77, 95, 161

governance (ethical, compassionate), 5, 6, 100, 113, 164, 179, 181, 191, 192-5, 199, 210
Greenberg, Spencer, 62, 116
Greene, Joshua, 12

Haidt, Jonathan, 15, 21
Harari, Yuval Noah, 70
Hare, R.M., 30, 34
Harris, Sam, 23, 115
hedons, 76-9, 106, 189
Herrán, Manu, 111
Hillel, Rabbi, 99
Hiroshima, 127, 162
holism, ethical, 9
human rights, 190-1, 193-5
Human Rights Council, 194

Impossible Burger, 164-5, 169
inequality, *see* equality
injustice, *see* justice
insect suffering, 5, 102, 149-55, 170
  see also invertebrate suffering
interests (in ethical sense), 22, 29, 40-1, 101-2, 175
invertebrate suffering, 5, 40-1, 51, 102, 149-55, 170, 172-4

Johnson, Mike, 8, 58, 66-7
justice (and injustice), 37, 62, 187

Kafka, Franz, 125
Kahneman, Daniel, 18, 53, 104-5
Kant, Immanuel, 31, 205
Keiper, Adam, 199
kidney stones, 45-6, 47, 54
killing,
  euthanasia of non-human animals, 176-7
  non-human animals, 102, 147, 155, 165, 169, 170, 173, 174-7
  oneself *see* suicide
  people, 31, 107, 111, 162, 163, 175
  sentient machines, 158
Knutsson, Simon, 69, 127
Koch, Christof, 156
Kolak, Daniel, 95
Kumar, Satish, 143
Kurzweil, Ray, 202

lab meat, *see* clean meat

Lancet Commission on Palliative Care and Pain Relief, 190
Lanier, Jaron, 98
Le Guin, Ursula, 107, 124
life satisfaction, 37, 39, 51-6, 58, 78, 119, 137, 189
lock-in (of a system), 191, 192, 201

MacAskill, William, 25, 29, 33, 187
Machine Intelligence Research Institute (MIRI), 198
Mankoski pain scale, 75, 83
Mayerfeld, Jamie, 27, 44, 45, 51, 77, 83, 91-2, 133
metaphysical truths, 9, 17, 97, 132
Metzinger, Thomas, 22, 39, 42, 67, 157, 200
migraines, 47
Mill, John Stuart, 29, 48
mixed states (hedonic), 45, 50, 53, 56
moral anti-realism, *see* moral realism
moral compensation, 144
Moral Foundations Theory (Haidt), 15
moral licensing, 144
moral nihilism, 26
  see also moral realism
moral objectivity, 21
  see also moral realism
moral realism (and anti-realism), 21-7, 30, 33, 44, 70, 159, 200
moral relativism, 23
morphine, 43, 82, 83, 91, 161, 178

Nagasaki, 127
National Institute for Health and Care Excellence (NICE), 188
nature, suffering in, *see* wild animal suffering
negative utilitarianism, 2, 29, 44, 67-71, 80, 81, 88, 92, 100, 122, 124, 129, 131-2, 134-7, 141-3, 159-60, 164, 186
negative utilitarianism *plus*, 2, 70, 132, 160
  xNU+, 70, 131-9, 141, 159, 192-3, 195, 198, 200
non-discrimination, substrate, *see* anti-substratism
Nozick, Robert, 37

octopuses
  evolution, 173-4
  suffering, 149, 155
  see also invertebrate suffering
Omelas (The Ones Who Walk Away from, story by Ursula Le Guin), 107, 110, 114, 124
open individualism, see personal identity
opioids, 178
opioid receptors (in invertebrates), 149, 154
  see also morphine
Ord, Toby, 68, 88
Organisation for the Prevention of Intense Suffering (OPIS), 47, 178
oysters
  evolution, 172-4
  suffering, 40-1, 149, 172-4
  see also invertebrate suffering

pain, chronic, 54, 85, 87, 119, 146, 178
Palliative care Outcome Scale (POS), 75
PANAS (Positive and Negative Affect Schedule), 75
panpsychism, 151
Parfit, Derek, 25, 82, 96, 118, 121, 124-5
Parliamentary model (for resolving ethical uncertainty), 33, 35
Pascal's Wager, 111-2
Pearce, David, 66, 78, 101, 126, 132, 138, 185
personal identity, 2, 9, 11-12, 19, 38, 41, 50, 64, 90, 91, 95-9, 100, 106, 112, 116, 132, 142-3, 145, 158, 175, 186, 193
  closed individualism, 64, 90, 95-9, 113, 135, 158
  empty individualism, 90, 96-7, 99, 100, 106, 113, 116, 135, 136, 143, 159, 175, 186
  open individualism, 96-7, 99, 111, 113, 186
PETA, 165
pigs, 101, 102, 147, 152, 154
Pinker, Steven, 190

plants
  growing for food, 155, 169-71, 172-3
  plant-based meat, 164-5
  sentience, 61, 150, 153
Plato, 63
Popper, Karl, 67
precautionary principle, 71, 111
preference satisfaction, 29, 39-40
prescriptions (ethical), 2-3, 12-14, 19, 20, 25, 27, 29, 51, 124, 133, 138, 139, 160, 187, 192
prescriptivism, 24
prioritarianism, 31, 79, 137
  negative prioritarianism, 137
  see also negative utilitarianism
psychedelics, 161, 178
purity (personal, ethical, moral), 15, 140, 141, 144, 169, 171, 172
Putin, Vladimir, 163

QALY (Quality-Adjusted Life-Year), 187-9

rationality (and irrationality)
  "big-picture", 17, 26, 186
  epistemic, 16-17
  instrumental, 16-17
rationalists, 3, 14, 29, 63, 67, 89-91, 94, 121, 126-7, 141
rats, 165, 169
Rawls, John, 100
Repugnant Conclusion, 118, 121-2, 188
Rethink Priorities, 149-50, 154
Robinson, Nathan, 162
Russell, Bertrand, 208
Russell, Stuart, 197-8

SALY (Suffering-Adjusted Life-Year), 190
scales (of pain and suffering), 51-2, 75-8, 86-7, 126
  cardinal, 76-7, 79
  logarithmic, 77, 126
  Mankoski, 75, 83
  ordinal, 76
  see also disability (metric), DALY, QALY, WELBY, SALY, YLS, YLSS, DLES

Schopenhauer, Arthur, 125
Schukraft, Jason, 150, 153
Schulman, Ari, 199
Security Council (UN), 194
signalling (social), 18
Silver Rule, *see* Golden Rule
Singer, Peter, 26, 40, 43, 92
slaughter, *see* killing
slaughterhouses, 42, 175
   see also killing
Smart, R.N., 67
snails
   evolution, 173-4
   suffering, 102, 149, 155
   see also invertebrate suffering
Soares, Nate, 198
Socrates, 63
speciesism, 101-2, 164, 166, 184
   anti-speciesism, 101-2, 164
spirituality, 12, 97, 142, 183, 186
sponges, 150
s-risks (and astronomical suffering), 127, 156
Stray, Jonathan, 208
suffering-focused ethics (term), 71
   see also negative utilitarianism
suicide, 46-8, 177-9, 189
   euthanasia, 177-9
   non-human animals, 48
   suicide headaches, *see* cluster headaches
superintelligence, *see* artificial intelligence
superrationality, 205
surveillance, 194
systemic change, 141, 159, 201

Tegmark, Max, 196
tinnitus, 146
tipping points, 88-9, 126
Tomasik, Brian, 47, 67, 73, 84, 109, 144, 149, 150, 152-4, 156, 160, 162
Tononi, Giulio, 156
Torres, Phil, 7, 126
torture, 26, 38, 45, 46, 50, 65, 69, 71, 86, 89-92, 99, 108-12, 118, 123-5, 127, 132, 145, 146, 162-3, 164, 197
   of non-human animals, 3, 4, 107, 139, 141, 144, 147-8, 152, 154, 164-8, 176, 183, 190, 197
   vs. dust specks (thought experiment), 89-91, 108
totalitarianism (and dictatorship), 4, 162, 191, 201, 203, 206
tranquilism, 57-8, 65
trolley problem, 12, 25, 197
Turing machine, 156
Tversky, Amos, 104

Ukraine, Russian invasion of, 4, 162-3
United Nations (UN), 193, 194
universal basic income (UBI), 181
Universal Declaration of Human Rights (UDHR), 193
utility, 29, 31, 79, 109, 125, 134, 141
   see also utilitarianism
utilitarianism (general), 5, 12, 28-36, 39, 67-8, 70, 74, 76, 78-80, 84, 112, 114-16, 128, 134-5, 139, 140-5, 158, 159-64, 166-8, 170-1, 176, 180, 182, 186-7, 200
   act, 29-30, 142, 203
   classical, 8, 29, 63-4, 66, 69, 70, 79-81, 92, 105, 106, 115, 118, 125, 128, 133-7, 188
   hedonistic, 29, 36-7, 81
   negative, *see* negative utilitarianism
   preference, 29
   rule, 29-31, 192, 203
   two-level, 30, 34
utopia (and utopian), 68, 107, 132, 181, 191, 197
   see also dystopia

vaccinations (of wild animals), 149, 183
value
   instrumental (extrinsic), 60-4, 71, 183
   intrinsic, 60-4, 93, 183
Varoufakis, Yanis, 163
veganism (and vegans), 3, 155, 165, 169-72
veil of ignorance (Rawls), 100-1, 103
Vinding, Magnus, 44, 66, 71, 89, 96, 176, 182, 195, 202
virtue ethics, 32

voting, 107, 158, 194, 204-5
Waldhorn, Daniela, 154
Wallace-Wells, David, 205
WELBY (Wellbeing-Adjusted Life-Year, also WELLBY, WALY), 189
wild animal suffering, 5, 42, 49, 144, 148-9, 156, 166, 171, 181, 182, 183-5, 209
Wilson, E.O., 142
World Health Organisation (WHO), 188
worms
  evolution, 173-4
  suffering, 149, 155
  see also invertebrate suffering

xNU+, *see* negative utilitarianism

x-risk, *see* existential risk

Yampolskiy, Roman, 157, 195-6
yin and yang, 10, 143
YLS (Years Lived with Suffering), 190
YLSS (Years Lived with Severe Suffering), 190
Yudkowsky, Eliezer, 7, 17, 89-90, 157

zoos, 148

www.ingramcontent.com/pod-product-compliance
Lightning Source LLC
Chambersburg PA
CBHW070940230426
43666CB00011B/2510